# Nature through Tropical Windows

# Nature through Tropical Windows

ALEXANDER F. SKUTCH

*Illustrations by Dana Gardner*

UNIVERSITY OF CALIFORNIA PRESS·BERKELEY·LOS ANGELES·LONDON

University of California Press
Berkeley and Los Angeles, California
University of California Press, Ltd.
London, England
© 1983 by
The Regents of the University of California

Library of Congress Cataloging in Publication Data

Skutch, Alexander Frank, 1904–
    Nature through tropical windows.

    Bibliography: p.
    Includes index.
    1. Nature history—Tropics. 2. Birds—Tropics.
3. Botany—Tropics. I. Title.
QH84.5.S58   1983        598.29'22'09728        82-8534
ISBN 0-520-04745-1                              AACR2
ISBN 0-520-04759-1 (pbk.)

Printed in the United States of America
1   2   3   4   5   6   7   8   9

*To Pamela and Edwin,*
*who for years have looked*
*through tropical windows with me*

# Contents

# *Preface*

THE shrinking tropical forests are a last home of mystery on a planet that is yearly more thoroughly investigated, from the upper limits of the atmosphere to the abyssal depths of the oceans and beyond, far into the solid Earth. For more than half a century in tropical America, I have tried to learn about the life of these forests, chiefly their birds and plants. The many dwellings that I have occupied were never within the forests' unbroken depths but nearly always near them, sometimes in a narrow clearing, usually no more than an easy walk from the woodland's edge. For uncounted hours I explored these forests, seeking plants, searching for the well-hidden nests of birds, and studying those that I could find. Although my chief endeavor was to learn about the forest birds whose lives were so little known— tinamous, trogons, motmots, jacamars, toucans, woodcreepers, cotingas, and many others—I often found myself devoting more time than I had intended to the more familiar birds around my various abodes. They were much easier to watch; their nests were sometimes so conveniently situated in front of a window that they seemed to invite observation, which was often richly rewarded with unexpected discoveries. Not infrequently one of the rarer forest birds emerged from the woodland depths to raise its family in the clearing where I dwelt, where its chances of success were somewhat better than in the predator-ridden forest. They, too, received my attention.

Indeed, it was by watching through a window of the two-

roomed wooden laboratory and office of the small research station that, years ago, the United Fruit Company maintained beside the Changuinola Lagoon in western Panama that I became a
dedicated student of tropical American birds. While, through a
microscope, I peered at thin sections of banana plants, a Rufous-
tailed Hummingbird[1] built her nest in a ramie plant just outside,
separated from me only by the fine-meshed screen. While she incubated her two tiny eggs and raised her young, I enjoyed so
many fascinating glimpses of avian behavior that I wished to devote years to the study of tropical birds, already so well classified
from museum specimens but so little known as living animals.
Since I have elsewhere told the story of this hummingbird, I
shall say no more about her here, other than to express my gratitude to this tiny bird who so influenced the whole subsequent
course of my life by introducing me to an absorbing study.

  In the following six years, I saw many birds through other
tropical windows, from the warm lowlands of Honduras and
Guatemala to the cool highlands of the latter country; but the
birds that I watched most carefully were farther afield. The next
window through which I made a prolonged study was in the
rough wooden wall of the thatched cabin that I occupied in the
valley of the Río Buena Vista, a mountain torrent tributary to
the Río Térraba in southern Costa Rica. In a gourd that I tied to
an orange tree in front of this glassless, screenless window, a pair
of Southern House-Wrens raised seven broods in two seasons. In
the second year, the young of each of the earlier broods helped
their parents to feed the nestlings of the following brood. This
surprising behavior, which had never to my knowledge been reported of house-wrens, kept me seated at this window, making
notes, for many hours that I might have spent seeking the rarer
birds in the forest on the ridge above the narrow valley. Nevertheless, I consider those hours well spent.

  The only window glass through which I have carefully watched

_____

  1 When the name of an animal or plant is capitalized, the scientific equivalent will be found in the index.

tropical birds was in a cottage at Montaña Azul, at the edge of the vast forest that four decades ago covered much of the deeply dissected northern slope of Costa Rica's Cordillera Central. Here, on a storm-beaten ridge 5,500 feet above sea level, the glass was helpful, but not adequate to keep out the wind-driven clouds, which seeped in through chinks in the double-boarded walls and dampened everything inside. Through this window I watched the aerial maneuvers of the Blue-and-White Swallows who raised their families on the ridge-beam of the roof above me, and saw many other birds of the wet subtropical forest, from little Golden-browed Chlorophonias and Common Bush-Tanagers to Emerald Toucanets and Resplendent Quetzals.

The windows through which I have watched most birds are those of the house that, forty years ago, I built close beside a tract of tropical rain forest in the valley of El General in southern Costa Rica. Because birds so often collide, sometimes fatally, with window glass or screens, these windows (with one exception) have neither. When the solid wooden shutters are opened, nothing separates us from the surrounding trees and shrubbery. Here, at an altitude of about 2,500 feet, the gentle breezes that pass freely through the rooms are refreshingly mild, and only rarely, in the months of heavy rains, would window glass increase our comfort.

The eastern windows of our home at "Los Cusingos" look over the birds' feeder and the rocky, tree-shaded channel of the Río Peñas Blancas, whose ceaseless clamor reaches me as I write, to a green ridge above which we watch the sun rise. On many a drizzly afternoon, a rainbow arches high above it. In the background, somewhat north of east, rises the ten-thousand foot rounded dome of Cerro Palmital, whose precipitous, forested hitherward face is often tinted by a glorious alpenglow, after the sun has dropped below the ridge close behind the house, on which jacaranda trees stand high above the steep, pastured slope. Our southern windows face the wall-like edge of the tract of ancient rain forest I have protected for four decades, now part of the national forest reserve. The northern windows look upon too many flowering trees and shrubs to permit a far prospect, but the area outside is not too crowded to attract birds.

From these windows I have, over the years, watched more birds than I can tell about in a single book, from Swallow-tailed Kites that soar overhead and lovely Turquoise Cotingas who perch on the highest exposed treetops to doves and Black-striped Sparrows who walk or hop over the lawn, sharing the chickens' corn with free Agoutis. In other books and in journals, I have told about many of these birds; for this one I have chosen a few that we most often see from our windows, especially those about which I have something new to relate.

What chiefly we see from our windows is trees. Here, where one hundred and twenty or more inches of rain fall in most years, nearly all in the long wet season that continues from March or April until December, tall forest not long ago covered all the landscape; in Parque Nacional Chirripó, visible from our eastern windows, it still flourishes almost unbroken up to the open *pá-ramo* above the timberline and the craggy summits of the Chirripó massif, the highest peaks between Guatemala and Colombia. If we did not continually pull seedlings from our lawn—which seems a pity—we would before long be so hemmed in by trees that we would enjoy no view and little sunshine. Moreover, tall trees might fall crushingly upon our house, blown over by one of the brief but violent windstorms that strike Los Cusingos at intervals of years. Accordingly, we try, not always consistently, to hold the trees as far from the house as they are high. Some are lovely when in bloom; all are interesting. In this book I tell about some of them and their interactions with birds and other creatures.

By holding the trees aloof and permitting more sunshine to enter, we encourage those unwanted, inadequately appreciated, mostly herbaceous growths commonly called weeds. Their strategies for survival where man does not want them make them no less worthy of study than such "aristocratic," highly esteemed plants as orchids and rhododendrons. Looking out of the window before which I write on this rainy November afternoon, I see several kinds that have escaped my wife's vigilance and seem worthy of a place in this book. A number of others, no less interesting, are visible from other windows.

Through intimate association with the living things around us, we reach out beyond the narrow human sphere into the larger natural world that surrounds and sustains us. We develop toward this world an attitude, often intensely personal, that with time and thought may grow into a world view or philosophy of nature; possibly, if held with fervor and capable of strongly influencing our conduct, it might be called a religion. Perhaps to have developed such a comprehensive outlook, especially if it be hopeful and sustaining rather than gloomy or despairing, is the most important outcome of long association with nature. Accordingly, it seems proper to share with the reader, along with studies of birds, plants, and other creatures, some of the thoughts that have arisen in my mind while I gazed through open windows upon tropical luxuriance, wandered through ever-verdant forests, or sat in a pensive mood beside mountain torrents.

# 1. *What Windows Reveal*

TO watch birds at their nests, I must often sit in a blind, which the British call a hide. The names are equally appropriate; the structure "blinds" the birds to my presence; it hides me from them. Made of stout brown cloth, my blind can be folded and carried in a knapsack. When I fit it around three slender poles tied together at the top, it has the form of a truncated triangular pyramid or, roughly, a three-sided wigwam, open at the top until I cover it with fronds or leafy boughs. In front it has two small rectangular windows, one above the other, each as broad as my binocular; on either side is a similar window. Each little window is covered by a flap of cloth, so that the opening can be made wide or narrow, or closed completely.

If the birds I am watching are not very shy, I may keep one or all windows fully open. If they are somewhat wary, I may open one window just wide enough to use my binocular. If they are extremely shy and observant, I peer with naked eyes through the narrowest possible slit. If the birds are very confiding, or their nest is high or distant, I may dispense with the blind and sit fully exposed, so that I might be said to have windows all around me. This is more pleasant but makes strict concentration on the nest I am studying more difficult than when I look out through only one narrow slit.

The windows in the sides of the blind give restricted views of

what is happening around me. But both through the side windows and while I have sat unconcealed, I have made incidental
observations of great interest—bonuses for my hours of patient
sitting.

Bird watchers often use a car as a blind, especially when
studying birds in open places. That birds are less shy of a big,
shiny automobile than of a person is a sad commentary upon
man's treatment of them. A house is also an excellent blind, but
has the disadvantage of not being portable. Most of our birds pay
little attention to what is happening indoors. If they obligingly
build a nest or occupy a birdhouse in full view of a window, we
could ask for no more favorable conditions for watching in comfort all that they do.

However, exceptions occur. Year after year, Garden Thrushes,
also known as Clay-colored Robins, have nested in the Caña de
India shrubs along the northern side of our house. One year their
behavior was exceptionally interesting. While we sat at breakfast
before sunrise on several mornings at the end of April, the male
thrush came and sang a few notes in the same place amid the
broad, red-and-green leaves just outside. He was evidently suggesting a nest site to his mate. Later, in this same spot, he helped
her to build their bulky, mud-lined nest, as few male Garden
Thrushes do. All this while these birds paid no attention to one
or more people watching through the wide-open window a few
yards away. Nevertheless, after the female laid her three brown-
mottled blue eggs, she became more shy. Even when I sat as far
back in the dining room as I could and watched through a partly
closed window, she would not continue to incubate. Likewise,
watching from a blind, I have noticed that, as their nesting advances, these thrushes become increasingly wary, until, when
their young are about to fly, it is sometimes hardly possible to
conceal oneself so well that they will approach their nest with
food while one watches.

Windows are the most revealing part of a blind—or a house.

The Author's Blind ▶

Obviously, they reveal to those within what is happening outside. Not so obviously, they reveal to a thoughtful observer the relationship of the inmates to the surrounding world. The width of my blind's front windows reveals the degree of wariness of the birds that I am watching. The width of the side openings indicates, among other things, how often I feel it prudent to glance around for the approach of venomous snakes in forests where they lurk.

We can learn much about social and ecological conditions by studying windows, without entering the dwellings to which they admit light and air. The narrow windows of a fortified medieval castle are signs of a turbulent society, in which the king is unable to preserve peace among his powerful subjects. The embrasures permitted defenders to aim their arrows over a wider angle, as well as admitting more light through a narrow aperture in a thick stone wall. Iron gratings at the windows on the ground floors of homes in Latin American cities reveal that thieves are feared. Unbarred or shutterless windows indicate a community where housebreakers are rare. The draperies at windows can tell us much about the people within. Hanging in ample folds of some costly stuff, they indicate wealth. Muslin or some other less expensive fabric suggests moderate means.

In addition to the thick curtains in which my mother delighted, the windows of the house in which I grew up in Maryland were equipped with more utilitarian shades, consisting of a stiff fabric rolled around a wooden rod with a spring inside it, placed at the top of the window. At the bottom of the shade was a strip of wood with a cord in the middle, for pulling the shade down as far as one desired. It did not need to be pulled up; the spring took care of that when by a touch on the string one released a catch. I cannot recall having seen such ingenious shades at tropical windows.

Besides these shades, the draperies that slid back and forth on a rod at the top when one pulled the proper string hanging beside the window, and glass windows that slid up and down in their frames, counterpoised by hidden weights so that they stayed just as far open as one wished, the windows of my childhood home had green shutters that swung out and in. They were composed of wooden slats that overlapped without touching, so that, although one could hardly see through them, they admitted air and a little light.

As though all this were not enough, in spring, when days grew warmer and the sliding curtains were taken down to be washed and stored for the summer, screens of hardware cloth that slid up and down were placed in the windows, to keep out houseflies and mosquitoes when the glass windows were left open in mild weather. The panes in these windows were single, not double with an air space between them, as where winters are more rigorous. The ecological implications of these arrangements were that we dwelt in a region of contrasting seasons, with cold, but not extremely severe, winters and hot summers. Likewise, that sanitation and drainage in our suburban community were inadequate, permitting houseflies and mosquitoes to breed.

It is probable that, square foot for square foot, the windows in this house, with all their accessories, cost considerably more than the solid walls that they interrupted. Certainly, they received much more attention, which was as it should be. The walls insulated us from our environment; the windows regulated our interactions with it, more or less efficiently excluding what we wished to keep out and admitting what we wished to enter, now increasing, now diminishing our insulation, both physical and social. Nothing is more important for any organism, animal or plant, than to have adequate control over its interactions with its environment.

The contrast between the windows of the house in which I passed my childhood and youth and those of my present abode is as great as that between the environments of these two dwellings. At all seasons, our windows at Los Cusingos are completely open when their solid wooden shutters are swung inward. We are surrounded by little that we wish to exclude; we have little

within that we wish to confine or conceal. Even at the height of
the rainy season, the outside air is never so chilly that a light
jacket does not keep us warm enough; except on afternoons at
the climax of a severe dry season, it is rarely oppressively warm.
Mosquitoes from the nearby forest, little black flies from the
river, and other blood-sucking insects are only occasionally both-
ersome, infect us with no diseases, and are never unendurable;
houseflies, those noxious carriers of filth, are extremely rare.

When we occupy a room in the daytime, the shutters are always thrown open, except for brief intervals on certain afternoons when wind would drive in rain. When we leave a room by
day, we often close the windows, chiefly to prevent an occasional
small forest bird from blundering in and dropping stains difficult
to remove on walls or furnishings (revealing that it has eaten
blue or purple berries). At night, when we light the lamps, we
close the shutters to exclude moths and other insects, as it is distressing to see them perish in the flame. To avoid this tragedy
when one occasionally finds its way into a room, we cap the lamp
chimney with wire mesh. These caps came with our Aladdin
lamps, the mantles of which are so delicate that even a moth's
wing would shatter them, and we bought a few extra ones to
place over our ordinary kerosene lamps.

When birds can see trees or shrubbery through the windows
in the opposite or adjoining walls of a room, they often try to fly
through the house. In all their experience, and that of their ancestors, they have been able to fly directly to what they can
clearly see. If glass or fine-meshed hardware cloth closes one of
these windows, they dash against it with such force that they are
often stunned or killed. The measures that are taken to prevent
such disasters reveal much about the character of the occupants
of a house surrounded by birds.

I know no better index of the benignity of an environment,
natural and social, than the way we treat our windows. If they
need panes of glass to exclude freezing air in winter and ener-
vatingly hot air in summer, the climate is one of uncomfortable

extremes. If these windows must be frequently washed, the atmosphere is laden with dust and pollutants. If they must at times be protected by stout wooden or metal shutters, violent storms are feared. If windows are barred against housebreakers, the social ambience is troubled. If they need screens to exclude noxious insects, the wider living environment is not as favorable as it might be. At the other extreme, if windows are no more than gaps in the walls, perhaps framed for adornment, that can be left wide open nearly every day in the year, the environment is as benign as one can find anywhere.

If the biblical account of Paradise is accurate, it was where guileless newly created man dwelt in perfect health and safety with nothing between his naked skin and his environment. This suggests an ecological definition of paradise as a habitat where we might thrive in such perfect harmony with our surroundings, living and lifeless, that no insulation of any kind would be needed. Although in our present troubled world you might search in vain for a place that is wholly paradisiacal, a tropical valley just high enough to take the edge off tropical heat, out of the path of hurricanes and shielded by a mountain rampart from persistent winds, covered with flourishing vegetation and not too densely populated by man, is as close to paradise as most of us can aspire to come. And if through his open windows the dweller in such a valley can watch flowering trees, lovely birds, and other creatures, what more can he reasonably desire?

## 2. *The House-Wrens' First Year*

IF anyone had suggested that in my first year in the valley of El General I would devote many hours to watching house-wrens through the window of my cabin, I might have replied somewhat as follows: "That would be a foolish waste of opportunities. I am going into a wild region with a rich variety of tropical birds about whose habits scarcely anything is known. The nests and eggs of many of them have never been seen by a naturalist. There will be tinamous, trogons, puffbirds, toucans, antbirds, manakins, cotingas, honeycreepers, tanagers, and a host of other birds, some of them belonging to species found only in southern Costa Rica and neighboring parts of Panama. These peculiarly tropical birds are those about which we need information, those that I have come so far to study. House-wrens similar to those in Costa Rica have received much attention from competent ornithologists in the north. Certainly, I cannot afford to give much time to them while so much remains to be learned about the other birds."

But most of the other birds that I so greatly desired to study were exceedingly elusive. Their nests were hard to find; and when, after long searching, I discovered one, it was likely to be far above my reach, or it would be destroyed by some predatory animal before I could learn much about it. The house-wrens, on the contrary, lived so close to me that I could not avoid paying some attention to them. Little by little, I found myself spending more time with them; and soon they were claiming more of the precious hours of my first nesting season in Costa Rica than I had intended to spare for them. But I had no reason to regret the time that I devoted to the wrens. Few of the many birds that I have studied in a half-century in tropical America have afforded me more amusement and instruction. With scarcely any have I become so intimate.

House-wrens spread over the Western Hemisphere from Canada to Tierra del Fuego. All are so similar that some ornithologists place them in the same species. However, there are good reasons for retaining the older classification, which recognizes several species. The Northern House-Wren breeds over most of the United States and much of Canada and migrates into Mexico in winter. The Southern House-Wren breeds from southeastern Mexico to the southern end of South America, and in the Lesser Antilles. It is permanently resident over most of this vast range. In the high mountains of Mexico, between the northern and the southern species, dwells a third member of this group, the Brown-throated Wren. Slightly less closely related are several species of wrens of the genus *Troglodytes* that inhabit the mountain forests of Middle and South America.

Southern House-Wrens are small, sharp-billed, brown birds that in plumage so closely resemble the well-known house-wrens of the north that only a keen birdwatcher can distinguish them, except perhaps by their songs. It is just this close resemblance of the Southern to the Northern house-wrens that makes the contrasts in their life histories so instructive to the naturalist. Many of the differences between these two closely related species, especially the smaller broods and more closely knit family life of the tropical wren, appear to be caused by the fact that it lives in the same area throughout the year, whereas its northern cousin undertakes migratory journeys that disrupt family ties and expose it to many dangers.

I was not surprised to find a pair of Southern House-Wrens around my thatched cabin beside the Río Buena Vista, for nearly

every dwelling that I had visited in seven years of wandering through Central America had its pair of wrens. I had found them in new clearings in the forest as well as in districts that had long been cultivated, in arid regions no less than in those of high rainfall, by the seacoast as well as high in the mountains. They accepted the rude hut of a squatter in the wilderness as readily as the splendid mansion of a prosperous planter. The only dwelling in Central America where I had spent much time without finding these hardy, adaptable birds was more than 9,000 feet above sea level in Guatemala.

The food of the house-wrens about my cabin consisted almost wholly of small insects, caterpillars, and spiders, which they hunted in the fruit trees growing in the dooryard, in the weedy pastures that bordered it, in my neighbor's garden, and in the densely tangled thicket across the rocky, grassy cart-road that passed in front. They liked nothing better than to find a pile of brush, or of stones, and to creep through it from end to end, searching every part for the tiny creatures with six, eight, or more legs that lurked in such places. They often entered a building, where all was quiet and promised safety, to peer into every cranny and crevice beneath the roof, looking for the small invertebrate creatures that were sure to be hiding there. Sometimes they even climbed up the trunks of trees with rough bark, ascending somewhat sideways, rather than upright like a woodpecker or a creeper, and plucked spiders or insects from the crevices. On the ground they either hopped with feet together or advanced with a few slow, walking steps.

While I sat writing, or rested on my cot gazing upward, I sometimes saw one of the wrens fly into the cabin through the open spaces beneath the eaves. Then, if I were careful not to move, I could watch the little brown bird explore the underside of the roof, clinging adroitly to the sugarcane leaves here and there, often upside down, while it sought the spiders, cockroaches, and other insects that hid among them. Often the wren

◀ Southern House-Wren

would pass across the whole cabin and leave at the other end; but if I made a sudden movement, it would quickly dart out through the nearest opening.

One evening, while I sat at supper on the porch in the early dusk, I heard a peculiar scratching and rustling among the leaves of the thatch above me. I could see nothing, and in less than a minute the noise stopped. The next evening, at about the same time, I heard the same rustling in the same place. Apparently, whatever made the sound was on the upper side of the roof; but before I could run out to see what it was, it had vanished. On the following evening, I watched the roof from the ground in front of the cabin. When the light was fading, a small brown bird flew around the corner of the house, alighted on the edge of the roof, and peered around cautiously to see whether it was safe. When it noticed me standing off in the dooryard, watching, it became alarmed and showed its annoyance by sharp, scolding *churr*'s and uneasy fidgeting. I retreated almost to the fence and continued to watch through my binocular. After a few minutes, the wren, reassured, crept up beneath the leaves near the edge of the roof and vanished. There it remained until, soon after the following dawn, I saw it fly out from the same spot.

This wren slept every night in nearly the same place in the thatch. Every evening it retired at the same time, almost to the minute by my watch, so that I never had to wait long for its arrival. On some evenings, it flew directly into its nook between the leaves; on others, it had trouble getting settled. For a minute or more, it crept over the sloping, uneven surface of the roof, before it found a comfortable cranny among the leaves and tucked itself away.

After watching for a few mornings, I concluded that the wren who slept in my roof was the female of the pair that lived about my cabin. The two sexes were so alike in size and plumage that I could distinguish them only by their voices. I knew that the wren who slept in the thatch was the female because her nearest approach to a song was a low, rapid twittering, sometimes followed by a slight, clear trill, making a little refrain that was pleasant to hear. She delivered these notes in response to the full, richly varied songs that her mate poured forth at dawn, as soon as he had flown from his sleeping place somewhere not far off—I had not yet discovered where. Like many other wrens, Southern House-Wrens live in pairs throughout the year. When the male sang, the female's responsive twittering was her way of acknowledging that he was her nuptial partner.

I was eager to learn where the male slept, but he was so secretive at nightfall that this was not easy. Near my cabin grew a few banana plants, left by a former occupant. One evening, a few weeks after I discovered the female sleeping in the roof, I happened to see the male fly to these plants and vanish. On the next evening, he did the same, giving me a clue. After much watching and waiting, and several games of hide-and-seek with the wren, I saw him slip into the center of a bunch of green bananas, to stay for the night.

I had already found house-wrens sleeping in the most varied situations, including little niches and pockets in steeply cut banks by the roadside, old woodpeckers' holes high in trees, and beneath the eaves of houses with corrugated iron roofs, but I had never before found one sleeping in a thatched roof, or in a bunch of bananas. Although I had discovered nests of several kinds of birds, including doves, flycatchers, and tanagers, on or in bunches of bananas hanging in plantations, I had never known a bird to roost in one. Such a bunch seemed an excellent dormitory for the wren, who was wholly invisible among the dozens of skyward-pointing green fingers, where he hung, snug and safe for the night, above reach of the tallest man.

As long as the fruit remained hard and green, the wren was not likely to be disturbed. After it began to ripen, its fragrance might attract such nocturnal visitors as raccoons, coatis, opossums, and other climbing quadrupeds, who, while feasting on

the fruit, might find the sleeping wren and include flesh in their meal—if the bird did not awake and fly out before an animal could reach him. However, in this small dooryard plantation, the wren was not permitted to jeopardize his life by sleeping amid ripe bananas, because, as soon as it approached maturity, the green bunch was cut and carried into the house to ripen. If he lost one of these hanging dormitories, he could easily find another, for he seemed not to care in which of several bunches he slept. If he noticed me watching one in the evening, he would fly to another into which he could slip undetected. This elusiveness made it difficult for me to discover where he hid away. In a week, I found him sleeping in three different bunches.

Since these two wrens lived so close to me, I thought it would be pleasant and neighborly to give them proper names. After long pondering, I called the songful male "Singing-Wren." His mate, who sometimes answered him with a simple little verse that sounded like *twit twit twit twit*, was named "Twittering-Wren."

One evening in February, when I watched too closely to see Singing-Wren retire into a bunch of bananas, he deserted the plantation and flew to the cabin, where, in the waning light, he crept under the cane leaves of the roof and remained out of sight. I admired his caution and adaptability in changing from one kind of dormitory to another very different one. Singing-Wren was far from stupid!

On the following evenings, Singing-Wren did not return to sleep in the bunches of bananas, but continued to pass his nights in the roof where Twittering-Wren slept. About this time, cows were turned into the enclosure where the bananas grew, and they proceeded to eat the plants, including their green fruits, their huge leaves, and their massive, but soft and woodless, "trunks," formed by tightly overlapping leaf bases. Soon only low stumps of the stately plants remained, making it impossible for Singing-Wren to return to his former dormitories. His sleeping place in the thatch was at the northern end, four or five yards from his

◀ Singing-Wren in the Bunch of Green Bananas Where He Slept

mate's nook near the southern end. At this season, he usually retired to rest a few minutes earlier than she did, sometimes churring noisily as he hopped over the roof to his preferred spot and crawled under the cane leaves.

I could never see these wrens while they slept, whether in my roof or in a bunch of bananas. In the highlands of Guatemala, a few years earlier, I had found Southern House-Wrens sleeping in niches, six or eight inches deep and too narrow to admit my hand, in steep, bare banks above a long, winding road cut into the mountainside. Often I peeped in at these wrens with a flashlight, just before dawn, so that if they awoke and flew out, they would not have long to wait for daylight in the cold mountain air. They always rested with their tails toward the outside. Their heads and wings were hidden amid their outfluffed plumage, which made them appear twice their usual size. Only a barred brown tail, projecting toward me from each little ball of down, could be clearly distinguished. At the bases of the feathers on the back were many whitish spots, which are concealed when the wren flattens its plummage, as in the daytime. After a walk through chilling mountain air, over fields white with frost, it was easy to imagine that the wren had flown into its sleeping niche through a flurry of snowflakes, which remained unmelted in its plumage.

### The First Nesting

One day in March, I found a calabash vine draping over a roadside tree. The owner readily gave me two of the fat, brown gourds that hung from it. They would make excellent bird houses for Singing-Wren and his mate, who, I supposed, would soon undertake to raise a brood. Although house-wrens can pass through a round hole barely an inch in diameter, they have trouble passing the materials for their nests through such a narrow doorway. To ease their task of filling the gourds, I cut into the side of each a rectangular opening, one and an eighth inches high and twice as wide, which would help them to take in sticks held crosswise in their bills. I carefully cleaned out the big, flat, white seeds and the dry pulp around them. Then I attached one of the smooth-walled bird houses to the front wall of the cabin, below the spot where Twittering-Wren slept in the roof. The other was tied in an orange tree where I could watch it from my window. The trunk and lower limbs of this tree bristled with sharp thorns, many as long as my little finger, which would make it more diffi-cult for small animals to climb up and plunder the nest.

I was far from confident that the wrens would accept my gourds when less conspicuous sites were available for their nest. Most often I had found Southern House-Wrens nesting beneath the eaves of buildings with corrugated iron roofs. While I dwelt in a narrow clearing in the forests of Panama, in a cabin propped high above the ground on posts, a wren built her nest beneath the floor, on the projecting edge of a foundation beam. On a beautiful Guatemalan coffee plantation, a wren nested in the hollow end of a stout bamboo crosspiece of a garden trellis. A neighbor told me that once, when he had left his saddlebags hanging for a long time unused on an outside wall of his house, a *zoterré*, as he called the house-wren, built a nest in them. One day, when he was preparing for a journey, he took the saddlebags from the wall and found four eggs in one of the pockets. Rather than break up the nest, he replaced the bags on the wall and left them there until the young wrens flew. On a Costa Rican planta-tion, house-wrens lined with feathers a bulky nest with a side en-trance from which much bigger Banded-backed Wrens had re-cently lost their nestlings to a snake, and laid their eggs in this borrowed structure.

Another strange situation for a house-wren's nest was be-neath a tall, cylindrical rain gauge standing in a shallow box on a post beside the office of a great coffee plantation. The planta-tion's timekeeper, who had noticed the wrens going in and out of the box, lifted up the bronze cylinder to show me the nest, which cradled three tiny, pink, newly hatched nestlings. The three pronglike feet of the rain gauge, between which the cup of fine sticks and straws had been built, were so close together that it appeared impossible to replace it without setting one of the feet upon a nestling. Because the box was so narrow, we could not replace the babies in their nest after the cylinder had been set above it. The man who had removed the gauge refused to lower it over the nestlings and left the delicate operation to me. I tried hard to replace the cylinder without injuring a nestling, but I could not see whether I had succeeded.

Farther from human habitations, house-wrens rear their families in holes and crevices in fence posts and trees, rarely as high as sixty feet; in tunnels beneath densely creeping pasture grass; and in shallow niches in steep earthen banks. The variety of their nest sites is as great as the variety of their sleeping places; wherever one finds them roosting, one may also expect to discover their nests. In Central America I have found them breeding from the warm lowlands up to 8,500 feet, where nights are often frosty.

The wrens who slept in my roof chose the gourd in the orange tree. While I was absent on a trip across the mountains, they filled the fat bottom of the gourd with fine sticks, straws, weed stems, and similar materials. Not satisfied with filling the capacious lower half of the gourd, they had continued to pile up the twigs against the rear wall. In the top of this mass of coarse materials, at the back of the gourd, they left a cuplike hollow, which they lined with fine rootlets and fibers, above which they placed downy feathers from my neighbor's chickens. Here Twittering-Wren laid her eggs, so high above the doorway that I could neither see them nor count them with my finger tips. I could not even view them in the little mirror, pivoted on the end of a stiff wire, that I used to see the contents of woodpeckers' holes and other nests in cavities, while they were illuminated by a small electric bulb connected by insulated wire with a flashlight. I surmised that Twittering-Wren had laid four eggs, the number that Southern House-Wrens most frequently lay in Central America, although often they lay only three, and rarely five.

Their eggs are densely speckled with brown, cinnamon, or pinkish cinnamon on a whitish ground, sometimes rather uniformly over the whole surface, sometimes chiefly in a wreath around the thicker end. They average 17.9 by 13.4 millimeters.

By the end of the first week of April, Twittering-Wren was clearly incubating, with no help from her partner, who remained nearby and sang profusely through much of the day. He had at least a half-dozen different songs, all bright and sweet and gladsome, but so swift and musically complex that I could not find words to help me remember them, the way I could paraphrase the verses of many of the other birds around my cabin. At intervals Singing-Wren went to the gourd to look through the doorway at his partner sitting on the nest. When she heard him singing not far away, Twittering-Wren moved forward to stick her head through the doorway, where she lingered, quietly looking from side to side, for a minute or two, before she drew back inside to resume incubation. When she emerged to search for food, he accompanied her; and often he followed her into the orange tree when she returned to her nest, sometimes with a downy chicken feather to tuck under her eggs. Unlike the Rufous-browed Wren of the highlands of northern Central America, and male birds of many other families, Singing-Wren was never seen to feed his partner.

Eight feet above the gourd in the orange tree, a pair of Blue Tanagers, working together, built a neat open cup, with thick walls of fibrous materials and a soft lining of fine fibers. Both sexes had blue-gray bodies and bright blue wings and tails. While Twittering-Wren incubated in the gourd, the female tanager warmed two pale blue-gray eggs, heavily blotched and spotted all over with brown. Although the male tanager never incubated, he was no less attentive to his mate than Singing-Wren was, accompanying her when she flew away to seek food and escorting her back to her nest, then perching beside her to sing while she settled on the eggs. His voice was not nearly as rich and powerful as Singing-Wren's; often it was almost squeaky. Nevertheless, his long, varied songs were sweetly appealing, like those that a little child sings in a quavering voice. Occasionally, when Singing-Wren proclaimed his presence in fuller tones, the bigger tanager flew at him and made him retreat. Most of the time, however, these two so different birds shared the same tree without conflict, although neither would tolerate another singing male of his own kind.

### The April-Wrens

In mid-April, Twittering-Wren hatched her eggs. It was as impossible for me to see the nestlings as it had been to see the eggs; but I was certain that nestlings were present, because the wrens now carried tiny insects and spiders into the gourd. Singing-Wren took his full share in bringing food to the babies, but their mother alone brooded them. Soon the chorus of soft peeps that greeted the parents each time one of them arrived at the doorway with food was additional proof that there were nestlings within. As they grew older, their soft, infantine *peep* changed to a harsher, louder cry. After enough feathers had sprouted to keep the nestlings warm, Twittering-Wren ceased to cover them by day. Then both she and her mate devoted all their time to hunting for food for themselves and their young, who had appetites that the united efforts of the parents seemed unable to satisfy. As long as they remained in the nest, Twittering-Wren slept in the gourd with them. As while she had incubated, Singing-Wren continued to lodge in the roof, about twenty feet away.

Early in May, the young wrens left the gourd. To my regret, I was not present to witness their departure. On the first night after their exit, their mother slept alone in the gourd. I did not learn where the nestlings passed the night, but apparently the only reason why they did not return to the gourd was that they still flew too weakly to reach it. On the following evening, the second after their emergence from the nest, they entered the gourd with Twittering-Wren.

Next morning, I watched the wrens begin their day's activities. Twittering-Wren awoke early and stuck her head through the doorway while the light was so dim that she failed to notice me standing only a few feet away. When she saw that day had scarcely arrived—even the Orange-billed Nightingale-Thrushes, who always started to sing much earlier than the wrens arose, had not yet broken their nocturnal silence—she withdrew into the gourd. There she remained until her mate flew from the roof where he slept and greeted the new day with his cheerful song, whereupon she immediately came out to join him. At this point, I thought it better to enter the cabin and watch from the window. Singing-Wren looked into the gourd, then flew off and promptly found an insect that he brought to a fledgling. Meanwhile, the young wrens inside proclaimed that they were alive and awake by their loud cries, which they uttered almost continuously and intensified when their father appeared in the doorway.

Nearly half an hour after their mother had left them, the first of the young wrens moved forward to the doorway, hesitated briefly, then flew boldly out to join its parents. Two more fledglings followed at short intervals. The three young wrens closely resembled their parents in plumage, but their tails were much shorter, and they had prominent yellow flanges at the corners of their mouths.

All day the fledglings followed their parents through the weedy pastures, constantly pleading for food. To satisfy those young appetites was a never-ending task for the hard-working adults. If I, a cat, a dog, a chicken, or any other creature that appeared dangerous came near the young wrens, the parents scolded with loud, harsh notes and led their family farther off among the bushes. Singing-Wren and his partner were so cautious and anxious for the safety of their young that they did not permit me to see much of them throughout the day.

As evening approached, I sat at the window, where, without disturbing them, I could watch the parents put the youngsters to bed. Soon after five o'clock, the wrens approached through the tall weeds beyond the orange tree, the fledglings buzzing, the parents making bubbling sounds, and Singing-Wren from time to time breaking into song. First, Twittering-Wren flew into the orange tree and entered the gourd, as though to make sure that no dangerous intruder lurked within and it was safe for the fledglings. Then she flew back to the young wrens, who had appeared at the edge of the short grass beside the cabin, and led them all into the orange tree. Although they had been out of the nest less than three full days, they could fly fairly well. Their mother went in and out of the gourd several times, while their father flew to the doorway and clung to the sill; both were showing the young wrens what they should do. Following their parents' example, two of the fledglings easily flew through the wide entrance from a convenient twig a foot or so in front of it. The third fledgling hung back, as though it found the flight to the gourd too difficult. The parents, still bubbling and churring excitedly, went again to look in; and one of them, clinging to the sill, fluttered its wings as it viewed its brood safe again within the sheltering nest.

Although the two in the gourd were not neglected, the fledgling outside, nearest the source of supply, fared best. Becoming hungrier, those inside looked out, stretching their necks through the doorway, until one hopped out; but with a little coaxing by its parents, it promptly returned. After a while, the third fledgling flew toward the doorway, but it was so unsteady on the wing that it missed the opening in the gourd's smooth side and alighted on a branch beyond and below it. Several other attempts to reach the entrance were equally unsuccessful. Nevertheless, the young bird, never discouraged, tried again and again, until it gained a toe-hold on the sill and pulled itself inside to join its nest mates.

Some of the orange tree's many thorns were nearly as long as the young wrens. I marveled that while flying and hopping among them in their weak, faltering fashion, they did not put out an eye, or otherwise injure themselves on the sharp points. However, they seemed never to suffer the slightest harm from them. Did they escape injury by chance, or because some pre-cocious instinct prompted them to be careful? Or was it rather that they weighed so little that, even if they did impinge against one of the points, the impact was too slight to cause serious damage, except perhaps to an eye? In arid regions, one sees wrens and other birds flitting among cacti and thorny bushes with an apparent lack of precautions to avoid the innumerable spines that excites the wonder of people, who can hardly touch such plants with impunity.

After all three of their fledglings were safe within the gourd, both parents continued tirelessly to bring them spiders, fat cater-pillars, and mature insects. Each arrival of a parent was greeted by a fresh outburst from the young. Their parents also cleaned the nest, carrying away the fledglings' droppings, each of which was still enclosed in a white, gelatinous sac that made it easy to pick up. Thus, in the last hour of the day, the fledglings were treated, and acted, just as though they were still helpless nest-lings who had never flown. Nest life continued as though it had not been interrupted by days in the outer world.

As the light grew dimmer, the parents ceased to bring food to the nest but went to the weedy pasture to find a little supper for themselves. Finally, nearly an hour after the first two fledglings had entered the gourd, Twittering-Wren joined them for the night. A few minutes later, with a final burst of song, Singing-Wren flew into the thatch of my roof, where he had slept so long.

The scene that I had just witnessed reminded me of another that I had watched three years earlier, high in the Guatemalan mountains. I had studied a family of Banded-backed Wrens, who nested in an oak tree in a bushy pasture, where they had built two bulky, roundish nests. Each had a thick roof of sheep's wool, moss, straws, and other materials that would shed rainwater. In the side was a wide doorway, shielded by a projecting roof. In the newer of these nests, five eggs were laid and three nestlings were raised. The three young wrens were attended by three grown ones, their parents and a helper.

After the young Banded-backed Wrens left their nest in the oak tree, they were led to sleep in the older nest on the opposite side of the crown, not by the parents but by their helper, who may have been the fledglings' elder brother or sister, hatched in the preceding year. It was extremely difficult for the young wrens, still shaky on the wing, to fly into the nest, which did not, like the gourd in the orange tree, have a convenient perch in front of the doorway. Their guardian flew back and forth, back and forth, between the entrance and a branch below it, showing them how to reach it, and by its own repeated example encouraging them to try again and again—just as Twittering-Wren and her mate went many times to the opening in the gourd to urge their fledglings to enter. After many failures, the young Banded-backed Wrens succeeded in following the example of their patient instructor and gaining the doorway. Later in the evening, when the parents and their assistant joined the three fledglings for the night, each was greeted by a chorus of hungry cries, for fledglings of all kinds have insatiable appetites.

The house-wrens gradually developed a routine for settling down in the evening. As soon as the family flew into the orange tree, Twittering-Wren would enter the gourd, while Singing-Wren sang on his favorite perch, a foot in front of the doorway. Twittering-Wren promptly emerged, and both parents flew to the entrance and left it again, while the young birds flew in, which after a few days they did promptly and easily. After the fledglings were safe within the gourd, the parents returned to the pasture to hunt supper for themselves. Twittering-Wren always joined her young before Singing-Wren was ready to retire. He looked in at his family, paused to sing to them from his perch near the doorway, then flew to the roof and crept out of sight.

In the morning, Singing-Wren was the first to arise. The moment that he emerged from the cane leaves, he announced his appearance by singing, sometimes on the end of the ridge-pole nearest his sleeping place, sometimes in a shrub in the dooryard. His first songs were often low and subdued, suggesting that he was still drowsy; but, as he repeated them over and over, his ardor increased, until he poured forth his loudest and brightest verses unstintedly. Occasionally, Twittering-Wren darted from the gourd as soon as she heard the opening notes of her mate's song, but usually she lingered with her fledglings three or four minutes longer. Soon after her departure, the young wrens joined their parents in the open and received breakfast.

As the fledglings grew older, they left the gourd earlier in the morning. Two weeks after their first flight, they delayed for only a few minutes after their mother's exit. Similarly, their time for retiring gradually became later, except on dark and rainy afternoons, when they would seek the sheltering gourd earlier than usual so as to remain snug and dry. Another change that I noticed as the days passed was that they received less food in the gourd, both before their departure in the morning and after their return in the evening. After they had been out of the nest for ten days, the parents rarely brought meals to them in the gourd, but fed them almost entirely while all were together in the open.

In the evening of the juveniles' twelfth day out of the nest, the parents neglected to lead them into the gourd. As a result, they stayed out twenty minutes later than on the preceding evening. Finally, becoming drowsy, two of the young wrens sought their dormitory spontaneously, without urging or guidance by their elders. The third juvenile delayed with its parents in the yard until Singing-Wren went to sing before the doorway, whereupon it entered the gourd to join its siblings.

A few days later, the young wrens went hungry to sleep. In the hard rain that had fallen continuously through the afternoon, their parents could not find enough food. As usual, two entered first, while the third delayed outside with the parents. Instead of waiting silently for the rest of the family to join them, as they now did on most evenings, they complained with much churring. When the third juvenile came to the gourd, the two within, perhaps mistaking it in the dim light for a parent, eagerly stretched forward gaping mouths, which blocked the doorway and delayed the entry of the third. Twice, in their eagerness for nourishment, the young wrens hopped out of the gourd when a parent passed in front; but neither their father nor their mother brought them a morsel after they retired. To give all that they could to their young that afternoon, the parents had probably deprived themselves of food, and were now trying to find a little for themselves before they went to rest. But all the rain that had fallen on that gloomy afternoon failed to dampen the buoyant spirits of Singing-Wren, who, as always, sang joyously in front of the gourd before he went to sleep in the dripping roof.

I passed many happy evenings in my cabin watching the wrens go to rest. It occurred to me that it would be convenient to have a desk in front of the window, where I could read or write until their voices announced their approach, then make notes on what they did. Since my room was so small, I hinged the "desk," a simple board, to the window-sill, so that when not in use it could be dropped against the wall, where it would occupy no space. On no two days did the wrens enter the gourd in exactly the same way; every evening afforded a different spectacle. Sometimes the young wrens were restless and went in and out repeatedly, until in the deepening dusk they were drowsy enough to settle down and sleep. One evening they stayed out late, dust-bathing with their mother on a bare spot in the yard. Then all three started toward the gourd as though moved by a common impulse. Arriving at the doorway together, the three tried to push through at the same time, which resulted in a jam. One perforce stayed behind until the other two had entered.

Throughout the month of May, the three juveniles continued to follow their parents on their daily rounds through the weedy pastures and bushy thickets surrounding the cabin. Before they had been out of the nest for two weeks, they began to forage for themselves, at first without much success. However, their skill increased so rapidly that by early June, when they were about six weeks old and had been in the open for twenty-six days, they were so well able to take care of themselves that their parents began preparations for a second brood. To distinguish these young wrens from those that I expected would soon enter the family, I called them the April-Wrens, from the month when they hatched.

### Expulsion of the April-Wrens

Although the adult wrens had stuffed the gourd very full in March, before their first nesting, they now carried still more material into it, building a new nest above the old one. Both Singing-Wren and Twittering-Wren hunted rootlets, fine twigs, and bits of fibrous material and took them into the gourd, but Twittering-Wren brought far more than her partner. He seemed so excited by what was happening that he was a poor helper, who could do little more than sing and sing and sing. Frequently he went to the doorway with empty bill, to peer in and watch his mate arrange the materials there, and even when he did a little work, he continued his songs, managing to pour forth sweet notes past the stick that he held in his bill as he approached the gourd.

The three April-Wrens still followed their parents and often begged for food with infantine cries and quivering wings, but they rarely received anything while the adults were at work. While their parents were busy with the new nest, they remained near, most of the time hunting insects in the grass, occasionally visiting the orange tree to see what was happening there. Anastasio Alfaro, a Costa Rican naturalist, had seen a young house-wren take straws to the nest that its parents were building for their second brood. Although I watched closely for the April-Wrens to help, I never saw any nest material in their bills.

When she began to prepare the nest for her second brood, Twittering-Wren went to sleep in the roof, as she had done before I provided the gourds. The three April-Wrens continued to pass the nights in the gourd without her. In the evening, Singing-Wren would perch in front of the doorway to sing profusely while the juveniles went in, and then go to look inside. Sometimes their mother entered with them, only to emerge and seek her place in the thatch.

Twittering-Wren slept in the roof for only a few nights, while the nest was being renovated. As soon as this task was finished, and the new nest was softly lined with chicken feathers, she returned to pass the nights in the gourd with the April-Wrens. In a few more days, she laid the first egg of her second set. Now, in early June, the weather was wet and gloomy. Gray clouds hung low over the deep, narrow valley of the Río Buena Vista; rain fell long and hard every afternoon; and often, too, the morning sky was darkly overcast and drizzly. Garden Thrushes, the chief choristers of the valley, had ceased to sing; White-throated Thrushes did so sparingly; and birds of many other kinds fell silent. But no amount of bad weather could depress Singing-Wren, who even on the darkest, gloomiest evenings perched in front of the gourd that his family had just entered and poured forth his cheeriest tunes for many minutes.

In spite of the fresh material that the wrens had heaped above their original nest, the new one was lower than the first had been. The sticks and straws in the bottom had become more closely packed, and the shrinkage in the lower layers was greater than the increase at the top. Now, by forcing my hand into the doorway as far as it would go and stretching my middle finger as far as I could, I felt the smooth surfaces of three eggs. The downy feathers on which they rested curled over them, making them difficult to glimpse in my little mirror when I lighted the gourd with an electric bulb.

Even after she began to incubate her new set of eggs, Twittering-Wren permitted the April-Wrens to sleep in the gourd with her. This surprised me, because most incubating birds are alone with their eggs through the night. Even in the case of the Banded-backed Wren, one of the most sociable of all the wrens, I found only the female passing the night with her eggs, while her mate and helpers lodged together in a neighboring nest. Now, instead of being the last to enter the gourd in the evening, Twittering-Wren was the first, for she returned from the day's final recess, when she found her supper, before the April-Wrens arrived.

On June 26 the three eggs hatched, and Twittering-Wren carried the three empty, speckled shells from the gourd. The tiny nestlings bore a few thin tufts of grayish down that quite failed to cover their pink skins. Their eyes were tightly closed. They were called the June-Wrens.

Everything moved along peacefully until the day when the eggs hatched. On that evening, the first two April-Wrens entered the gourd quietly, as usual. As the third flew to the orange tree, it was pursued by Singing-Wren, who seemed to be trying to drive it away. The young bird eluded its father and slipped into the gourd. Singing-Wren sang just once in front of the doorway, then entered the gourd—the first time I saw him do so at this late hour. His purpose seemed to be to drive out the juvenile whom he had been chasing. How I longed to see what was happening within those smooth, brown walls! After watching intently for a minute or two, I saw Singing-Wren emerge alone and cling to the sill. He had failed to expel the third April-Wren but would not admit defeat. While he hung in front of the gourd, an April-Wren came to the doorway and pecked at him. Singing-Wren pecked back, and for a while they fought. The bird on the outside, at a disadvantage, was soon forced to drop away from the sill.

On the twig in front of the gourd, where every evening he had perched to sing to his family, Singing-Wren rested for many minutes in sullen silence, while the shadows grew black around him. At last he flew up to the roof where he slept, but after a minute he returned to perch in front of the gourd. He went again to the roof, only to come once more to the orange tree. Apparently, the situation distressed him so much that he could not rest, for it was well past his usual bedtime. Finally, in the deepening dusk, he flew for the third time to the roof, where in silence he crept up among the cane leaves.

Probably the April-Wren whom Singing-Wren tried to expel was a young male, now becoming old enough to be regarded as a rival. In spite of the bold front that he had put up, on the following evening the third April-Wren did not approach the gourd, and the next evening he also failed to appear. I surmised that during the day Singing-Wren had driven away the young bird, who in the open could not resist his father as he had done in the gourd.

Now only two April-Wrens slept in the gourd with their mother and three little brothers and sisters. Nevertheless, Singing-Wren seemed not to be satisfied. In the evening, after the two juveniles had joined their mother inside, he came as usual to perch in front of the gourd, but, instead of singing as he had always done, he rested there in silence. He went to look in the doorway, then returned to his perch, where he sat for a while longer without uttering a sound. At length, he went to the roof, without ever a parting note for his mate.

I was curious to learn whether the April-Wrens would feed the nestlings with whom they were so closely associated. I knew that among Common Gallinules or Moorhens, Groove-billed Anis, Barn Swallows, and bluebirds of several species, the young of early broods sometimes give food to later broods in the same year. I had watched unmated Banded-backed Wrens and Brown Jays, apparently yearlings, help parents to attend their young— and similar cooperation has since been reported of birds of the most diverse families all over the world. Would the April-Wrens be equally helpful? I spent many hours sitting at the window, watching the parent wrens carry food into the gourd, without ever seeing an April-Wren visit it in the daytime.

While I looked for the April-Wrens to feed the June-Wrens, I kept a record of how many times each parent brought food. Almost always Singing-Wren paused to sing on the clothes-line, or in the orange tree, as he approached the gourd with something in his bill; or else, after feeding the nestlings, he sang before he flew out of sight. Twittering-Wren always came and left in silence, which served to distinguish her from her tuneful mate. But even if Singing-Wren went to the nest silently, as he occasionally did, I could recognize him by the large amount of yellow on his lower mandible. Twittering-Wren's bill was wholly black.

In three hours of the morning when the June-Wrens were nine days old, they were fed seventy times, which was twenty-three meals for each of them. Singing-Wren brought food thirty-six times, Twittering-Wren thirty times, and four times I was not alert enough to distinguish which of them flew rapidly into the gourd with food. Twittering-Wren brooded her nestlings for intervals of a few minutes. They were much bigger than when they had hatched, but their skins were covered only by bristly pinfeathers.

In the evening of the following day, the two April-Wrens alighted in the orange tree near the gourd and perched for several minutes in tense, motionless attitudes. Twittering-Wren was already inside with the nestlings. After a while, an April-Wren flew to the entrance, only to dart away more rapidly than it had come. Then the second young wren advanced to the doorway. Their mother, on the inside, moved forward to peck vigorously at the juvenile, who returned thrust for thrust with spirit. Soon, to avoid the full force of Twittering-Wren's pecks, the April-Wren, still clinging to the sill, leaned far backward, then retreated to a nearby perch. The April-Wrens were now old enough to find shelters for themselves, and their mother would tolerate them in the gourd no longer.

The parents' long indulgence had strengthened the young wrens' attachment to the gourd. They refused to be evicted from the dry shelter where, as nestlings and then as fledglings and adolescents, they had slept for nearly three months. Again and again, the April-Wren flew to the doorway to exchange pecks with its mother. Once it almost pushed inside, only to be forced back into the opening.

While this bout was raging, Singing-Wren arrived, perched on his favorite branch, and sang profusely. While the young wren, clinging tenaciously to the doorsill, parried its mother's thrusts, he dashed at it from the rear. This double attack made the April-Wren flee. After its departure, Singing-Wren went to look into the gourd, perhaps to see whether the nestlings had been injured in the scuffle. Probably mistaking her mate for an

April-Wren in the dim light, Twittering-Wren greeted him with pecks no less vigorous than those that she had just showered upon the juvenile.

The April-Wrens were so determined to sleep in their customary shelter that, despite harsh rebuffs, they returned again and again to try to force their way in. Daylight was fading fast; it was well past the wrens' usual time for settling down, and difficult for me to follow their movements amid the dark foliage of the orange tree. Singing-Wren had already gone to his cranny in the roof, but still the young wrens struggled to gain admission to the gourd. As dusk deepened, the mother's opposition seemed to weaken, until in the end both young wrens succeeded in entering, to sink into peaceful sleep close beside the parent with whom they had so recently engaged in fierce combat. Six wrens slept in the gourd: the mother, three helpless offspring that she shielded with tender care, and two older ones, whom she had tried to drive from their sheltering birthplace into a hostile or indifferent world.

Next morning the two April-Wrens emerged from the gourd while the light was still too dim for house-wrens normally to be abroad, before their father's song had announced his rising. Doubtless, when they awoke at daybreak and remembered the enmity of the mother who rested so close beside them, they felt unsafe and fled. Or possibly she had already resumed her attacks upon them.

That evening I watched to see whether the April-Wrens would come again to·sleep in the gourd. As night approached, Twittering-Wren brought a final meal to the nestlings and stayed to brood them. Soon an April-Wren flew into the orange tree and advanced stealthily to the doorway, only to dash away in a trice with its mother pursuing it. This time she did not merely oppose the young wren at the entrance, but continued to chase it quite out of the tree. Then she returned to her nestlings. After a short while, an April-Wren (I could not tell whether it was the one who had just been driven away) came to enter the gourd, but at the threshold its courage failed and, without trying to push in, it darted away more hurriedly than it had approached. Finally, when it was almost dark, a single wren flew to the gourd and crept in without opposition, to remain through the night. Perhaps, after a strenuous day, Twittering-Wren had already fallen asleep.

After this, the April-Wrens did not try to force their way into the gourd, where they so obviously were no longer welcome. A month earlier, when the parent wrens were preparing the nest for another brood, I had moved the second gourd from the wall of the cabin, where it had been consistently ignored, to a place in the orange tree a few inches below the occupied gourd. I thought that, since the nesting gourd was destined for younger and tenderer occupants, the April-Wrens, or Singing-Wren himself, might sleep in the other gourd in its new situation. But here, too, they all neglected it. Even when they were ready to struggle so hard to enter the gourd where they had grown up, the April-Wrens showed no interest in the other so close by, although it offered a safe, dry lodging. Perhaps it did not attract them because it was quite bare. I could not learn where the April-Wrens slept after their eviction from the nesting gourd.

On the evening following that on which Twittering-Wren had driven the April-Wren from the orange tree, a single wren joined her in the gourd unopposed. I suspected that the dimly seen figure was Singing-Wren, whom I had not seen go to the roof. Watching as the night ended, I saw a wren fly from the gourd and sing in a neighboring shrub. Then I was certain that Singing-Wren had departed from the male house-wren's almost invariable custom of sleeping apart from his incubating or brooding mate. Probably he did so the better to keep the April-Wrens out.

Through the last week of the June-Wrens' nestlinghood, they were accompanied by both parents every night. These young wrens, now growing apace and becoming well feathered, became increasingly clamorous for food. Singing-Wren and Twittering-Wren toiled tirelessly from dawn to nightfall to satisfy the huge appetites of the growing nestlings. Singing-Wren lost much of his former ebullience; he seemed too busy to sing. After leaving the gourd at daybreak, he delivered only one or two songs before he began his serious day's work of hunting insects and other small creatures. When evening came, he seemed to be weary after a long, toilsome day, for he sometimes joined his partner in the gourd without a vesper song.

When I prepared the gourds for the wrens, I threw the seeds on a bare spot in the dooryard. After the rains began, they sprouted and soon grew into vines that, unable to reach a support for climbing, trailed over the ground for many yards in every direction. The lobes of their big, heart-shaped leaves curled upward to give them the form of broad, shallow cups, which did not hold water because they were not completely closed. In June these vines began to flower. The buds remained closed throughout the day, to expand after sunset into splendid white blossoms, with five broad petals spread out in a circle as wide as the palm of my hand. All through the night they displayed their pure beauty to the moths and the bats, to close and wither after the return of the morning light.

### The June-Wrens Leave the Gourd

On the morning of July 14, I awoke with the feeling that something important was about to happen. Arising at the first peep of day, before the Orange-billed Nightingale-Thrushes began to sing, I slipped into my clothes and threw open my window's rough wooden shutter. When the cold, damp wind that almost every morning swept down the troughlike valley from the high Cordillera de Talamanca at its head blew boisterously through the glassless window, I added a jacket to my thin garments. Then I sat at the window desk, placing within reach the breakfast that Miguel, my young assistant, had prepared on the preceding evening. The June-Wrens would be just eighteen days old. Some years earlier, another brood of Southern House-Wrens had flown from their nest at this age, and I expected that

Twittering-Wren's family would do the same. I wished to watch the gourd without interruption, so as not to miss anything that occurred.

As usual, Singing-Wren left the gourd first and sang a few times before Twittering-Wren emerged to join him. They lost no time finding food for the nestlings, and returned with their breakfast before the light was strong enough to reveal what they brought. To keep count of how many meals the young received, I laid a matchstick on the right side of the desk every time Singing-Wren brought food, one on the left every time Twittering-Wren did so, and one in the center if I failed to recognize the parent who fed the nestlings. A bank of dun clouds loomed up above the forest on the eastern ridge, intercepting the sun's rays and making the early morning very dark. At first, most of the matches went into the central pile, because Singing-Wren was often silent and it was too dark to detect the yellow on his bill. Half an hour after the nestlings received their first meal, I had laid out sixteen matches, so many in the center that it seemed best to lump them all together and start anew to keep the record.

For the next three hours, I continued to keep tally with the matches; and now that the light was stronger, only one went into the center. In the first hour, Singing-Wren brought food only eight times, while Twittering-Wren did so thirteen times. In the second hour, Singing-Wren fed the nestlings eleven times and Twittering-Wren twelve. In the third hour, Singing-Wren, as though to make the score even, worked unusually hard and brought sixteen meals, while his partner seemed to tire and came with food only eleven times. When I counted all the matchsticks, there were thirty-five for Singing-Wren and thirty-six for Twittering-Wren. If I had given the one in the center to Singing-Wren, it would have made their scores exactly even. The three nestlings had been fed eighty-eight times in the first three and a half hours of the day, which was twenty-nine times for each of them, or at the rate of eight or nine times per capita per hour.

As on other mornings when I watched, the nestlings received only animal food, including hairless caterpillars, small moths, small grasshoppers, and other creatures that I failed to recognize. Sometimes a parent brought two or three items together, as was most evident when a green and a brown caterpillar hung side by side from its bill.

Like myself, Singing-Wren seemed to anticipate some exciting event, for he was more songful than he had been of late. He even managed to pour out a snatch of song past the insect that he held in his bill; and almost always, after he had delivered the meal, he flew to the clothes-line to sing more fully, with less encumbrance, before he flew away to search for more food. Twittering-Wren also seemed excited. Approaching the gourd with food, she sometimes fluttered her wings, and after leaving the doorway she rested on a nearby twig and vibrated her relaxed wings for a longer while. She churred and rattled a good deal. Sometimes she entered the gourd to stay with her nestlings for a few minutes, which their father never did. Usually, however, both parents clung to the sill while they passed food to the nestlings, who eagerly reached forward to receive it.

The June-Wrens were noisy and took their meals with loud, sharp *churr*'s. Often they appeared in the doorway, each revealing a head and neck well covered with brown feathers, a sharp black bill, and conspicuous yellow flanges projecting from the corners of its mouth. When they gaped widely to take food, the bright orange-yellow of the mouth's interior drew the eye from the duller shades of the plumage and helped the parents to place the food where it should go, especially while the nestlings were inside the dimly lighted gourd. Sometimes the heads of all three June-Wrens were framed together in the dark rectangle of the doorway. When one was very hungry, it would push through the opening as far as its shoulders to spy from side to side for the return of a parent; but none ventured to perch on the doorsill. Toward mid-morning, when they were satiated, they appeared less often in the doorway. I surmised that, although eighteen days old and well feathered, the young wrens would not leave the gourd until the morrow.

I prepared to leave the cabin to visit another nest, but before closing the door I glanced again through the window at the gourd. All three June-Wrens were in the entrance, stretching outward, while both parents were hopping around in the orange tree in front of them, highly excited. It appeared that something momentous was about to occur. I was not kept long in suspense, for in a few moments the nestling at the right of the doorway tried to leave by climbing out on the side of the gourd. The hard, smooth, bulging surface offered no foothold to the little bird, who prudently retained a hold on the sill, clinging by one foot. Its stubby tail was outside the edge of the opening; its position was awkward; and its two nestmates pushed from behind. For a short while, it struggled to regain the safety of the nest, but in vain. Becoming exhausted, it released its grasp on the sill and fluttered helplessly downward through the thorny branches of the orange tree, on one of which it managed to catch a foothold and stop its fall, a short distance above the ground.

Scarcely had the first June-Wren left the gourd when the second fluttered weakly forth to join it. The third hesitated two or three minutes, then launched out in the same clumsy fashion and, like the other two, fell about a yard through the spiny boughs before it succeeded in halting its descent.

Now the greatest bustle and excitement prevailed in the lower third of the orange tree. The father and mother flitted around restlessly near the gourd, the former singing continuously, the latter churring and fluttering her wings, while the young voiced their sharper *churr*. Both parents flew into and out of the gourd again and again, just as they had done more than two months before when they coaxed the young April-Wrens to return for the night. They also repeatedly entered the second gourd, which six weeks earlier I had fastened below that in which they nested. Until this morning, I had not seen them show the slightest interest in this empty shell.

Meanwhile the fledglings, as we may now call the June-Wrens, were rapidly learning how to use their feet for clinging and perching, their wings and tails for flying and balancing themselves. The sharp, two-inch-long thorns of the orange tree, which I had feared might injure the wrens, were, on the contrary, helpful, offering close-set, convenient footholds and perches along the smooth, upright branches, to which the fledglings would not otherwise have been able to cling, for twigs were widely spaced in this part of the tree. Aided largely by these long thorns, which formed a kind of ladder, the young wrens managed to flit, flutter, and scramble up toward their parents, who continued to go in and out of the gourds, especially the one with the nest.

For a while, it appeared that the parents would induce the June-Wrens to return to their nursery, but, just as the fledglings drew near it, the adults changed their procedure. Perhaps they had urged the young to climb higher to give them altitude for their first long flight. Since fledglings just out of the nest often trace a descending course, the higher the point from which they start, the farther they can go before they strike the ground. Now Singing-Wren and his mate, one singing and the other churring, flew down into some low weeds about thirty feet from the orange tree, and then returned. They repeated this several times, thereby inciting the June-Wrens to follow. One of the latter flew bravely in the direction they had taken, but beyond the point they had indicated, on its first flight covering a distance that, when measured later, proved to be fifty feet. The other two fledglings promptly followed, but flew only thirty-three feet.

For a small songbird, the Southern House-Wren's nestling period, usually eighteen days, less often nineteen, and rarely twenty, is long. Since the young are often raised beneath the eaves of a house, or in a hole high in a bare trunk, with no convenient perches in front, they need to be old enough to fly well before they emerge. Moreover, since many of their nests are not readily accessible to predators, they increase their chances of survival by remaining safely inside until they are well developed, instead of departing when only ten or twelve days old and still unable to fly well, as many altricial birds raised in vulnerable open nests do, including some considerably bigger than house-wrens.

After they had rested for a short while on the exposed perches where they first happened to alight, the June-Wrens dropped down into the low herbage. When, a few minutes later, I left the window and went out to look for them, they were nowhere to be seen. They had hidden in the weeds and were quite invisible. Their parents, on the other hand, made themselves conspicuous by flitting around me at a distance of a few yards and scolding loudly to divert my attention from their fledglings.

As night approached, the June-Wrens were led by their parents to sleep among the fibers of an old banana stump, all that remained, after cows had eaten leaves and trunk, of one of the plants in whose bunches of fruit Singing-Wren had formerly slept. I did not see the fledglings enter, but was led by the parents' activity to investigate the stump. I peered into the hollow center, then examined the leaf bases around it, without detecting a single fledgling. When I gently kicked the stump, a slight movement revealed that one of the dark objects at which I had been gazing was a young wren, and continued scrutiny disclosed two more, whose brown bodies blended well with the brown fibers amid which they crouched immobile. Here the parents fed the fledglings, and carried away their white droppings. After a day of roaming through the fields, they were again treated like helpless nestlings, not in their proper nest but in a temporary shelter.

As the night ended, I visited the June-Wrens in their banana stump. My flashlight's beam revealed that they had climbed up among the disarranged fibers around the hollow center, where they were sheltered by the remnant of a flat leaf-base that bent inward, forming an elfin canopy that had kept them dry through the night's heavy rain. Each wren had its feathers fluffed out, transforming it into a tuft of soft down, amid which its head was wholly hidden. Only a stubby tail projected plainly from it. Presently a fledgling awoke and gazed steadfastly into the yellow beam, evincing no sign of alarm. Twittering-Wren was not present with the June-Wrens.

On the following evening, the fledglings retired into a different banana stump, where the bent-over base of a leaf-sheath also formed a roof above them. Repeatedly disturbed by a cow with a broken horn, who perversely persisted in grazing close to the stump although there was no lack of grass elsewhere, they finally hid where I could not find them. On the next night, too, I failed to discover where they slept. On the fourth evening after their departure from the gourd, their parents led them to lodge in the thatched roof of my cabin. Here their father and mother also retired, after bringing them a little more food, including insects and spiders that they found among the cane leaves around them.

With so many nooks and crannies to choose from amid the leaves that sheltered me, it took the wrens many minutes to settle down for the night. In the evenings, a chorus of sharp, bubbling *churr*'s above my head would advise me that the family had arrived, and I hurried outside to watch them retire. When, after a few nights, they had selected permanent dormitories, Twittering-Wren slept with the three June-Wrens in a fold among the leaves at one end of the roof, while Singing-Wren lodged alone at the other end.

On most mornings, the wrens remained silent until they flew from the roof. But sometimes, if I continued to lie on my cot below them until daybreak, I would hear them begin to *tuck* and *churr* at the first light. They continued to talk quietly among themselves in their pocket between the leaves until it was time to fly forth into the new day.

When I looked into the gourd after the June-Wrens' departure, I found it infested with lice, legions of which crawled over my hand. This explained why, during the June-Wrens' final days in the nest, the parents had plucked invisible objects from their feet every time they clutched the doorsill to pass in food, then continued to clean themselves after they left. Doubtless this plague of vermin was the reason why the parents did not lead the June-Wrens to sleep in the gourd, as they had done with the April-Wrens. They chose the banana stumps, so near the ground, as a temporary lodging for their fledglings until the latter gained the strength and skill to reach a nook in the high, slippery thatch, then promptly led them to the greater safety of the roof that had so long been their own shelter. Unless they used foresight, it is difficult to explain their admirable provision for the young wrens' safety and comfort.

### The August-Wrens

At the beginning of August, Twittering-Wren started to prepare for her third brood. While Singing-Wren sang tirelessly, but gave little substantial help, she once more covered the old nest with rootlets and bits of weed stems, then with a soft lining of downy chicken feathers. She also brought a few broad scales from a cast snakeskin, probably not, as some have supposed, as a talisman to hold plundering serpents aloof, but simply because they were soft and pliable, like scraps of transparent cellophane, which house-wrens and other birds sometimes place beneath their eggs. Then she laid four eggs, around sunrise on four consecutive mornings. She laid the first of these only twenty-three days after the June-Wrens' departure from the gourd, although thirty-four days had elapsed between the April-Wrens' exit and the start of laying for her second brood. The weather was much more favorable in July and early August, with less rain and more sunshine, than it had been in late May and early June, just before the second set was laid. This appeared to be the reason why the third set was laid so much more promptly, and contained one more egg than the second set. Omitting an exceptionally short interval presently to be mentioned, fifteen intervals between the departure of one brood of Southern House-Wrens and the start of laying for the next brood ranged from fourteen to thirty-six days, with an average of twenty-four and one-half days.

By August, when Twittering-Wren began to incubate her third set of eggs, nearly all the other birds that had started to nest early in April, when she did, had finished breeding for the year. Moreover, most of these other birds laid only two eggs in a set, so that, even if they successfully reared three broods, they could have only six offspring, whereas Twittering-Wren had now laid eleven eggs. However, in a region with a rapidly expanding human population, like the valley of El General at that period, there was each year room for more house-wrens. Each year more families moved in and made cabins for themselves, while the older children of earlier settlers married and built dwellings of their own, with more thatched roofs where wrens could sleep. Yearly more of the ancient rain forest, where house-wrens are never found, was cut and burned to make cornfields and pastures and weedy clearings in which house-wrens could thrive. Even when no cabins were built in these new clearings, the wrens could find sleeping places and nesting holes in the charred and battered trees that remained standing in them, or among the stumps and half-burnt logs that littered the ground. Twittering-Wren's progeny could go forth and colonize some of these lands newly opened to settlement by house-wrens.

In the Caribbean lowlands, on the opposite side of the mountains that rose like a verdant rampart at the head of the valley where Singing-Wren dwelt, the situation was quite different. Great banana plantations that had been abandoned because of the ravages of the Panama disease were overgrown with thickets that soon became woodland, while buildings had been dismantled or were falling into ruin. Here house-wrens were being forced out, while forest-dwelling wrens were regaining their ancient domain.

Now Twittering-Wren remained in the gourd, warming her third set of eggs more constantly than she had done in April when she incubated her first set. She seemed to be tired from the hard work of rearing two broods of young wrens and preparing for the third, and content to sit quietly in her nest, resting and looking out over the small part of the green valley that she could see, framed in the little rectangle of her doorway. When I timed her movements in April, she stayed away from her eggs slightly more than she covered them in the daytime; now in August she was in the gourd almost twice as long as she was absent. Once she sat continuously for forty-four minutes, the longest interval in the gourd by day that I timed; in April, her longest session was only twenty minutes. Her shortest session on the nest was now fourteen minutes, whereas in April she had sometimes sat for only eight minutes. Her recesses now ranged from eight to twenty-nine minutes, and on the average were slightly shorter than they had been in April. In nearly ten hours of watching from the window while incubation was in progress, I timed fourteen of Twittering-Wren's sessions on her eggs, which totaled three hundred and sixty-one minutes. Her fourteen recesses added up to two hundred and one minutes.

When, after sitting for a while, Twittering-Wren was ready to leave the gourd, she moved forward to the doorway, pushed out her head, and looked lingeringly from side to side, frequently continuing this for a whole minute before she flew away. Sometimes she came to her doorway to gaze out in this fashion, as though about to leave, but instead of flying out she finally withdrew into the gourd and continued to warm her eggs. Returning to her nest after an outing, she often brought a downy feather, as she had done in April. Singing-Wren was still attentive to his mate in the mornings, but in the afternoons he rarely came near the gourd. The June-Wrens were out of sight all day. Now foraging for themselves, they were busy trying to find enough to eat.

While Twittering-Wren hatched her eggs, Singing-Wren abandoned my roof to sleep in the weedy cornfield across the road that passed in front of the cabin. Here stumps that had not been consumed by the fire that had been set to prepare the field for planting offered a variety of niches in which he could find shelter. I often heard his first and last songs of the day coming from the cornfield, but I never found the cozy nook or cranny where he slept amid the tangled growth. The June-Wrens continued to lodge at the southern end of the roof, where their mother had formerly slept with them. For a while, only two were present; the third had gone to try its fortune elsewhere. After a few nights alone, however, it returned to the familiar roof and lodged with its siblings.

After Singing-Wren moved to the cornfield, I found four sleepers in the thatch, for about this time another young wren began to take shelter there, and each evening tucked itself away among the leaves at the front. In the mornings it darted out and went off alone, paying no attention to the other wrens. I surmised that this was one of the April-Wrens, who had returned to sleep in its parents' domain; but I could no longer distinguish the April-Wrens from other young wrens that had grown up in the neighborhood.

Twittering-Wren hatched one of her eggs fourteen days after she laid the last of them. Two more hatched on the following day; one was infertile. The Southern House-Wren's incubation period, counting from the laying of the last egg to the hatching of the last nestling, is usually from fourteen and a half to fifteen and a half days, rarely as long as seventeen days. Twittering-Wren's three tiny, pink nestlings were called the August-Wrens. As they grew older, they demanded just as much food as the earlier broods had received, and their parents toiled as strenuously to nourish them. But the adults were not so full of energy as they had been earlier in the year; Singing-Wren devoted so much of his strength to providing for his family that he rarely had enough left for singing.

Soon after the August-Wrens hatched, some boys showed me a house-wrens' nest beneath the thatched roof of a shed where maize was stored. The birds had stuffed their nest into a cranny between the dry sugarcane leaves and a pole that supported them. In a shallow pocket made of small sticks, weed stalks, and fine rootlets, the female was incubating three speckled eggs as late as the end of August. Perhaps, if I had not provided a gourd for my wrens, they would have made their nest beneath my roof.

At this time, a tiny Bananaquit was incubating two spotted white eggs in the orange tree that held the gourd. Her nest was a hollow ball of grass blades and similar materials, with a round doorway at the edge of the underside. One morning, while at recess, the sharp-billed, yellow-breasted female Bananaquit preened her feathers directly in front of the gourd. Twittering-Wren was absent, hunting insects for her nestlings. When she returned with a caterpillar in her bill and found her neighbor trespassing, she flew at the smaller Bananaquit to drive her away. The latter resisted, and the two fluttered down through the branches. Coming to rest on a lower twig, the Bananaquit defiantly stayed. Twittering-Wren flew again at the yellow-breasted bird; the two grappled and dropped downward again. The Bananaquit freed herself and flew to her own nest, leaving the wren on the ground. Both combatants lost feathers in this encounter.

Before the August-Wrens were well feathered, I went to San José to mail botanical specimens that I had collected, and in my absence they left the nest. On the evening of my return, Twittering-Wren and two August-Wrens slept at the southern end of the roof in the nook where the three June-Wrens had lodged up to the time of my journey. The third August-Wren and the June-Wrens vanished as obscurely as the April-Wrens had done. Doubtless, they left to seek new homes for themselves and mates with whom they could raise families of their own in the coming year.

My roof had developed many leaks, and since the rainiest months of the year had arrived, it was necessary to repair it with new sugarcane leaves. It was patched up in many places, including the very spot where Twittering-Wren had slept with her two youngest offspring. This caused her to abandon the roof and take the August-Wrens to sleep across the road in the cornfield, where the maize had been harvested long ago. It was now so overgrown with tall weeds and vines that I despaired of finding where the wrens hid themselves away. Singing-Wren still slept there, too, and only a single April-Wren, if such it was, continued to sleep in my roof.

October, the wettest of the twelve months, was now at hand. Except for a few pleasant days in the middle of the month, and some fine, bright mornings, it was rainy and gloomy. Clouds hung low over the valley. Swollen by afternoon downpours, the Río Buena Vista rose over its banks and thundered down its rocky channel. Scarcely any birds sang.

Singing-Wren and his partner continued to lead and feed the August-Wrens for a month after they left the nest. Rarely Singing-Wren looked into the gourd, but otherwise the adults showed no interest in it now. They were molting all their feathers and looked exceedingly shabby, for much of their plumage was missing, and what remained was faded and frayed. After Singing-Wren had renewed his body plumage and was again decently clad, he lost all his tail feathers at one time, becoming even more stubby-tailed than a fledgling that has just left the nest. The young August-Wrens in new feathers were much more presentable and handsome. Nevertheless, Singing-Wren continued to voice his cheery songs, not nearly as often as earlier in the year, but now and again through the day, just enough to prove that he was not wholly downcast and wretched. To sing during the October rains, and in the midst of the molt, revealed greatness of spirit. His name was well deserved.

When the August-Wrens were nearly two months old and had been out of the gourd for five or six weeks, the parents drove them away. One returned to sleep in the roof, where the bird that I supposed to be an April-Wren still lodged. But I knew that neither of them would stay there long; for Singing-Wren and Twittering-Wren, who still kept together as a mated pair, would want to be alone in their territory around my cabin when they were ready to resume nesting in the following year.

# 3. The House-Wrens' Second Year

WHILE I dwelt beside the Río Buena Vista, I paid the boys in the neighborhood for reporting to me nests that they found and left undisturbed. Early in my second year there, these helpers and I discovered many rare nests in the thickets around my cabin and in the forest up on the ridge. In a hollow high in a great tree was a nest of the Laughing Falcon, whose diet consists almost wholly of snakes, so that this member of a family that preys heavily upon smaller birds is one of their best friends, for it reduces the number of their most destructive enemies. Likewise, we found a nest of the Marbled Wood-Quail, built on the ground in the forest and roofed with dead leaves, which shielded the four white eggs from rain and the eyes of prowling creatures. Equally interesting was a nest of Olivaceous Piculets, smallest of woodpeckers, smaller even than house-wrens, who had carved in soft, decaying wood a hole that was a miniature of those made by their larger relatives.

With nests of these three unusual birds and many others to study, I did not intend to devote as much attention to the house-wrens as I had done in the preceding year. But it is not always true that things new and strange yield a richer harvest of knowledge than those we have known so long that we believe we have nothing more to learn about them. So it was with the wrens. In the second year that I lived with them, they did so many unexpected things, the course of their nestings was so different from that of the first year, that I was soon convinced that I had scarcely begun to understand them. Of the many rare and fascinating birds whose habits I studied in this second year in the valley of El General, the house-wrens that I had already watched so long proved to be the most exciting and entertaining of all.

In this second year, the dry season was so much wetter than it had been in the first year that it hardly deserved this designation. Rains were frequent in December, January, and February; only in March did we enjoy some continuous dry weather. Despite the rain, or possibly because of it, the several species of wrens that lived in the thickets and along the riverside all began to breed early, in December and January, long before most other small birds. Twittering-Wren and her partner returned to sleep in my thatched roof in November, and before Christmas they tidied up and covered with fresh material their old nest in the gourd, in which they had already raised three broods. Twittering-Wren found many broad scales from the white underside of a snake and mixed them with the white feathers that lined her nest. On December 27, she laid the first egg, and that evening she slept in the gourd instead of the roof. She laid an egg on each of the following mornings, and when she had four she started to incubate, fully three months earlier than I had found her nesting in the preceding breeding season.

In many species of birds, it has been found that older individuals lay earlier in a season than those just starting to breed. Probably Twittering-Wren laid her first set of eggs so much earlier in this second year because she was now more mature. Apparently, when I first became acquainted with her, she was a year or less of age, and the April-Wrens, the first brood that she raised in the gourd, were her very first offspring. Several things helped to strengthen this belief. One was her voice, which had gradually changed. When I first knew her, she had answered her mate's animated songs with only a simple, tuneless little twitter. After a while, she added a slight trill to the twitter. At first only the shadow of a trill, it acquired strength and prominence as the months passed, until in the second year it became an important part of her utterance. Although brief, the trill was full, soft, and pleasing. Sometimes it was introduced by the twitter that had at first been her only song, but on other occasions it was delivered alone. If I had not already named her, I might have called her "Trilling-Wren" instead of Twittering-Wren.

### The Precocious January-Wrens

After the usual fifteen days of incubation, Twittering-Wren hatched three of her four eggs. Apparently because their parents were more mature and attended them more efficiently, the January-Wrens gained strength and skill more quickly than did any of the broods of the preceding year. Compared with the previous occupants of the gourd, they were a precocious trio. Most of the differences in the history of the wren family during the second year seemed to result from the more rapid development of the young.

For the first seventeen days of the January-Wrens' lives, I had nothing new to record about them. They rested quietly in the nest, and were attended by their parents much as the former broods had been cared for. Although they remained in the gourd until they were eighteen days old, just as their predecessors had done, on the very day of their departure they gave unmistakable indications that they were an unusual set of fledglings. In the first place, they emerged from the gourd much earlier in the morning than the June-Wrens had done more than six months before. The first January-Wren flew into the open while I was at breakfast. When I began to watch the wrens at seven o'clock, I found it perching in the orange tree, while the other two were still in the gourd, with their heads framed in the doorway. One tried to climb out on the side of the gourd, but finding this too hard and slippery to afford a foothold, it attempted to return to the security of its nursery. Since it had retained a firm grasp on the sill, it managed to pull itself inside after a brief, vigorous struggle.

Soon one of the twain made the short flight to a branch in front of the gourd, and the other promptly followed. They dropped down through the thorny branches, but soon caught themselves, well above the ground. Now the parents, highly ex-

cited, went in and out of the gourd many times, while the father sang, the mother tucked and churred, and the fledglings uttered slight, sharp notes. Following the example of its parents, a January-Wren worked its way up to a twig in front of the gourd, and, with surprising ease and perfect poise, flew through the doorway on its first attempt. Already, less than an hour after its introduction to the outside world, it could enter the gourd as well as the April-Wrens had been able to do at the end of their third day in the open.

Now Twittering-Wren and her mate behaved most unexpectedly. Some parent birds favor with food the fledglings who first leave the nest, neglecting the stay-at-homes until growing hunger impels them to join the others who are being fed in the open. Not so the parent wrens, who lavished attention on the fledgling that had returned to the gourd, bringing to it all the food they found, and quite neglecting the other two, who perched nearby, watching their elders carry morsels past their gaping mouths. Before long, one of these two young wrens, tired of calling and pleading in vain for its fair share of the good things that passed so temptingly before it, flew down to the tall weeds a few yards away, whence their parents were bringing the insects. Now it in turn became the sole object of its parents' attention. The fledgling who had re-entered the gourd, finding itself alone and neglected, soon flew out to rest beside its nestmate who had remained in the orange tree.

The morning was cool and brilliantly clear. A strong, chilling wind blew down the valley, shaking the few tufts of natal down that still adhered to the full new plumage of the young wrens. Nearly half an hour passed before one of the parents, the father, again brought food to the orange tree. From force of habit, he took it directly into the gourd, but, finding this deserted, he promptly emerged and delivered the insect to one of the fledg-

◀ Nestling January-Wrens in Gourd

lings who waited hungrily nearby. Soon their mother also fed them. After a while, all flew down into the weedy field to join the third fledgling, and there they continued to roam with their parents through the remainder of the day.

The January-Wrens were so skillful and capable that their parents led them to sleep in the gourd at the close of their first day in the open. Soon after five o'clock, when the heavy afternoon shower had ended, Singing-Wren and Twittering-Wren came to the orange tree and inspected the gourd. Then they flew back and forth between the weeds and the gourd, urging the young wrens to follow, which one promptly did. As soon as it arrived in the orange tree, they started to flit in and out of the gourd, demonstrating to the fledgling the next step to take. This January-Wren, exceptionally strong and skillful for its age, flew through the doorway without the least difficulty. Another fledgling soon arrived in the orange tree; but the third, more backward, delayed among the weeds and called. Now the parents divided their time between passing back and forth between the weeds and the orange tree to bring on the laggard and going in and out of the gourd to show the second fledgling how to reach it. After the third fledgling arrived in the orange tree, they ceased to visit the weeds, but continued to pass back and forth between the gourd and the branch in front, and to flit among the neighboring boughs. All this while, the father sang frequently. Before long, the second fledgling managed to enter the dormitory.

The third January-Wren was far less precocious than its two nestmates. While trying to reach the opening in the gourd's side, it fell to the ground, then laboriously struggled up the thorny trunk until it regained the branches. Repeatedly it missed the twig to which it tried to hop and fluttered down again, losing several precious feet of hard-won altitude, but with undaunted persistence it would work its way upward. Once, after repeated failures, it gained a toe-hold on the sill, with its little body leaning far backward, its head above the upper edge of the doorway. This was an awkward position, which it lacked the skill to improve. Instead of continuing to struggle until it could slip its head inside, it took the easier course and fluttered upward to catch hold of the string that encircled the gourd's neck and fastened it to the tree. With this aid, the fledgling raised itself to the top of the gourd and paused to catch its breath. After a short rest, the clumsy but persevering January-Wren returned by a roundabout course to the branch in front of the entrance, for still another attempt to fly in. This time it struck the gourd slightly too low and, unable to cling to the smooth bottom, it again fluttered earthward.

Meanwhile the light had grown dim; and the parents, who all this while had been flitting in and out of the gourd to encourage their weakest fledgling to enter, flew from the orange tree. They had been so busy showing the third young wren how to reach its bedroom that they had failed to bring food to the other two, as in the preceding year they had always fed the fledglings after they had gone to rest. When the dusk had become so deep that I could scarcely see her as she flitted through the dark foliage of the orange tree, the mother returned to the gourd to sleep with the two January-Wrens who had been strong and skillful enough to enter. As long as it could stay awake, the third fledgling continued to struggle valiantly toward the doorway, but in the fading light it was overcome by drowsiness and fell asleep where it happened to be, on the short, winged petiole of an orange leaf, a scant foot below the baffling doorway that it had tried so bravely but vainly to enter. Here it turned its head back among its feathers and slumbered.

Since the night promised to be cold, before going to bed I went out to bring the lone January-Wren into the cabin and keep it warm until dawn. With a swift movement, I plucked it from its orange leaf and was approaching the door, when it slipped through my fingers and rose into the air until it vanished in the darkness. After a fruitless search, I left it under the open sky. The night was clear and starry, and before dawn it became very cold—at least, it felt cold to one who for years had lived where snow never falls. Fitful gusts of boisterous, chilling wind blew down the valley from the high cordillera and loudly rustled the dry cane leaves that thatched my cabin.

At dawn I went out, as I so often did, to watch the wrens begin their day. At half-past five, Singing-Wren flew out of the thatch, and a moment later Twittering-Wren sallied forth from the gourd. Soon weak little calls, issuing from the tall weeds at the edge of the dooryard, told me that the January-Wren in the open had come safely through the night. I was delighted to receive this assurance of its well-being. It seemed to claim most of the food that its parents could find, for it needed much nourishment to replenish the energy it had spent to maintain its body temperature through the chilly night. It was long before a single meal was taken to the fledglings in the gourd. Half an hour after their mother left them, one of these young wrens pushed its head through the doorway, then hopped out and called sharply in the orange tree. Eight minutes later, the other followed; then both joined their parents among the tall weeds and received breakfast.

Although the afternoon was continuously bright and sunny, instead of wet and gloomy as on the preceding day, the parent wrens led their family earlier to the gourd. Two January-Wrens entered promptly, with hardly any urging. One had become so skillful on the wing that, starting from a perch behind the gourd, it flew around the bulging side and curved into the doorway in perfect form. The third fledgling, doubtless the one who had passed the preceding night under the stars, did not even try to enter the dormitory. It lingered in the top of the orange tree until the parents went to hunt insects on the roof, then promptly followed them there and claimed much of the food they found among the cane leaves. The January-Wrens in the gourd at first remained quietly out of sight, but ere long, feeling neglected, they looked out, peering around the sides of the gourd to see where the others had gone. Soon one hopped out, just as the parents returned to the orange tree. When Singing-Wren found it in the open, he flitted back and forth between the entrance and the branch in front, while Twittering-Wren entered, which was the routine way of inducing the young birds to go inside. Like an obedient child, the January-Wren promptly returned to its nursery.

Before long, the third fledgling followed its parents to the orange tree, where they continued to fly to the doorway, occasionally entering. So encouraged, it tried valiantly to reach the opening, but repeated all its errors of the preceding evening. Its trouble was not that it could not fly well, but that it lacked skill and control; it was clumsy. Again and again it started toward the doorway, only to lose confidence at the last moment, veer aside, and alight on a twig beyond. Thrice it actually secured a hold on the sill, without being able to pull itself through the doorway. It climbed to the top of the gourd, or fell away below, then returned for another attempt to enter. While it was engaged in this fruitless effort, its mother brought it a green caterpillar, as though to encourage it. To compensate for its lack of dexterity, it had dauntless persistence that kept it trying until, at long last, it succeeded in joining its siblings in the gourd. Twittering-Wren did not accompany them that night, but crept into her old cranny among the cane leaves.

While in the gourd in the evening after they were led to rest, and before their departure in the morning, the January-Wrens were quiet. They did not call loudly as the April-Wrens had been in the habit of doing, but voiced only a few low, sharp *tick's* and *tuck's*, although no food had been brought to them after they entered. They seemed to have received enough before they retired, probably because the parents foraged more skillfully than in the preceding year. The adults devoted the last minutes of daylight to finding food for themselves.

### The Young Helpers
Before the January-Wrens had been in the open for ten days, Twittering-Wren and her mate showed renewed interest in the gourd by day, as though they intended to raise still another brood

in it. When I noticed this, I decided that, after sheltering four sets of young wrens, it deserved a thorough cleaning. I took it down and removed all the varied materials that the birds had carried in over an interval of nearly a year. That at the bottom was far advanced in decay. Then I washed the gourd in the river, and tied it up in its former place in the orange tree with stout new cord.

After the empty gourd was replaced in the orange tree, Twittering-Wren and her mate came many times to inspect it, and Singing-Wren sang much from his perch above the doorway. On the following day, he entered and sang with his head pushed out through the orifice. Soon after this, the pair started to fill the bottom with coarse sticks. Sometimes while Twittering-Wren was absent, Singing-Wren brought a twig, but more often he just sang in front of the gourd, or entered to utter low notes of contentment, then rested on the sill with head outward and sang again. When his partner joined him, the task proceeded more rapidly. Usually she worked more efficiently than her partner, who devoted so much of his energy to singing, even when he had a stick in his bill. Both had difficulty passing long pieces through the doorway. Sometimes, after Twittering-Wren had pushed one partly inside, she released her grasp while she entered to arrange it, and meanwhile it fell to the ground. At other times a long stick caught at both ends and, after ineffectual efforts to push it in, was dropped. Such a slight mishap could not depress Singing-Wren's high spirits enough to stop his singing. Instead of descending to retrieve a fallen piece, the wrens went off to seek another at a distance. They seemed to derive so much pleasure from filling the gourd, and I so greatly enjoyed watching them, that I regretted that I had not emptied it after each nesting.

"What can be more unsuitable, untractable, for a nest in a hole or cavity than the twigs the house wren uses? Dry grasses or bits of soft bark would bend and adapt themselves easily to the exigencies of the case; but stiff, unyielding twigs!" So wrote John Burroughs with reference to the Northern House-Wren. But stiff twigs, although obviously troublesome to pass through a narrow opening, serve the wrens' purposes far better than soft, pliable materials would. In the first place, if the cavity is deep, the wrens do not rear their family in the dark bottom but near the doorway, where the nest receives more light; and for filling the bottom and raising the level of the nest, stiff unyielding twigs are more efficient than pliable materials that pack together and shrink in volume. If rain enters the cavity, as sometimes happens, it will drain through sticks more rapidly than through leaves or fibrous stuff, which become waterlogged and sodden. Moreover, twigs afford better ventilation of the nest's foundation. In this case, as in many others, animals have adapted means to ends far better than appears at the first glimpse. The Sulphur-bellied Flycatcher and its near relative the Streaked Flycatcher, who often nest in a deep woodpecker's hole or other cavity in a tree, yet prefer to incubate their eggs and brood their young at the top where they can look through the doorway, face the same problem of filling a large space economically, and they solve it in the same way the house-wrens do, by building up a foundation of twigs or stiff petioles rather than of soft and pliable materials that would be easier to pass through the orifice.

The January-Wrens, only eleven days from the nest, appeared to be largely self-supporting, hunting food for themselves and rarely begging for it. Although they followed their parents through much of the day, they were frequently alone; they did not come to the orange tree to pester their elders with demands for food while the latter were busy filling the gourd, as the April-Wrens had done after they had been out of the nest twice as long.

In four days, Twittering-Wren and her mate filled the bulging bottom of their gourd with fine sticks to above the level of the doorsill. Then Twittering-Wren began to make the nest proper in the hollow that she had left in the top of the pile of stiff twigs, and for this she brought only flexible materials, including rootlets and fibers of various kinds. But her mate, still working almost as hard as she did, stupidly brought only sticks, which certainly were no longer needed. It was even more difficult than at first to pass the longer pieces through the doorway, partly blocked by the excess of material that had already been brought. However, Singing-Wren struggled resolutely with his burdens, and with much shoving succeeded in forcing most of them inside, dropping few. Twittering-Wren devoted a good deal of effort to arranging these superfluous contributions of her well-meaning co-worker, so that they would be out of the way. At times his masculine lack of perception in domestic matters must have strained her patience. When she flew off for more rootlets or fibers while he waited in front of the gourd to take in another unwanted stick, he sometimes followed her, still bearing his burden. Male birds of many kinds do the same, more eager to be with their mates than to finish the nest.

For five days, Twittering-Wren continued to line the nest, bringing first rootlets, plant fibers, and horsehairs, then downy feathers and scales from the bellies of snakes, while Singing-Wren still came with sticks and stiff, dry petioles. Once I saw her deliberately remove from the gourd an exceptionally long stick that Singing-Wren had maneuvered inside, where there was no longer room for it. If he happened to be resting directly in front of the doorway when his mate came forth, he made haste to remove himself from her way. Possibly she had pecked him for his stupidity. Another female house-wren pulled a feather from the back of her mate when he took an unwanted stick to the nest that she was lining.

When the new nest was completed, or practically so, Twittering-Wren and the three January-Wrens left the roof to sleep in the gourd once more. As formerly, Singing-Wren caroled before the doorway while they entered, then clung to the sill and peeped in to see how they had settled down to rest. Finally, he flew up to sleep in the roof.

Exactly three weeks after the January-Wrens left the nest, Twittering-Wren laid the first egg of a new set. This was, so far, the shortest interval between the departure of one brood and the laying of another set of eggs. Again she deposited four speckled eggs on the white chicken feathers and snake scales that softly lined her nest.

While Twittering-Wren incubated her eggs, the January-Wrens continued to roam about the vicinity, sometimes with their father. Once I saw Singing-Wren and a January-Wren accompany Twittering-Wren as she returned to her nest. Her mate sang in front of the gourd while she entered, but the young wren went in with her and stayed a short while. Later, while Singing-Wren poured forth his verses, I heard a January-Wren, resting near his father, sing for the first time. The young wren's song was higher in pitch than that of the adult, more warbling and less definite in phrasing, as is true of the first songs of other kinds of wrens. He repeated it several times, while Singing-Wren continued to sing. When the young male flew to a neighboring tree, his father pursued him closely. After they alighted, the January-Wren sang a few times more, practicing his first songs only four weeks after he had left the nest, when he was forty-six days old.

Two of Twittering-Wren's eggs inexplicably vanished. The remaining two did not hatch until the sixteenth day after the last was laid. Possibly whatever was responsible for the loss of the other two eggs also caused a temporary interruption of incubation, and so delayed hatching by one day. The two latest additions to Twittering-Wren's family were called March-Wrens.

On a living post near the wrens' orange tree I had set up a small gourd with a wide round doorway for a pair of Yellow-crowned Euphonias that had been trying unsuccessfully to build a covered nest amid the sprouts that had grown up around the top of the post. The euphonias ignored the gourd, but the wrens promptly inspected it. On the night before Twittering-Wren's eggs hatched, all three January-Wrens slept in it, leaving their mother alone in the larger gourd for the first time since the new nest was finished. On the following night, they returned to the old gourd to sleep with Twittering-Wren and the two nestlings that had hatched meanwhile.

About the time the March-Wrens hatched, I noticed that one or two of the January-Wrens hesitated to enter the gourd in the evening, probably because their mother pecked at them from within. Their delay in entering was never long, whence I inferred that their mother's opposition was mild. On the second evening after the eggs hatched, Twittering-Wren appeared to try harder to exclude one January-Wren. Because she stayed wholly within the gourd, not even showing her head in the doorway, I could not see what she did; but the behavior of the young wren showed clearly that it was repulsed when it tried to enter. After a January-Wren had joined its mother without difficulty, the second approached the gourd in a cautious, distrustful manner, and alighted on the doorsill, only to dart away. Repeatedly it flew toward the entrance, but lost courage and veered off to the side. Several times, too, it alighted on the sill, only to hang there with its head outside, hardly trying to push in. Finally, it flew to the doorway and slowly forced its way inward, against what opposition I could not see. While the young wren tried to push into the gourd, its father rested quietly in front, a passive witness to the dispute. He seemed less eager to keep these young birds out than he had been to expel the April-Wrens the preceding year.

That night only two January-Wrens slept with their mother, far back in the gourd, where it was difficult to glimpse them through the doorway. The third passed the night alone in the new gourd that I had put up for the euphonias. Yet, a few nights later, all three readily entered the old gourd again to sleep with their mother and the nestlings. The three rested side by side in a row on the front rim of the nest, breasts toward the doorway, heads turned back and snuggled into out-fluffed feathers.

By day, too, the January-Wrens occasionally entered the gourd that sheltered their younger siblings. Twittering-Wren hardly opposed these diurnal visits; on the contrary, she permitted one of the juveniles to rest beside her while she brooded the March-Wrens. But Singing-Wren, who did not try to exclude the January-Wrens from the gourd in the evening, became excited when they approached it in full daylight. When he found one within, he would quiver his wings, then pursue it as it flew out. Or, if a January-Wren tried to enter in his presence, he attacked and drove it away. The young wrens were most persistent in visiting the gourd by day; when driven off, they soon returned. Singing-Wren's objection to their presence was neither strong nor consistent; although at one time he chased them off, if he found one of them beside the gourd a few minutes later he might ignore it.

By dint of great perseverance and stubborn refusal to be excluded, the January-Wrens won the right to enter the gourd at any time. They used this privilege to good purpose, helping to feed the nestlings and to carry away the little white packages of waste. By this time, one of the March-Wrens had vanished, leaving only a single nestling, already nearly feathered. One January-Wren had also inexplicably disappeared. The other two now so closely resembled their parents that I could distinguish them only by lingering traces of the yellow flanges at the sides of the mouth, which had been growing fainter ever since they had left the nest nearly eight weeks earlier. I could also, in a favorable light, distinguish the two remaining January-Wrens from each other, for the bill of one was wholly black, like that of its mother, while the lower mandible of the other was extensively yellowish at the base, like that of Singing-Wren. The first was evidently a young female, whom I named "Blackbill"; the second, a male, became "Yellowbill."

Blackbill brought food to the nestlings much more often than her brother. Although he frequently entered the gourd for a short while, usually he came with empty bill. In two and a half hours of the morning when the remaining March-Wren was thirteen days old, Singing-Wren fed the nestling fifteen times, Twittering-Wren nine times, and Blackbill seven times. Yellowbill brought nothing, although two days earlier he had fed his younger brother, for the March-Wren also proved to be a male. Although in this interval Twittering-Wren did not feed the nestling as often as Singing-Wren did, at other times she brought more than he, and always kept a watchful eye on her nestling. At intervals she visited the nest without food, and, if the March-Wren's loud cries informed her that he was hungry, she went off and in a minute or two returned with something for him. When she needed an insect, she found it promptly. One afternoon she carried a rootlet into the nest, then a broad snake scale. Since she rarely took such things into the gourd while she had babies to feed, I suspected that she was already inclined to raise another brood. Singing-Wren carried out one of the white snake scales, perhaps mistaking it for a white dropping.

Approaching the nest, the January-Wrens frequently revealed their youth by uttering a short, low fragment of a *churr*, such as I never heard from a parent. When they began to feed the nestling, they often flew into the far side of the orange tree or alighted among its lower boughs, and then advanced stealthily, by an indirect course, to the gourd, as though fearful of being detected and driven away by their father. After Singing-Wren stopped trying to keep them away, they adopted a more direct approach. Although Twittering-Wren did not, as a rule, try to keep the January-Wrens out of the gourd when they brought food, once, while brooding, she pecked at one of them when it came to the doorway with an insect in its bill.

After feeding their younger brother, the January-Wrens often lingered in the gourd for several minutes, and sometimes for nearly half an hour. Whether they brooded the nestling, or only rested beside it, I could not see. However, the March-Wren was now so well feathered that it hardly needed to be warmed by day. Sometimes the two young helpers stayed together in the gourd for a short while; or either of them would delay inside with Twittering-Wren. It surprised me to find Yellowbill, the young male, tarrying in the nest, as his father never did, whether it held eggs or nestlings. When Singing-Wren came with food, he delivered it and promptly left.

If either parent arrived at the gourd with food while Blackbill or Yellowbill was within, the young wren would come to the doorway and take the item for delivery to a nestling. Once Blackbill flew up with an insect in her bill and found Twittering-Wren in the gourd. With quivering wings, she passed it to her mother, who in turn gave it to the March-Wren; then both left together. A little later, when Yellowbill was in the gourd and tried to take a spider that his sister had brought, she refused to yield it to him and pushed past him to deliver it directly to the nestling. Once Blackbill was resting amid the foliage near the gourd when her father arrived with a caterpillar. She opened her mouth and fluttered her wings, like a young fledgling pleading to be fed. When Singing-Wren refused to give her the food, she hurried into the gourd before him and, with her head in the doorway, once more begged for the caterpillar with vibrating wings and gaping mouth. This time she received the caterpillar and withdrew into the nest to pass it to her little brother. The next time that Blackbill tried to take a morsel from her father at the doorway, he carried it off. But in a minute he returned and, after hesitating, relinquished it to her.

The wrens' habit of passing food from one to another for delivery to the March-Wren, instead of always giving it directly to him, recalled the behavior of the big Brown Jays that inhabit the Caribbean side of Central America and southern Mexico. When a pair of mature jays establish a nest, they are often assisted by from one to five full-grown individuals, hatched in the preceding year, if not earlier. I could distinguish these helpers from one another and from the breeding adults by the various patterns of black and yellow on their curiously pied bills; breeding adults usually have less yellow, and sometimes their bills are wholly black. After feeding the nestlings, a jay frequently delayed on the rim of the bulky open nest, composed of sticks and rootlets, received food that the other attendants brought, and placed it in the gaping mouths of the baby jays. Sometimes a parent passed food to a helper; sometimes a helper delivered food to a parent; and sometimes one helper gave it to another. Most of this food was promptly transferred to the nestlings; but rarely, when a helper was very hungry, he carried away and ate what was intended for the babies. Likewise, parent Common Gallinules often deliver food to their older offspring, who in turn place it in the mouths of their downy brothers and sisters of a later brood.

### A Troubled Day

For three days, the parents and the two January-Wrens continued to attend the single March-Wren amicably. Then Twittering-Wren, finding that her two young helpers could nourish the nestling, began to prepare for still another brood. Probably she was prompted to nest again so soon by the poor success of this second brood, of which only one nestling survived from four eggs. Since the gourd in which she had always nested in the past was still occupied, she chose for her new nest a smaller gourd with a wide round entrance, which ten days earlier I had tied up in a young guava tree, about sixty feet from her orange tree. Here she slept alone, leaving Blackbill to stay with the March-Wren through the night. Yellowbill, probably forced out by his increasingly aggressive sister, took shelter in the cabin's roof, where Singing-Wren continued to sleep.

Early on the following morning, March 28—a memorable day in the history of Singing-Wren's family—he and his mate visited the small guava tree. Both sang profusely, he his sweetly varied verses, she her simple twitter followed by a musical little trill, from which it seemed ungenerous longer to withhold the name of song. Then they began to pick up twiglets from the ground and carry them into the empty gourd. They worked with tremendous energy and flew up with stick after stick. Singing-Wren brought as many as he could without interfering with his singing. Many of the pieces were so long that they spanned the wide round doorway; and the builders, after vainly pushing and tugging to take them in, dropped them and went off for others.

Meanwhile the January-Wrens, principally Blackbill, kept the nestling supplied with food. Nor did the parents wholly neglect their youngest offspring; after their first energetic bout of building, they remembered to bring him something to eat. With a nest to be built and a nestling to be fed, they were apt to become confused and carry a billful to the wrong place. One took an insect to the guava-tree gourd, where only sticks, straws, and rootlets were required. Later, after placing a number of twigs in this gourd, Twittering-Wren carried one to the orange-tree gourd, whither she should have brought a caterpillar or spider for the nestling. Throughout the morning, both parents continued occasionally to make the mistake of offering sticks to it. Usually they deposited these pieces in the orange-tree gourd with the March-Wren, but sometimes they awoke to their error and carried them to the new gourd.

For an hour, Blackbill continued faithfully to attend her baby brother. Then she started to act strangely. Indeed, her queer behavior had first drawn my attention the preceding afternoon, when all four of the grown wrens had gathered in a low bush. Blackbill uttered the simple twittering verse Twittering-Wren used to deliver before she acquired her pretty, clear trill. While Blackbill called, she quivered her drooping wings. Twittering-Wren, perching close to her daughter, was meanwhile throwing up her wings momentarily above her back and occasionally voicing her *twit twit twit*, followed by her own peculiar trill. Singing-Wren and Yellowbill merely looked on, and the former sang from time to time. All flitted through the low bush in a restless, excited manner.

Now, at seven o'clock in the morning, Blackbill resumed her strange conduct. After feeding the nestling, she left the gourd, but immediately turned around and reentered. Soon she emerged and flew to a bush about midway between the two gourds. Here she twittered sharply and rapidly for a minute or two, then continued to the guava tree and tried to enter the gourd, while her mother strove to drive her away. The excitement now became intense; the birds flitted around so swiftly that it was hardly possible to distinguish the parents from their daughter. Blackbill, still perching in the guava tree, vibrated her relaxed wings and twittered for a long while. Twittering-Wren flitted nervously about and threw up her wings with a rapid, twitching motion; while Singing-Wren sang loudly and continuously. After this had continued for a while, all flew together to the roof.

Soon after this first encounter, Twittering-Wren carried food into the orange-tree gourd, then delayed inside to arrange the sticks that she and her mate had absentmindedly taken in. While she was within, Blackbill arrived with food and peaceably gave it to her for delivery to the nestling. It appeared that the orange tree was recognized as neutral ground, but it it was not long to remain so.

After four minutes in the orange-tree gourd, Twittering-Wren emerged and flew to the new gourd, whither her mate followed. They resumed their work of carrying in sticks; but soon Blackbill came and interrupted them a second time. This resulted in another scene much like the one just described, with the difference that when Blackbill again tried to enter the gourd, Twittering-Wren grappled with her and the two tumbled to the ground. Soon they separated without serious injury to either. Blackbill flew up to a convenient perch, where she continued to shake her wings and twitter.

After a while they remembered the nestling, who was crying loudly for food, and all three went to hunt insects for him. After taking a meal to the March-Wren, Blackbill lingered for a few minutes in the gourd. While she was there, Yellowbill, as was his habit, arrived without food and was about to enter. Blackbill pecked savagely at her brother as he came to the doorway. He withdrew for a few moments, then again tried to enter, to be rebuffed in the same rude fashion. Blackbill was developing an ugly temper.

All through the morning, the quarrel continued. Blackbill was clearly the cause of it. Twittering-Wren did not object to her daughter's presence at the old gourd, but would not tolerate her at the new gourd. Blackbill persisted in going to the new gourd and, moreover, pertinaciously followed her mother through the dooryard, quivering her wings and calling *twit twit twit twit*. The mother frequently tried to avoid her daughter by flying away, but Blackbill naggingly followed. All the set fights started at one or the other of the gourds, where Twittering-Wren could not easily avoid her daughter without total surrender of her status as Singing-Wren's mate and mistress of the territory. Singing-Wren took no part in the struggles, in this resembling birds of many other kinds, among which males dispute only with males and females with females. He merely looked on and sang while they fought. But once, when Blackbill entered the new gourd in the absence of his mate, he continued to dart at the doorway until she retreated.

The first really fierce encounter started when Blackbill tried to exclude Twittering-Wren from the orange-tree gourd. When the latter forced her way in against all opposition, the violent conflict began. At first I could see through the doorway that they were fighting; but soon they vanished into the back of the chamber, and for what seemed an age the battle raged unseen. Singing-Wren flitted about restlessly just outside and sang. Yellowbill, with youthful curiosity, tried to enter the gourd and see what was happening, but Singing-Wren would not permit this. At last, one of the combatants appeared in the doorway, then hung over the edge, but could not fall because she was clinched with her opponent. Finally, she dragged the other out. Both fell to the ground, where at first they tumbled about, but soon lay motionless, fiercely grappling each other with bills and feet. When, after a long while, they separated and flew up, neither appeared much the worse for the affray.

Blackbill never had enough. Not long after this, she went again to the new gourd and came to grips with her mother inside. Soon they rolled out and dropped to the ground, where they tumbled about, then lay for minutes clutching each other. One cried out in pain, then they remained nearly motionless so long that I feared one had been killed. At last they separated, and

Twittering-Wren was victress. She flew away without difficulty; but Blackbill could only flutter up to a dead weed stalk, where by one foot she hung upside down from a round, dry flower-head, while the other foot clutched spasmodically upward at the empty air. Half her tail feathers were missing, and blood stained her chin. Nevertheless, after a minute she had recovered sufficiently to perch upright, and before five minutes had passed she was once more pursuing her parent, twittering and shaking her wings as before.

It was remarkable how, after these struggles, Twittering-Wren, fresh and showing no signs of battle on her plumage or of fatigue in her bearing, would go to the orange-tree gourd, look in, hear the hungry pleading of her nestling, then fly away and within a minute or two return with an insect for it. It appeared that she could have disabled or even killed Blackbill, had she tried. As the morning grew older, Singing-Wren gave less time to carrying sticks into the new gourd and more to feeding his nestling. Yellowbill, too, brought food more frequently. His specialty was long, green caterpillars, while the parents came chiefly with small cockroaches from my roof.

It would be tedious to recount all the conflicts between mother and daughter during that long, troubled day. None of the later fights was quite as fierce as those already described. As the hours passed, both Twittering-Wren and Blackbill tired and fought with less energy. In the afternoon, all four grown wrens brought much food to the nestling, more than on past afternoons, to compensate for their neglect during the morning. Yellowbill in particular distinguished himself by feeding the March-Wren more frequently than he had ever been seen to do before. Twittering-Wren, very weary, drowsed while perching in the orange tree near the gourd, closing her eyes for a few seconds at a time. Blackbill, sitting with her head in the doorway a few feet from her mother, nodded in similar fashion.

Yet, until late in the afternoon, Blackbill continued at intervals to behave as she had done all day, shaking her wings and twittering, following her mother as though to pick another fight, which Twittering-Wren tried to avoid by moving away. As sometimes happens with creatures much bigger than wrens, freedom to engage prematurely in adult activities had made Blackbill offensive. An extremely precocious wren, she was not content with being permitted to feed and brood the nestling, but tried to drive her mother away and make herself mistress of all the gourds and the territory around them, just as though she had been an adult bird.

As evening approached, Twittering-Wren and Yellowbill, worn out by their exciting day, retired early into the orange-tree gourd. Blackbill delayed outside until it was almost dark, then came to join her mother and brother in the gourd. Twittering-Wren did not oppose her daughter's entry; and the two who had fought so bitterly through the day slumbered innocently side by side through the night. Singing-Wren, perching in front of the gourd, delivered a parting song that seemed like a hymn of peace, then flew up to sleep alone in the roof.

What a day it had been! What endless excitement and fighting! In all my years of watching birds, I have never seen another conflict, whether between individuals of the same or of different species, a tenth so fierce and prolonged as that between Twittering-Wren and her daughter. The small birds of tropical America are, on the whole, mild and pacific, less given to fighting than many of the feathered kind in lands where a severe winter and scarcity of food disrupt family bonds and make it necessary for birds hurriedly to seek mates and territories when spring returns. Their disputes tend to be protracted rather than violent, like that between two pairs of Masked Tityras that for weeks contended for a nest tree without attacking each other, as described elsewhere (Skutch 1969). Watching through the cabin window the oft-repeated clashes between the two female wrens, I sometimes felt like a war correspondent witnessing a battle.

When the day was done, my admiration for Twittering-Wren was greater than ever. What a strong, capable bird she was! Most

birds build their nests at one time and feed their young at another; she did both in one day, yet only exceptionally became
confused and took the object in her bill to the wrong place. Even
the necessity of defending her home against usurpation by her
unfilial daughter and the exhausting struggles in which she was
forced to engage did not fluster her or make her forget to attend
her nestling. Finally, she seemed to be without malice, and
charitably permitted her enemy to join her in the gourd at the
close of their wearying day.

### Yellowbill

After her departure from the gourd next morning, Blackbill
went off alone and did not reappear through most of the day.
With this disturbing element absent, the wrens' lives went on
serenely as before her outburst. Singing-Wren devoted most of
his energy to filling the new gourd with sticks. He worked very
hard, both morning and afternoon, but not too hard to sing
cheerily at this task. He carried up so many sticks that I lost
count of them. Some were so long that they would not pass
through the doorway while held crosswise in his bill, but he
pushed with a will to force them inward. If he succeeded, it was
only by accident, for despite all the building he had already done
he showed little understanding of the mechanics of the situation.

Singing-Wren worked alone most of the day. With her best
helper absent, Twittering-Wren had to give much attention to
the nestling, but at intervals she found time to go to the new
gourd, skillfully arrange the materials her mate had left there in
disorder, and even to bring a few more pieces. While she tidied
up the gourd, her partner rested near the entrance and sang
joyously. By evening, the guava-tree gourd was so full of sticks
that it was hardly possible to add another.

Like a child with a new toy, Singing-Wren was so absorbed in
the apparently delightful occupation of filling the new gourd that
he neglected the nestling. If it had not been for Twittering-
Wren, aided by Yellowbill, the March-Wren might have starved.

Twittering-Wren, as has been said, gave most of her attention to the nestling and devoted only odd moments to the new gourd. Because of this division of labor, I saw none of the mistakes, such as bringing sticks to the hungry nestling and food to the un-tenanted guava-tree gourd, that had occurred repeatedly on the preceding day.

Now for the first time the nestling showed his head, with its conspicuous yellow flanges at the corners of the mouth, in the gourd's doorway. Since he received more attention than the day before, he did not cry so much. The relations between the two attendants, Twittering-Wren and Yellowbill, remained un-changed. When the mother, arriving with food, found her young helper in the nest, she entrusted it to him for transfer to the nest-ling. Each at times tarried in the gourd for brief intervals of rest, frequently together. Twittering-Wren brought much more food than her son. Both cleaned the nest.

That afternoon I went to the orange tree and made a clucking sound with my tongue to learn which of the grown birds was in the gourd by calling it to the doorway. On hearing the sound, both Twittering-Wren and Yellowbill came out and began to scold. The young bird became highly excited, churred harshly, and ventured closer to me than his mother dared. He approached so near the hand that I raised toward the gourd above my reach that I surmised that if I touched it the wren would strike me. I brought a stool from the cabin and stood upon it to place a hand upon the doorway. Thereupon, Yellowbill flitted wildly among the branches of the orange tree, scolding vehemently, but not daring to approach much closer than a yard from the offending hand. Twittering-Wren remained a little more aloof and became less agitated, possibly because she was more accustomed to my visits. Other small birds, including a Gray Catbird in Maryland and a Slaty Antshrike in the forest of Panama, have not hesi-tated to peck the hand that touched their nests, but no wren of any kind has been so courageous. Likewise, house-wrens have never tried to lure me from their nests by simulating injury, a ruse more common among birds with open nests than among those that breed in holes and other closed spaces.

As soon as I withdrew the hand that blocked the opening in the gourd, the March-Wren, frightened more, perhaps, by the cries of his attendants than by my intrusion, jumped out and fluttered to the ground. Still unable to fly, he hopped away over the short-cropped grass and was easily caught. I replaced him in the gourd, and to make him stay I loosely stuffed the doorway with a handkerchief. As soon as I left, the attendants returned and, completely mystified by the white object that blocked their doorway, flitted excitedly back and forth in front of it. Four were present, for Blackbill, attracted by the hubbub, had reappeared. During the ten minutes that I left the handkerchief in the entrance, none of the four wrens touched it or made a move to pull it out; although, in a similar predicament, a Bananaquit removed the tuft of cotton that blocked the entrance to her nest (see chapter 7). When I took the handkerchief from the gourd, the March-Wren stayed inside.

During the night that followed, Twittering-Wren again slept in the guava-tree gourd, and only Yellowbill remained with the nestling in the orange tree. Blackbill did not appear in the evening, and I failed to discover where she slept. I never to my knowledge saw her again.

Singing-Wren had worked so hard filling the gourd in the guava tree that by the following morning, the third since the new nest had been started, Twittering-Wren could begin to make the nest proper of softer materials, in the deep hollow that had been left for it at the back of the pile of fine sticks. Repeating a former error, she came once, with a sheaf of slender petioles in her bill, to look into the orange-tree gourd, and when the March-Wren pushed his gaping mouth through the doorway, she stuck the whole billful of indigestible stuff into it. The March-Wren promptly drew back into the gourd, making it impossible for me to see what he did with the petioles. Singing-Wren appeared to have completely forgotten the nestling. Less level-headed than his mate, more apt to be absorbed by a single activity, he could not keep so many things in his mind at once. His interest now centered on the new gourd, and he continued to sing incessantly.

On the last morning of the month whose name he bore, the March-Wren left the nest at the age of eighteen days. Like the January-Wrens, he made an early departure, before seven o'clock. Then he roamed through the dooryard and surrounding weedy fields with his parents and older brother. The lower mandible of his bill was almost wholly yellowish horn-color, which seemed to indicate that he was a male.

Only six days after the March-Wren made his first flight, Twittering-Wren deposited the first egg in the guava-tree gourd. Again she laid four and began to incubate them. Still too young to nourish himself, the March-Wren followed Singing-Wren, incessantly clamoring for food, while his mother sat in the nest warming the eggs. Probably Yellowbill helped to feed him. Before he was quite a month old, and only ten or eleven days after he left the nest, the March-Wren began to hunt insects for himself. When only thirty-four days old, he started to practice singing, in a voice much softer and weaker than his father's. In the evenings, he would leave Singing-Wren and go alone to join his mother in the guava-tree gourd. Yellowbill soon ceased to accompany them at night. Before the eggs hatched, he vanished; and I never learned what became of him.

When I first knew Singing-Wren, he had slept in the midst of a bunch of bananas. Since birds frequently build their nests in the same kinds of places as they choose for sleeping, I was confident that before long I would find a house-wren's nest in the center of a bunch of bananas. About the time that Twittering-Wren was hatching the March-Wrens, another pair of wrens built their nest in a cluster of green bananas growing beside a neighbor's cabin. These wrens, like mine, had slept in the cabin's thatched roof until the female started to incubate her eggs among the bananas. After the young wrens left the nest, they were taken each evening to sleep in the bunch of fruit, just as Twittering-Wren's fledglings were often led to rest in the gourd where they had grown up.

### The Guava-Wrens

Late in April, Twittering-Wren hatched all four of her eggs in the guava-tree gourd. All her other young had been named for the month of their birth; but since an earlier brood had been called April-Wrens, I named the latest brood "Guava-Wrens" to avoid confusion. When the four nestlings were eleven days old, well clothed with feathers, and able to call loudly for food, I moved their home from the guava tree to the orange tree in front of my window, so that I could watch them more conveniently. I removed the old gourd, in which Twittering-Wren had raised so many nestlings, then fastened the smaller gourd in exactly the same place, where I was sure that the parents would soon find it.

When Singing-Wren, Twittering-Wren, and the March-Wren returned to the guava tree and failed to find the gourd, they were bewildered. They did not search for their nest, for when nests, eggs, or helpless nestlings vanish, they are almost always irretrievably lost to the parents, who, accordingly, seldom seek them. For over an hour, the Guava-Wrens called loudly without attracting their attendants, who now seldom visited the orange tree.

I went to bathe in the river, intending to replace the gourd in the guava tree if the parents had not found it before I returned. When I got back, however, the parents and the March-Wren were busily bringing food to the nestlings, who had grown exceedingly hungry. Miguel, who was present when the wrens discovered the gourd in its new position, reported that all three grown birds had seemed overjoyed, and the father had sung profusely.

That evening, after much indecision, the March-Wren retired into the gourd that I had set up for the euphonias. Here he fell asleep, but not to enjoy a tranquil night. At dawn the gourd was vacant; horses grazing around the post had probably frightened him out in the dark. Twittering-Wren entered the gourd that had been moved to the orange tree with her nestlings, but not feeling at ease, she flew out in the gathering gloom and finally went to sleep in the roof. Although the nestlings remained unbrooded, they were already so well feathered that they did not suffer. On the following night, both their mother and the March-Wren slept with them, as before the gourd was moved.

Just as the March-Wren had been fed by his older brother and sister hatched in January, so he in turn now helped to nourish the Guava-Wrens. Less than two months old when the Guava-Wrens were themselves ready to fly from the nest, he did not bring nearly as much food as the parents did; nevertheless, considering his immaturity, he did very well. Thus, in two hours of the morning following the transfer of the Guava-Wrens to the orange tree, Singing-Wren fed them twenty-one times, Twittering-Wren eighteen times, and their young helper five times. After delivering what he had brought, the March-Wren frequently delayed close beside the gourd, and with open mouth and quivering wings begged for items that the parents brought. Usually he received them and passed them to the nestlings.

Often the March-Wren entered the gourd and stood for several minutes above the Guava-Wrens. Since they now took their meals through the doorway, their mother rarely went inside by day and never stayed long. He was always eager to clean the nest. Once, when a nestling delivered a white dropping into Twittering-Wren's bill, the March-Wren tried to take it. He seized an end of the gelatinous lump, pulled it off, and flew away with it, while the mother carried off the larger part. He reminded me of a child who, eager to show how grown-up it has become by sharing its mother's tasks, gets in the way and slows up the work. Still young and unskillful, he was often careless with the pellets that he was so eager to take, sometimes dropping them on the foliage below the gourd. When Twittering-Wren arrived, she always noticed these white objects, conspicuous on the dark leaves, and carried them to a distance, so careful was she of the cleanliness of her nest and its surroundings.

Since the old gourd had a narrow doorway, I could never watch the activities of the nestlings it sheltered. The new gourd from the guava tree had not been intended for wrens and had been given a wide round entrance. From my window, I could look right into it and see the four Guava-Wrens resting in their dimly lighted nest. It was especially interesting to watch them at the moment when one of the three attendants arrived at the doorway with food, and try to learn how the grown birds decided in which gaping mouth to place the item, so that one nestling did not receive more than it needed while the others went hungry.

The instant one of the attendants reached the gourd, four widely opened, orange-yellow mouths stretched forward to greet it. As soon as it alighted in the doorway, the attendant placed its billful into one of the four mouths that gaped so prominently in front of it, probably the nearest. I never noticed a moment's hesitation to suggest that the parent was weighing the needs of the several claimants for the meal; nor did the adult remove food from the mouth of a nestling who swallowed it sluggishly and place it in another, as birds who raise their families in open nests often do. Probably because house-wrens so often breed in dark crannies, where it is difficult to watch the food disappear, they have not adopted this method of ensuring its equitable distribution among the members of a brood.

Thus, when the nestlings were all equally prompt to open their mouths when food arrived, which of them received it appeared to be fortuitous. But when they were well fed and drowsy, as they often were after the first spurt of feeding in the early morning, the one whose hunger appeared to be sharpest was usually the first to stretch forward its open mouth, and its alertness was almost always promptly rewarded.

Only three of the Guava-Wrens could find room at the front of the nest, and one of these three was usually forced to remain well to one side. The fourth rested at the rear, looking over the heads of its nestmates, where it was at a great disadvantage when food arrived. When hungry, it struggled, sometimes successfully, to push into the front row. Likewise when, after receiving a meal, a nestling turned around to deliver a dropping to its attendant, it often lost its place at the front. No member of the brood could continue indefinitely to occupy the most favored seat at the dinner table and receive most of the food.

At the age of twelve days, the Guava-Wrens were well feathered and began to preen their plumage. When fifteen days old, they occasionally ventured beyond their nest into the front of the gourd; and by the following morning some had become bold enough to push their heads through the doorway and look around for the approach of a meal. They had begun to peck at spots, or perhaps small crawling insects, that attracted their attention inside the gourd. When an insect flew past their doorway, two who were looking out tried to snap it up, but were too slow to catch it. Now some of them perched on the rim of the nest-cup to sleep like grown birds, instead of crouching down in the hollow to be brooded, as they had done while younger. Twittering-Wren ceased to sleep in the gourd several days before the Guava-Wrens were old enough to leave, but the March-Wren still kept them company by night.

One morning while I was absent, some mischievous children beat on the gourd with a stick until they drove out all four Guava-Wrens. The oldest was only seventeen days of age, the next two were sixteen days old, and the youngest only fifteen days old, so that it should have stayed in the nest three days longer. The older ones could fly for short distances, the youngest scarcely at all. I wished to replace the young wrens in their nest; but the parents, ever watchful, had already led them off through the weeds and bushes, where I could not find them. This was the first time that Twittering-Wren had given promise of raising a brood of four, and I was vexed with the children who had jeopardized the nestlings' lives by driving them prematurely from the gourd.

Heavy showers fell on the young wrens during their first afternoon under the open sky. At about five o'clock, the parents and their helper led them to the edge of the bare ground beside the kitchen. Without guidance, one of the Guava-Wrens entered the passageway between the kitchen and the living quarters, where it stood on the ground and uttered sharp little calls that drew my attention to it. Then it flew up the kitchen wall and clung to the rough boards. It continued to flutter along the wall, around the corner of the building, until it almost reached the low roof. It appeared to be seeking a cranny in which to rest, but found none. Soon it flew to a castor-oil plant behind the kitchen, where it received food from the March-Wren. This fledgling, who could take better care of itself than the others, was probably the oldest of the Guava-Wrens.

Later, another young wren climbed up the kitchen wall in the same way. These birds showed me that fledgling wrens spontaneously seek a cranny as night approaches, and that this impulse develops even before the normal time for leaving the nest. Accordingly, they would look for a dormitory without parental guidance; but they would be unlikely to find a shelter for their first nights out of the nest if the parents did not lead them to a suitable nook that they had already selected.

While one Guava-Wren rested in the castor-oil bush, two more sought shelter from the slow rain among the dense foliage of sprouts at the base of the spiny trunk of a Lagartillo tree. Soon, following their parents' calls, they passed behind the kitchen to a low, red-flowered shrub on the other side. The fourth, evidently the youngest, had until then lurked unseen amid low weeds. Laboriously hopping through the herbage, it made its way to the bush where the others had gathered, and at last all four Guava-Wrens were united.

Now the parents and their helper flew back and forth between the red-flowered shrub and the kitchen roof, which was much lower than that over the rest of the cabin, trying to guide the young wrens to the thatch. But the fledglings made no move to follow, perhaps because the flight was beyond their power. Next, the parents remembered the low gourd on the living post, which was little more than five feet above the ground, and they flew several times to that, then back to the fledglings. This gourd was a good way off; the fledglings were now very tired; and only one, probably the oldest, started toward it. The young wren went less than halfway, became discouraged, and stopped among some bushes, whence I heard its weak calls until dusk descended and it fell asleep, all alone.

The other three Guava-Wrens settled down to pass the night in the red-flowered shrub. They all perched in a row, side by side, on a slender branch not two feet above the ground. From time to time one hopped upon the back of a neighbor. They tried to huddle together as though they were in their nest or some snug cranny. This move frequently unbalanced the fledgling who was hopped upon, and it fell from the perch together with the other who clung to it. Then they fluttered up to the twig again, and arranged themselves as before.

It seemed a pity to permit these fledglings to pass the night in the rain in such a low, exposed situation, when they should be tucked away in some snug shelter. I thought that as they grew drowsy I could catch them and take them inside for the night. Cautiously I approached and extended my open hands, one above their perch and the other below; the three little wrens would make just a double handful. Then I quickly brought my hands together—on the bare twig. The fledglings had slipped away at the last instant. They vanished into some denser bushes that gave better protection, and there, doubtless separate now, they passed their first night in the open air. And a cold, wet night it proved to be.

On the second evening after they were driven from the gourd, the Guava-Wrens did not appear in the vicinity of the cabin, and I could not discover where they or their mother slept. On the third evening, Singing-Wren, Twittering-Wren, the March-Wren, and three Guava-Wrens flew up to the roof of the cabin.

The fourth Guava-Wren, probably the youngest, failed to accompany the others. Driven from the sheltering gourd prematurely, it had succumbed.

For a long while, the old wrens and the young hopped and flitted over the thatch, pushing up under the cane leaves here and there, but never remaining long out of sight. It took them over an hour to settle down. After their arrival on the roof, the young wrens neither received nor begged for food, although in the preceding year fledglings only a few days out of the nest had almost always been fed after they were led to their sleeping place.

When I looked into the gourd on the living post before daybreak, my flashlight revealed that, during all the moving around on the preceding evening, a Guava-Wren had left the roof to sleep there with his elder brother. The March-Wren was lying beside the fledgling in the bottom of the gourd, in a strange, unnatural posture. Not wishing to disturb the birds, I did not investigate. My next inspection of this gourd, in the early afternoon, showed the March-Wren lying just as I had found him as night ended, with no sign of injury to disclose why he had died. I hoped that Death had blown his cold breath upon the wren while he slept, painlessly. I wrapped the little body in tinfoil and buried it at the foot of the orange tree that had sheltered so many members of his family.

On the evening of their brother's burial, the three surviving Guava-Wrens were again led to sleep in the thatch, but on the next evening their parents installed them in the gourd on the post where the March-Wren had died. This low gourd with a wide entrance was for a long while their nightly shelter. Here they slept alone, for both parents preferred the thatch. The three climbed as far as they could up the sloping side of the gourd, where they rested in a row.

The season of heavy rainfall had now returned, after a dry season that had been brief and far from dry. Rain fell almost every afternoon, sometimes in torrents. At times, when a shower began late in the afternoon, the young Guava-Wrens hastened to their gourd for shelter well before their usual hour for retiring. Often they emerged again when the worst of the downpour had passed. Sometimes a single Guava-Wren went to escape the rain in the gourd. If none of the others followed, it would be restless, coming to the doorway again and again to look out and see what the weather was doing. After five minutes, it could endure confinement and solitude no longer, and flew forth to seek its companions in the rain, which was still falling just as fast as when it had entered. None of the wrens ever took shelter from a shower that began much before five o'clock in the afternoon; and the hardest downpours made little difference in the time when the adults went to rest. The well-oiled plumage of birds protects them so well from getting wet to the skin that few of the species that have holes or covered nests take advantage of such shelter in the daytime. Of all the birds in the valley, the ease-loving woodpeckers were most likely to be found in their dormitories during a daytime storm.

Late in May, Twittering-Wren and her mate covered the nest in which the Guava-Wrens had been raised with fresh material. There, in early June, she laid four eggs, her fourth set since December. If she continued to breed as late in the second as in the first year, she may have raised five broods, laying a total of about twenty eggs, an exceptionally large number for a bird in tropical America. But I could not tarry to learn whether Twittering-Wren would lay a fifth set of eggs, for my sojourn in the thatched cabin by the Río Buena Vista had come to its end. Regretfully, I took leave of the wrens and all the other birds that I had studied so long, and went to pass a year at Montaña Azul, farther to the north and higher in the wild mountains, where rain fell more continuously than in the valley of El General and most of the birds were of kinds that I had not seen there. But here, too, I found Southern House-Wrens, who sang cheerily in the gloomiest weather, reminding me of the ebullient little bird who had so long slept in my roof and fed his nestlings in the gourd outside my window. The more I thought about him and his family, the more I admired their energy, versatility, and ability to adjust rapidly to changing situations, which is the mark of intelligence. These were the factors that had enabled the species to establish itself firmly in the most varied environments over the immense territory stretching from Mexico to Tierra del Fuego.

*Postscript*

In the years that have sped by since I left Singing-Wren, I have looked for young helpers in many other families of house-wrens, especially those who nested beneath the newly laid tiles of the house at Los Cusingos even before it was finished and, later, occupied boxes that I attached to guava trees in view of a window. Despite much watching, I have never again seen a juvenile house-wren attend its younger siblings. Sometimes the wrens at Los Cusingos led their fledglings to sleep in open nests deserted by other birds, in thick crotches of trees, or amid clustered foliage, instead of in the bird house where they had been raised, so that they lacked the intimate association with subsequent broods that seems necessary to induce juveniles to feed them. In other cases, young wrens who tried to sleep with their mother while she incubated a later set of eggs were expelled from the nest box, and sometimes chased to a distance and vigorously attacked by their intolerant parent. Finally, ten years after I left Singing-Wren, I had a box in which one juvenile of the first brood continued to sleep with its mother until she hatched the next brood. Now, at last, the stage was set for another instance of juvenile helping; but, alas! two days later the nestlings vanished, apparently taken by a predator.

Twenty years have passed since house-wrens, formerly a familiar presence here, have nested near us. At intervals one appears, sings while he forages through the shrubbery, then, disdaining the box that I have prepared for him, inexplicably vanishes. The reason may be that I have great difficulty keeping these bird houses free of ants and little, black, stingless bees of the genus *Trigona*, which build nests in them. Or perhaps the greater abundance of nest-robbing Cinnamon-bellied Squirrels than when I first came discourages the wrens. I doubt that the continued presence of Riverside Wrens and Rufous-breasted Wrens, who forage amid denser vegetation and build their own covered nests, sends the house-wrens elsewhere. Both of these wrens sing delightfully, but we miss the house-wrens' very different songs.

It is not surprising that I never again found young helpers among house-wrens, for, as the history of Singing-Wren's family clearly showed, their habits are not appropriate for cooperative breeding, such as one finds in Banded-backed Wrens and many other birds permanently resident in mild climates. Among the big Banded-backed Wrens, and numerous other cooperative breeders who are also dormitory-users, only the mother sleeps with eggs and nestlings, while the other members of the family lodge apart, thereby avoiding the risk of breaking eggs or injuring tender nestlings in a crowded nest. If, instead of trying to expel juveniles from the gourd where Twittering-Wren incubated a later brood, she and her partner had consistently installed them in another shelter, much conflict might have been avoided, and perhaps they would have raised four March-Wrens instead of only one. Such fighting as erupted between Blackbill and her mother appears never to occur in a family of true cooperative breeders, where admirable harmony prevails. This is because the yearling, and often older, helpers that are the distinctive feature of cooperative breeders are not precocious but just the reverse. They might be said to prolong adolescence, for they refrain from breeding at an age when at least some of them are physiologically able to reproduce. They remain subordinate to the parents, whom they assist with later broods, thereby enjoying the advantages of an established territory, instead of hazardously abandoning their natal spot. They gain experience that will later help them to become competent parents.

# 4. Miniatures and Giants

OTHERS may go to Africa to see elephants, giraffes, lions, and ostriches, or to Yellowstone Park to meet grizzly bears and bison; to me, the much smaller creatures that surround me are more attractive and interesting. Their activities tend to be more varied; they are more creative; and they can be watched at close range with less danger. A comparison of great and small animals gives the advantage to the latter on almost every point except size and power.

Let us begin with a matter of the greatest importance, their relation to the plants that support all animals, whether directly, as in vegetarians, or indirectly, as in carnivores. Large grazers and browsers can be most destructive of vegetation, even to the point of ruining their habitat, as happened on Arizona's Kaibab Plateau when the deer multiplied too freely after the removal of their predators, and as elephants tend to do in African parks where they are protected. With sharp hoofs and great weight, they break the ground cover and increase erosion on steep slopes; they impact level ground.

Only small creatures benefit the plants that nourish them. All the pollinators are small, from scarcely visible insects up to birds about the size of thrushes; no great bird or mammal could play this essential role in nature's economy. In tropical America, bees of many kinds, above all the small, stingless meliponine species, are probably the most important pollinators. Although

American Bison and Barn Swallows ▶

in the larval stage butterflies can be very damaging to vegetation, as harmless winged adults they compensate by pollinating the flowers whose nectar, and sometimes pollen, they seek. The multitudinous moths appear to perform this service far more seldom, because so many are nocturnal, while most flowers open by day; exceptional are the hawk moths, which become active in the evening twilight. Small beetles are primitive pollinators, chiefly of such structurally simple flowers as those of palms.

Pollinating birds are nearly all slender-billed and small. In the Americas, three hundred species of hummingbirds, ranging from Patagonia to Alaska, are the chief avian pollinators. Long-billed honeycreepers, sharp-billed orioles, and an occasional wood warbler, such as the Tennessee, also pollinate flowers as they search for nectar. In the African and Oriental tropics, small, brilliant sunbirds play this role. In Australia, the many kinds of honey-eaters, along with some of the smaller parrots, such as the colorful lories with their brushy tongues, and certain small marsupials are effective pollinators. Among the few mammals that transfer pollen while seeking nectar are some of the smaller bats.

Large mammals transport many seeds in fruits that stick to their hairs, and clothed man is an important disseminator of such seeds, frequently of the very plants that he least wants in his fields and gardens. But, aside from man, only small mammals, especially rodents, deliberately plant seeds. In northern lands, squirrels bury more seeds than they retrieve. In Costa Rican forests, the chief planters of larger seeds are Agoutis, who, when they have eaten enough, dig little holes for them, then cover them with earth and litter, frequently leaving them until they germinate into seedlings of great trees. Among birds, jays and nutcrackers store underground great numbers of seeds, which, especially for the latter, are a principal source of nourishment through the winter and following spring. But the forehanded bird may die, or forget some of its seeds, which, if they escape rodents, may grow into trees. By far the most important disseminators are frugivorous birds, who not only spread through woodlands and over fields the seeds that they swallow but do not digest, but on long migratory flights may carry them great distances. Ducks and other birds that frequent ponds and marshes may transport seeds in the mud on their feet, which helps us to understand why many aquatic plants are so widely distributed. Although grazing and browsing animals may seriously injure their habitats, the nectar-drinkers and fruit-eaters benefit the plants that support them.

Only small creatures are skillful builders of nests for reproduction or shelter. In David Hancocks's fascinating book *Master Builders of the Animal World*, the largest animal credited with outstanding constructive ability is the beaver. The bigger the animal, the less its need of shelter to preserve body heat at night or in inclement weather, and the less adequate its organs for making anything more intricate than a burrow in the ground or a rough heap of vegetation. Of the larger mammals, only the primates have limbs that might be applied to skillful building, but none appears to construct anything noteworthy with its grasping hands. By pulling together branches or other vegetation, high in trees or on the ground, the great apes quickly finish open nests for sleeping, but their work is crude indeed compared with the exquisite constructions of countless smaller creatures. The only mammals whose nests can compare in neatness and delicacy with those of birds are certain small rodents, such as the Harvest Mouse and the Dormouse, whose compact balls of grasses and vegetable fibers, each with a hidden doorway in the side, win admiration.

To give even a fair sample of the wonderful fabrications of avian builders would require a book. Outstanding are the felted nests of hummingbirds and American flycatchers, the woven nests of Old World weaverbirds and New World orioles and their relatives, the domed clay ovens of South American horneros, and the intricate castles of interlaced twigs built by other members of the same great neotropical family. The neatly carved holes of woodpeckers reveal skill of a different kind. In addition to receptacles for eggs and young, many birds build closed nests specially for sleeping. Birds' nests are often tastefully decorated with lichens, mosses, or other bits of vegetation, like the exquisite downy cups of hummingbirds and the pendent pouches of bushtits, perhaps only for camouflage, but perhaps also to satisfy a nascent aesthetic sense. The largest feathered creature that shows much architectural skill is the Hammerhead of Africa, a twenty-inch-long stork that builds, of sticks and other vegetation, a closed chamber three or four feet in diameter, which it lines with mud or dung and provides with an entrance tunnel at the side. The nests of nearly all large birds are crude constructions of sticks, which, as in the case of eagles that add to the same structure year after year, may become enormous without revealing much taste or skill. Or the big birds simply deposit their eggs on the ground, perhaps in a shallow depression that they scratch out.

Among insects, the outstanding builders are wasps. The tropical American species make such an enormous variety of nests, usually of a papery material composed of wood fibers cemented together with saliva but sometimes of felted plant hairs, that I continue to find new examples to admire. Some are great top-shaped structures hanging high in trees, some are elongated and stringlike, some the most delicate little chests fastened beneath leaves. Some have corrugated walls for greater strength. Other wasps' nests, like those which *Metapolybia* spreads over our walls, contain countless tiny windows, each closed with a transparent material to admit light to the brood cells, which, like those of most, if not all, paper-making wasps, are as neatly hexagonal as those of honeybees. Far less irascible than northern hornets, many tropical wasps can be watched at reading distance without inciting them to sting.

To small creatures we owe most of the pleasing sounds of the animal world; large ones rarely do more than bark, croak, roar, howl, or bellow. The monotonous sounds of grasshoppers, crickets, and other orthopterons are pleasant accompaniments of our walks through fields and woods, or relieve the silence of night. The voices of certain small frogs are pleasingly bell-like, or resemble the twanging of a small stringed instrument. Softened by distance, the klaxonlike call of the toad *Bufo marinus* is not unmusical. But the outstanding musicians of the animal world are, of course, the songbirds of the Oscine suborder, which includes the greater part of the familiar birds of parks and gardens. Most of the best songsters are small to very small; among Oscines, crows and ravens seem to have become too big to sing well, although some of their relatives, the jays, give pleasing medleys, sotto voce. Among the sub-Oscines, lyrebirds have won fame as accomplished mimics, and a number of others have pleasant or even beautiful songs, which tend to be simpler than those of Oscines. Among other orders of birds, some of the tinamous, which hardly exceed a domestic hen in size, are outstanding for the purity of their notes, combined in quite simple phrases. Larger birds tend to have shrill or raucous voices, devoid of melody.

Recently we have heard that some of the great whales sing. I had read so much about the remarkable performances of the Humpbacked Whale that I asked a friend to bring me a recording from the United States. When the record-player began to turn, we listened with great expectations, which were all too soon disappointed. Doubtless whales' notes sound sweet to these huge mammals, but I much prefer the songs of tiny wrens. Probably it is no accident that the smallest of the anthropoid apes, the gibbons, have the clearest, most pleasing voices.

When we think of beautiful animals, birds and butterflies come first to mind, followed perhaps by beetles and moths. Few of the world's loveliest birds are larger than pheasants and parrots, most considerably smaller, down to glittering, gemlike sunbirds and hummingbirds. Nature seems to delight in concentrating her brightest colors on small surfaces. As a base for pure colors, fur appears to be far less favorable than feathers, and scarcely any mammal can vie with birds for brilliance. Many, especially among the smaller antelopes, are supremely graceful; but the biggest mammals, such as the elephant, rhinoceros, hippopotamus, and grizzly bear, sacrifice beauty and grace for mere bulk. Among marine vertebrates, the most colorful and graceful are small fishes, above all those of coral reefs.

Finally, especially among the warm-blooded vertebrates, the smaller species take the most elaborate care of their young. Few great mammals prepare for the reception of their offspring, which they drop wherever they happen to be. Their parental care consists of little more than permitting them to suck, and defending them when they can. Small mammals, notably rodents, build more or less adequate nests, dig burrows, or find holes for their litters; and marsupials (including even the big kangaroos) carry them in their pouches or on their backs. For nearly all birds, the production and rearing of young involves more laborious attention than it does for any other animals, except perhaps the social insects and a few others that care for their progeny. Instead of growing inside a parent who is possibly unaware of their presence, in the manner of mammals, avian embryos develop in eggs—themselves often beautiful objects—that must be warmed by long hours of patient sitting, or, as in megapodes, in an incubator mound that the birds laboriously make and attend. After the nestlings or chicks emerge from the shell, they are, in most birds, fed for weeks or months from the parents' bills, or guided by them while they pick up their own food. This parental care, laborious and prolonged for nearly all birds, is most complete in the smaller kinds, the passerines, woodpeckers, and others placed near them in our systems of classification, who make the most adequate nests, feed and brood their young, and diligently attend to the nest's sanitation, a refinement rare among the bigger birds. Moreover, many of them lead their fledged young to sleep in snug, covered nests—as, to my knowledge, no great bird does.

On the negative side, small creatures, multiplying excessively, sometimes become destructive pests on farms and in homes.

They are most likely to cause great losses where man has destroyed the ecological balance, and above all where he practices monoculture on a vast scale. It takes a great many small creatures to do as much damage to standing crops as a few big animals can do in little time.

One of the triumphs of modern technology is miniaturization, the development of small models of such objects as radios, calculators, and many other things, usually electronic, which can do whatever the larger early models did, with great saving of materials and energy—no small advantage in a world that uses both too lavishly. Nature tried miniaturization ages ago, with notable success. A miniature is not merely something small, but a small object that embodies the essential features of a bigger one that preceded it, like a miniature portrait. The earliest living things were doubtless very small, probably one-celled, but they were not miniatures, for they did not copy anything larger. A small songbird is a true miniature, for it has all the organs that the biggest birds have and can do almost everything they can do, except tasks requiring great strength. Indeed, it does many things better; it builds neater nests, takes better care of its young, sings more sweetly, and is often more beautiful. One of the most amazing accomplishments of this birdling, which may weigh less than an ounce, is its ability to migrate back and forth, year after year as long as it lives, between two definite points, thousands of miles apart—a feat for which an aviator needs a chart, a compass, and a whole panel of instruments. Such a feathered mite is a marvel of miniaturization. Economical of energy, it demands little of nature's productivity, and, if a nectivore that pollinates flowers or a frugivore that disseminates seeds, it earns its food by serving the plants that provide it.

The earliest known feathered creature, *Archaeopteryx lithographica*, half bird and half reptile, lived more than 125 million years ago and left its imprint in the lithographic limestone of what is now Bavaria. It was about the size of a crow, could climb trees with the aid of claws on its wings, catch insects in its toothed beak, and glide downward by spreading its wings and long bony tail, feathered to the end. Only about 70 million years later, in the Eocene, small songbirds, including ancestral titmice and starlings, appear in the geological record. Although the wide gap in this record does not permit us to trace in detail the evolution of songbirds, existing evidence points to the conclusion that it proceeded from fairly large predecessors to much smaller descendants—that it was true miniaturization. The evolution of the smallest birds, the hummingbirds, is still less known, for fossils of their ancestors appear not to have been found, but they undoubtedly sprang from larger forebears.

For the flowering plants, or angiosperms, so closely associated with songbirds and hummingbirds, the evidence for miniaturization is strong. According to Alfred Gundersen (1950), "Among dicotyledons *Magnolia, Sassafras, Populus, Liquidambar, Platanus* and others [all trees] may not have been very different in the days of the dinosaurs from what they are today, but most herbaceous plants seem to have originated since that time." Like true miniatures, the small herbs can do everything that great trees can do—they have green leaves capable of photosynthesis, absorb water and minerals from the soil, transpire, flower, and set seeds—except produce wood, which they do not need. To compensate for this lack, they are our best natural sources of strong fibers. They supply most of mankind's food. Without them, it is doubtful whether man would have developed agriculture and the civilizations that it supports. Many of them produce food in one growing season, sometimes in a few weeks, whereas trees do not fruit for years after they germinate, which would have been long for primitive man to await a return for his labor.

Evolution commonly modifies its earlier productions in diverse directions—the phenomenon known as adaptive radiation. Although in some lines of descent it produces miniatures of its early models, in others it takes the opposite course, creating giants. This is most evident among the vertebrates, whose internal skeleton and circulatory system can support much larger masses of flesh than are viable, for example, in insects with exo-skeletons and less efficient systems for supplying oxygen to their tissues. Over the geologic ages, each major division of the verte-brates has produced gigantic animals. Among the fishes, mantas twenty feet long, and almost equally large sharks, still swim in the oceans. By the Triassic period, the amphibians had produced the gigantic, crocodilelike *Cyclotosaurus*, about fourteen feet long, and many somewhat smaller species that were much larger than any existing members of the class. Most famous for titanic size are the reptiles, which by the Upper Jurassic had developed such huge monsters as the fifty-ton, eighty-foot-long, vegetarian *Brachiosaurus*, and by the late Cretaceous had evolved the for-midable *Tyrannosaurus rex*, forty-seven feet long, capable of standing nineteen feet high on its hindlegs, and tearing its prey with teeth six inches long—the most powerful terrestrial preda-tor that Earth has borne. In the air the great reptiles were repre-sented by *Pteranodon*, with a wing-span that may have reached fifty feet, by far exceeding that of any existing bird.

The largest feathered creatures were flightless giants, includ-ing the powerful, seven-foot *Diatryma* from the lower Eocene of North America and Europe, and the Miocene *Phororhacos* of South America, which stood six feet tall and had a head as large as that of a horse. Both of these monsters were evidently power-ful predators. Much taller and much more recent were the vege-tarian moas of New Zealand, of which the largest species were ten feet high, and the equally tall elephant birds of Madagascar, which may have weighed up to one thousand pounds, and laid eggs with a liquid content of two gallons.

After the disappearance of the great dinosaurs at the end of the Cretaceous period, the mammals, who until then had been quite overshadowed by their reptilian neighbors, began to domi-nate the land. Before long they produced their share of giants, one of which, the rhinolike *Baluchitherium*, whose remains were found in deposits of Oligocene age in Asia, was eighteen feet high at the shoulder, the largest mammal ever to live on land.

Later, in the Pleistocene, the edentate mammals gave rise to the giant ground sloth, *Megatherium*, about twenty feet long, which invaded North America from its South American home after the closure of the Panamanian land bridge. It was contemporary with the bulky mastodons and mammoths, and like them became extinct in relatively recent times. Although titanic whales, up to the eighty-foot Blue Whale, still swim in diminishing numbers in the oceans, the land no longer supports the great variety of gigantic mammals that it once bore, and the largest extant species, the elephants of Africa and Asia, are inferior in size to terrestrial mammals that have vanished.

Among the factors leading to gigantism, predation appears to be the most influential. If an animal becomes too large to elude its enemies by hiding, and is not swift enough to escape them by flight, its best course may be to become so large and powerful that, aided by horns, sharp hoofs, other weapons, or protective armor, it can resist them. The predator, in turn, must become bigger and stronger to overcome its prey. This gives rise to an evolutionary race between predator and victim to outdo one another in size and strength. It is significant that the largest terrestrial predators that ever existed were contemporary with the largest herbivores, upon which, in late Mesozoic times, they evidently preyed.

Competition for mates and territories, in which the larger individual may have the advantage, may also lead to increase in size. When food is scarce, browsing animals, like the gigantic *Baluchitherium* and the modern giraffe, which can reach the highest twigs, are likely to survive while shorter individuals of their species starve. To support such long necks, large bodies are needed, so that natural selection would promote gigantism. Like giraffes, the moas evidently browsed heavily on leaves and twigs of shrubs and trees. Since they appear to have been numerous in species and individuals, the ability to reach higher probably favored the evolution of the tallest species, *Dinornis maximus*.

Oceanic islands, including New Zealand; Madagascar; the

Mascarene Islands, where the turkey-sized Dodo and Solitaire lived; and Cuba, which in the late Pleistocene supported exceptionally large owls, eagles, and a vulture as big as the Andean Condor, have been favorable for the evolution of large birds. Islands often favor rapid divergent evolution by early colonizers that find abundant food and little competition. A not infrequent consequence of such radiation is gigantism. South America was an island continent when it gave birth to the formidable *Phororhacos*.

The wholesale extinction of reptiles great and small toward the end of the Cretaceous period remains an unexplained mystery. The mammals, which were destined to replace them, were still too small and weak to have affected them seriously, except, perhaps, by eating their unguarded eggs. The Cretaceous was an age of fluctuating climates, and possibly, in an interval when cold or drought depressed the production of food, the huge consumption of the gigantic saurians so depleted habitats that widespread extinction resulted. A similar interval of multiple extinctions occurred when the mammoths, mastodons, giant ground sloths, sabre-toothed tigers, and other great mammals that dominated the continents during the Tertiary and early Quaternary eras went the way of the dinosaurs. In this case, man, who had become a powerful predator and now thinly covered all the continents and many islands, may have been largely responsible for many extinctions. The moas all vanished after the Maoris, who hunted them, colonized New Zealand, about one thousand years ago. To be sure, small no less than large animals have become extinct in great numbers throughout the geologic ages, but gigantic ones appear to be exceptionally vulnerable. When small ones go, others soon replace them if habitats remain favorable, but the great ones leave gaps that may long remain unfilled.

As we survey the history of animals through the ages, it is difficult to resist the conclusion that gigantism is a miscarriage of evolution, perhaps a misfortune. In contrast to many small animals that pay for their food by serving the plants that produce it,

great animals devour huge quantities that they have done nothing to earn. By large-scale destruction of vegetation or devouring
many weaker animals, they are more likely to injure than to improve the environment. They find it more difficult to adapt to
changing situations. Unlike smaller, less specialized, creatures,
they are nearly always evolutionary dead-ends, unable to evolve
into different forms that may carry their lineage through suc-
ceeding ages.

The value to itself of any life depends wholly on its psychic
aspect. It could make no slightest difference to a creature quite
devoid of sentience whether it continued or ceased to exist. Unfortunately, our most profound zoological investigations fail to
yield the information about the inner lives of animals that we
need for an evaluation of their consciousness. Nevertheless, we
know enough to point to certain probabilities. We know that the
evolution of human brains and intelligence was closely linked
with that of our hands and manipulative skill. If man is the most
intelligent animal, it is because he has the most versatile execu-
tive organs in the whole animal kingdom. The reason for this
close alliance of intelligence and manipulative skill is clear:
without intelligence to direct them, our supple hands could not
realize their full potential for the preservation and enrichment of
our lives; and, conversely, without organs to make its ideas effective, the most brilliant mind could hardly promote our survival.
Accordingly, neither large brains of high quality, nor skillful
hands would without the other have much "selective value" and
be promoted by evolution.

The human example shows that the quality of brain is posi-
tively correlated with the number of things an animal can do.
This seems to apply with equal force whether its skills are learned
or follow innate patterns; for all learning rests upon an innate
foundation, and the perfection of complex innate patterns of behavior often requires practice that involves learning. I emphasize
the quality rather than the size of the brain because the former is
more important, although the latter certainly affects a brain's

total capacity. Neither in man nor in other animals is intelligence closely correlated with the brain's size; big animals with large brains are often more stupid than smaller animals with smaller brains; and among humans we find small-brained geniuses and big-brained dolts. Moreover, we are often told that much of our brain remains unused, so that with far fewer cerebral cells we might be equally intelligent, learned, and capable. From these facts we may conclude that small creatures with diverse skills, often combined with an advanced social life, have brains of higher quality than great animals whose activities are much less varied. I surmise that their psychic life is correspondingly richer, more satisfying or enjoyable.

In the vegetable kingdom, great size is less unfortunate than in the animal kingdom. Gigantic trees not only elaborate all their own food but often offer much to animals, and, in the tropics, their trunks and limbs support many epiphytic plants. Until man began to covet their timber, their chances of survival, as individuals and as species, were much better than those of gigantic animals. Mammoth, mastodon, and giant ground sloth, probably even dinosaurs, coexisted with trees not greatly different from some that flourish today. We can enjoy their impressive presence, which draws our gaze skyward, without fear that they will attack us, as great animals are likely to do. We can wander through majestic groves without risk, but in African parks visitors are warned not to leave their cars because of the danger of attack by big quadrupeds.

Not only in the animal kingdom is great size a disadvantage. In every category, from stars to animals to man-made artifacts, moderate or small size is often best. Our Sun is a rather small star. Our middle-sized Earth is covered with abundant life, while its huge sisters, Jupiter, Saturn, and Uranus, appear to be lifeless. In *The Breakdown of Nations* (1957), Leopold Kohr pointed out the benefits that might be gained by separating huge countries, with huge problems and great capacity for destructive wars, into smaller, more homogeneous nations, with problems more amenable to limited human intelligence. In *Small Is Beautiful* (1973), E. F. Schumacher pleaded for an "intermediate technology," simpler, smaller-scaled, less dehumanizing than the huge corporations with vastly complicated installations that create such an excess of merchandise with so great a sacrifice of human values. The widespread notion that bigger is always better is a delusion. The vulgar mind applauds bigness; the refined mind appreciates the beauty of small, finely organized things. To admire bigness and power, as such, is a barbaric trait that has been responsible for a large share of human ills; as when men adulate, and die for, the ruthless, egoistic conqueror who, at a vast price of slaughter and devastation, builds a huge, often evanescent, empire.

We might ask in passing what might be the optimum stature for man. I would say, no bigger than is necessary to carry his large-brained head with ease and grace, perhaps not much over five feet, certainly no more than six. A person of moderate size can do everything a bigger one can do, not only of mental work but also of tasks that require great physical strength and endurance. The increase in average height that has occurred in some populations in the last century may be a consequence of improved nutrition rather than genetic changes. However this may be, any tendency toward gigantism should be carefully watched and, if possible, halted; for, as the whole history of animals shows, gigantism can have disastrous consequences. Moreover, the bigger person needs more food, larger garments, bigger beds and motorcars; his heart works harder. The difference between the material needs of a five-foot person and a six-foot person may seem trifling, but, multiplied by millions, it can make a vast difference in a world already pressing hard upon its natural resources. And not only is it highly desirable to prevent human stature from becoming excessive, it is even more urgent to hold human populations at moderate density.

Gigantic animals have all but vanished from the land and their numbers are diminishing in the oceans. Even those of moderate size yearly become rarer as forests are destroyed, wetlands drained, and environments polluted. Perhaps we must resign ourselves to seeing ever fewer birds large enough to adorn the landscape, like egrets and ibises. But we might find consolation in the thought that the adaptable small birds, the true miniatures, which should long be with us, have the most varied plumage, the sweetest voices, the most charming nests, the most fascinating habits, and least avoid our presence. To lose them would be the greater tragedy.

In addition to some of my happiest, most instructive hours, the small creatures that surround me have given me a model for my own life; for one wishes to become like that one admires. I try to live like those that are most peaceable and have achieved the best relationship with the vegetable world that supports them, to be creative in my own way, as they are in theirs. Since I am much bigger than they are, with correspondingly greater needs, I have not succeeded as well as my models. Although I sow and cultivate some of the plants that support me, I must often resist and destroy other plants, including those that threaten to overwhelm my crops or to make a thicket of my dooryard. I have been guilty of the destruction of stately trees whose timber I needed for my house and its furnishings. The small creatures that live most harmoniously with plants benefit but never destroy them. Nevertheless, by trying to live like a small rather than a great animal, I have dwelt in greater harmony with creatures of all kinds, reduced my demands upon Earth's bounty, and created to the best of my ability.

Intermediate in size between the miniatures and the giants, man shares, often in intensified form, the traits of both categories. On the whole, he resembles small animals more than those of his own size or larger. Like many of the former, he serves the plants that nourish him, more thoroughly than any of them does. On the other hand, he tends to be extremely destructive of unwanted vegetation, as small pollinators and frugivorous disseminators are not. In the constructive ability that allies him to small creatures, he is infinitely more versatile, and has no parallel whatever among large animals. Like many small creatures, he can sing, but he far exceeds them in the variety of the music that he can produce, not only with his voice but with the instruments that he devises. The indications of an aesthetic sense, which we detect in small animals rather than great ones, flower in him. His many-faceted care of his babies resembles that of the most careful avian parents more than it does that of any animal as big as himself. In all these ways, man is more similar to small than to great animals. Nevertheless, he has been, and on the whole remains, as ruthless to other animals as any of the great carnivores. Multiplied by his inordinate numbers, his demands upon the planet's productivity far surpass those of the greatest of the giants. Man's future appears to depend upon which side of his ambivalent nature he chooses to cultivate and which to suppress. If he continues to squander Earth's resources like a thoughtless giant, he will probably follow the giants to extinction. If he cherishes and perfects the traits that he shares with the best of the small creatures, he may long continue to enjoy the Earth they adorn.

# 5. Blue-and-White Swallows

AT Montaña Azul, where I studied Resplendent Quetzals, Prong-billed Barbets, Emerald Toucanets, and other birds of the mountain forests, strong contrasts in the weather were reflected in the changing moods of a mind sensitive to nature's varying aspects. When for many days together a strong north wind drove chilling gray clouds through the treetops, until everything dripped with condensed moisture and the birds I most wanted to watch seemed to have gone elsewhere, it was difficult to preserve a hopeful outlook. But when the sun rose into the bluest of skies, setting aglow the gardens of flowering epiphytes that heavily burdened the massive trees, I could imagine no fairer abode. It was on such smiling days that, through an open window or from the porch, I chiefly watched Blue-and-White Swallows circling over the pasture on the ridge where my cottage stood, or above the deep, wooded ravines on either side.

These small swallows had dark, violaceous steel blue upper plumage. Below, they were white, except for their grayish brown sides and flanks, their blue-black undertail coverts, and, on some individuals, a few dusky spots on the chest. Their short tails were slightly forked. Their bills were black, their eyes brown, and their feet dark. I could not distinguish the sexes by their plumage.

These Blue-and-White Swallows on the northern slopes of

Costa Rica's Cordillera Central were near the northern limit of their far-flung breeding range, which covers much of South America to Tierra del Fuego. Of the two subspecies, the southern nests in Chile and much of Argentina. Individuals that breed at high southern latitudes, where winters are severe, migrate northward in the austral autumn, rarely as far as southern Mexico. The other race, which nests from northern Argentina to Costa Rica, appears to reside permanently wherever it is found.

Blue-and-White Swallows are amazingly tolerant of climatic extremes. In western South America I found them on the rainless guano islands off the desert coast of Peru, where in the evening they circled around catching insects above the Guanayes, who had settled in compact, innumerable masses to pass the night on the ground. They are the common swallows of the Ecuadorian Andes, present in the high, cold *hoyas* nearly ten thousand feet above sea level, and over the rainy eastern foothills. Voyaging along the upper Amazon and its great tributaries, I watched them skimming over the turbid water with White-winged Swallows, White-banded Swallows, and wintering Barn Swallows, but they were less abundant here than in the mountains. Since my visits to these regions were during the winter and early spring of the southern hemisphere, I could not tell whether these Blue-and-White Swallows were residents or migrants from southern Chile and Argentina. Probably those on the guano islands and along the Amazon were migrants from the south mingled with Barn Swallows from the north, for the Blue-and-White Swallows that breed in the tropics prefer higher altitudes. In Costa Rica I have found them from about fifteen hundred feet up to the mountaintops at ten thousand feet. At higher elevations, this is the most abundant swallow, but at low altitudes it is far less numerous than the ubiquitous Rough-winged Swallows.

In this country, Blue-and-White Swallows are most often seen in settled regions where there are many buildings for their nests and open fields above which they can forage. In their man-

Blue-and-White Swallow ▶

ner of life, they differ little from other swallows. They subsist largely, if not wholly, upon insects they catch in the air as they weave back and forth over open fields, housetops, and expanses of water. When tired, they rest in company with swallows of their own and other species upon exposed perches—leafless branches in wilder country, telegraph and electric wires where these are available. Their song is a thin, weak, prolonged trill that slides upward at the end. In Costa Rica I have heard it more or less frequently at all seasons, but chiefly from March until June, when they nest. Apparently, over their immense range, Blue-and-White Swallows vary as little in voice as in plumage. Hudson (1920), who knew them in the La Plata country, described their song as "a single weak trilling note, much prolonged, which the bird repeats with great frequency when on the wing. Its voice has ever a mournful monotonous sound, and even when it is greatly excited and alarmed, as at the approach of a fox or hawk, its notes are neither loud nor shrill." This description would apply equally well to the utterances of Blue-and-White Swallows in Costa Rica. When alarmed, they voice full, plaintive monosyllables, and when defiant, as when disturbed at their nests, low harsh notes.

### Nesting

In its selection of a nest site, this little swallow is as adaptable as in its choice of a habitat. The closed space in which it always builds may be in the most diverse situations. Within a half-mile of the cottage at Montaña Azul, I found these swallows breeding in a cavity formed by decay in a dead trunk standing in a pasture; in tunnels in roadside banks, made by other birds or left by the decay of a stout root; and beneath the sheet-iron roof of my cottage. The two nests in burrows were ten and twenty-three inches back from the mouth. Elsewhere, I have found nests beneath roofs of tiles and thatch. One pair laid four eggs in a deep cranny among the roots of a tree at the top of a high bank. Another pair fed nestlings in a niche above the lintel of the doorway of a lawyer's office, opening directly upon the narrow sidewalk of a busy street in the heart of the city of San José, Costa Rica, years ago when the air was purer. Several pairs appeared to be feeding nestlings in crevices in the masonry abutments of the highway bridge over the Río Verde in the Pastaza Valley of eastern Ecuador.

Hudson, who knew the southern race as a summer resident in central Argentina and called it the "Bank-Martin," found it nesting in holes in the banks of streams, in the sides of artificial ditches, and in the walls of wells. But on the flat, open pampas, its favorite nest site was a hole the Miner or Little Housekeeper had bored into the wall of one of the great burrows dug by the Viscacha, which the swallow claimed after it had been abandoned by the bird that made it. Hudson believed that Bank-Martins, or Blue-and-White Swallows, never dig into the earth themselves, which agrees with my experience in Costa Rica. In Chile, however, these swallows usually nest in small colonies in yard-long burrows they excavate for themselves in exposed earthen banks, but, as farther north, they choose a wide range of different sites (Goodall *et al.* 1957). In the wild Sierra Nevada de Santa Marta of Colombia, Blue-and-White Swallows select inaccessible crannies in cliffs (Todd and Carriker 1922).

In Costa Rica permanently resident Blue-and-White Swallows live in pairs at all seasons. Toward the end of January, a pair that flew over the mountainside at Montaña Azul began to be interested in my roof. Day after day, they circled on tireless wings around the cottage, and often they fluttered up beneath the eaves, apparently seeking a nest site so early in the year. The arrival of a third swallow, and sometimes a fourth, was the occasion for animated aerial pursuits, accompanied by loud, sharp notes. Sometimes pursuer and pursued struck together in the air. More rarely, they grappled and fell to the ground, to rise in a few moments, apparently none the worse for their tussle. After a while, the intruders would withdraw, leaving the two who claimed the house to gyrate in peace around their chosen shelter.

By early March, this pair had not begun to build, and I had

not discovered where they slept. On the evening of March 6, when they continued to fly around the house on the ridge until after sunset, I expected that they would pass the night with me. While I stood waiting for them to enter beneath the eaves, a fierce little Bat Falcon swooped down, seized one of the swallows in its talons, and bore it off to devour high in a dead tree. The survivor flew off over the profound wooded gorge of the Río Sarapiquí and vanished through the dusk. Next morning it returned for a brief visit to the scene of the tragedy, but did not tarry. Three days passed before I again had a pair of Blue-and-White Swallows flying around the cottage. Without much doubt, the survivor had returned with a new mate.

Late in the afternoon of March 12, one of the pair, who had been winging together about the house, entered the narrow space above the ridgeplate, beneath the corrugated iron sheets at the northern end of the roof. Here it chirped loudly, while its mate continued to circle around outside. After an interval, the second swallow heeded the other's entreaties, fluttered up to the roof in a tentative fashion several times, then entered the cranny. While the two rested side by side upon the two-inch-wide beam, twittering softly, the white breast of one shone out from the dusky nook. A third swallow, who had been flying around nearby, darted up to the entrance as though to join the two inside, but it was promptly, in a subtle manner that escaped me, made to understand that it was not welcome. Immediately dropping away, it continued its tireless flight. As day waned, the pair sallied forth several times for an excursion over the mountainside, then returned to their nook. The third swallow, fluttering up under the eaves, repeatedly looked in as though it longed to join the two who rested so contently there, yet dared not. As daylight faded, rain fell, and the third swallow vanished, leaving the two together on the ridgeplate. I was confident that they would at last sleep above my head; but suddenly one shot out and vanished through the deepening gloom, leaving its partner alone in the niche.

On the darkly overcast morning that followed, the solitary swallow lingered on the ridgebeam, its white breast gleaming in the narrow cranny, while other birds flew and sang and sought breakfast. Half an hour after daybreak, the other two swallows flew up from the east and, to my surprise, both joined the bird in the niche. Then all three flew out and circled around, until two returned to the nook, to stay less than a minute.

This little drama continued for about a week. One member of the pair wished to sleep on the ridgeplate; its mate preferred a distant shelter; and the situation was complicated by the intrusion of the third individual. In late afternoon, the pair would rest close together in the nook, the male sometimes singing his fine, sharp trill with a rising inflection at the end. After a while, one would fly out; its mate would call with loud, full-toned, pleading chirps; then either this swallow would follow the first into the open, or the latter would rejoin the other in the niche—a reunion followed by contented chirpings. Finally, dusk falling, one would fly out of view, leaving its protesting partner alone on the ridgeplate. After a night without a companion, it would linger in the confined space next morning until its mate flew back across the ravine and entered beside it, sometimes with the third swallow following. Soon the two would fly out together to break their fast. Before March ended, the swallow who slept beneath the roof, finding that it could not persuade its mate to keep it company there, abandoned this dormitory. Yet both continued to rest on the ridgeplate in the late afternoon, sometimes at the northern end, sometimes at the southern.

Thus it happened that this pair had not settled upon the niche above the ridgebeam as a dormitory when they began to build there on the last day of March, at the more sheltered southern end, three days after a neighboring pair had finished a nest in a roadside burrow. As in other pairs that I have watched, the male and female shared the task of nest-construction, picking up bits of straw from the bare ground of the flower beds, instead of from the adjacent pasture, where such material was more abun-

dant. This was probably because bare earth was easier to alight on, and to take off from, than uneven, yielding grass. After finding a satisfactory piece, each swallow flew directly to the nest, sometimes with a grass blade trailing far behind its tail. In the intervals between carrying things to the roof, they traced erratic courses in the air in their usual fashion.

So many pieces fell from the sides of the two-inch beam that the swallows probably would not have completed their nest if I had not given them a broader support by closing with cardboard the spaces between the ridgeplate and the underside of the roof. Before long they had straws scattered from end to end of the long beam. In the afternoon, their day's work done, the pair rested side by side on the beam, sometimes creeping along until they were above the center of the house, far inward from their nest. They were not disturbed when I climbed up into the dark attic to view them from below with a flashlight. Often the male sang, his finely trilled song penetrating the thin ceiling above me while I wrote my notes on rainy afternoons. Before their nest was finished, the pair began to sleep inward from it on the middle of the ridgeplate.

After a week's work, the shallow cup of grass blades, straws, and dry herbaceous stems was finished and warmly lined with downy chicken feathers. Now the swallows slept upon the nest or close beside it. Another week passed before the female laid the first of four spotless, glossy white eggs. In Costa Rica I have found one other set of four eggs, four sets of three, and two sets of two, both laid by the same female. Beyond the tropics, in Argentina and Chile, Blue-and-White Swallows lay three to six eggs—another example of the widespread "latitude effect."

In the nine hours that I watched the swallows incubate beneath my roof, I timed twenty-five sessions on the eggs, ranging from 3 to 50 minutes and averaging 18.6 minutes. The nest was neglected for eleven periods ranging from 1 to 14 minutes and averaging 6.9 minutes. The eggs were incubated 85.9 percent of the time. During the early morning and in rainy weather, they

◀ Blue-and-White Swallow over the Cottage at Montaña Azul

were constantly attended by both members of the pair, sitting alternately; but later in the day, when the sun heated the iron roof, even through the coffee sack that I draped over the ridge above the birds for their greater comfort, they were neglected for brief intervals, while both swallows flew around together, catching insects.

When ready to return to the eggs, a swallow would often fly up in front of the niche as though about to enter, only to veer aside at the last moment and continue to circle in the air a few times more, catching additional insects before it settled down for a period of quiet sitting. Usually a swallow's entry was promptly followed by a departure. More rarely, the two stayed together in the nest for a few minutes before one flew out. I could not watch the birds change places on the nest in the dark cranny; but once I clearly saw the swallow that had been sitting brush past the other as it emerged, leaving the new arrival to take charge of the eggs. Each evening both members of the pair retired early into the niche, where one slept upon the eggs, the other on the nest's rim, his white breast upon his mate's dark blue shoulder.

One morning while I watched these swallows, the green lizard who dwelt in the wall of the cottage climbed up to the end of the ridgeplate and started in toward the nest. After a few seconds, it scuttled out and hurried down the wall, evidently driven out by the swallow in charge of the nest. Then the bird moved forward to a point near the beam's end, where I could see it clearly. It stretched up its neck and widely opened its mouth, probably emitting a hissing or rasping sound too slight to reach me. After repeating this several times, it returned to its eggs.

On May 2 and 3, after the usual fifteen days of incubation, four tiny, pink-skinned nestlings hatched. They had sparse, light gray down and tightly closed eyes. The insides of their mouths were pale flesh-color. When they were four days old, the rudiments of their feathers became visible as dark spots beneath the skin, and at nine or ten days their plumage began to expand.

When two weeks old, one of the nestlings fell from the nest and died on the ceiling boards below before I found it. The other three lived to fly. While they were very small, their parents slept in the same manner as during incubation, one warming them in the nest and the other resting on the rim. But after the nestlings were two weeks old and well clothed with feathers, and their sharp notes penetrated the whole cottage each time they were fed, they were no longer brooded. Now one of their parents roosted on the beam inward from the nest, the other in some un-discovered situation.

When twenty days old, the nestling swallows began to wan-der along the ridgeplate, and at night they rested on the bare wood behind the nest rather than in it. Now the second par-ent deserted them in the evening, flying away with loud cries through the dusk, apparently to join its mate in that other sleep-ing nook they had found so hard to abandon when they decided to nest under the roof. It was strange that this earlier dormitory still attracted them so strongly. By day both parents continued to bring food to the young at short intervals, but they began very late, an hour after neighboring birds had become active.

During their last week in the nest space, the young swallows were thus alone through the nights. When, at the age of twenty-six and twenty-seven days, they flew out, their upper plumage was dark gray instead of deep blue, and their underparts were clouded with gray instead of being pure white, as on their par-ents. Their tails and longer wing feathers were black. After the young swallows' emergence, their parents led them to rest on the ridgeplate, at the northern end rather than by the nest at the op-posite extremity. Now, at the end of May, afternoons were usu-ally rainy, and the fledglings retired early. On the day the last of them flew out, they took shelter in the nook at half-past three. The following day, when a hard shower fell early, they entered at 1:20 in the afternoon and remained until nightfall. While they rested there, warm and dry, their parents flew around in the rain catching insects for them. Each return of a food-bearing parent was greeted by a chorus of loud chirrups. At intervals the adults, tired by so much flying under a wet sky, would rest for fifteen or twenty minutes beside their offspring, the male sometimes singing his high-pitched trill and also low, bubbling notes. Then the two would dart forth into the rain together, to collect more insects for their young.

As evening approached, the parents rejoined their fledglings for the night. The five slept pressed close together in single file on the ridgeplate, the three young swallows in the center and a parent at either end, as I could clearly see when I climbed up into the attic with a flashlight. Their slumber was not sound, and, being somewhat wakeful myself, I repeatedly heard their weak chirps above me in the night. In the morning, the whole family lingered late, not leaving the roof until a few minutes before sunrise. The young were not fed before they left their sleeping nook, but sallied forth after their parents had been circling around the house for five minutes or less, then flew swiftly out of view with them.

After they had been in the open for three days, the young swallows formed the habit of going to rest between four and half-past four in the afternoon, depending upon whether it was raining hard or only drizzling. Ten days after their first flights, they no longer received food from their parents after their early return to the ridgeplate. A day later, the adults started to renovate the nest, carrying up bits of grass from the yard, then feathers, to cover the old structure with a layer of fresh materials. Then they slept upon the refurbished nest, leaving their offspring to roost alone at the opposite end of the long ridgeplate. Now thirty-nine days old, the juveniles appeared already to be quite independent of parental care; in the morning, while the parents lingered on the nest, they emerged and flew rapidly away. When, finally, the adults came out, they did not go in search of their offspring, but circled around the cottage hawking for insects. Two hours later, the three young swallows returned and joined in these aerial gyrations, catching their own food and receiving none from their parents.

On June 17, eighteen days after the departure of her first brood, the female swallow laid the first egg in the renovated nest. In the next two days she laid two more, completing her set of three. Soon after this, two of the young birds ceased to sleep under the roof. The third continued to pass the night alone at the northern end of the beam until early July, when it, too, vanished, aged a little over two months. The parents were not so fortunate with their second brood as with their first; two nestlings succumbed at an early age during a prolonged rainstorm; the third, when half grown, died when a horde of army ants ransacked the cottage from foundation to roof. Despite their loss, the adult pair, now thoroughly attached to the house, continued to sleep side by side upon the ridgeplate, at least until August, when my sojourn in this stormy region ended.

On an evening a short while before my departure from Montaña Azul, when it was already nearly dark, a strange combination of sounds above my head continued until I climbed up into the attic with a light to investigate. By day a number of bats, hanging head downward, slumbered in this dimly lighted space beneath the roof. Now that its dark day was dawning, one of these creatures had tried to reach the outer air by creeping along the ridgeplate, but found its passage blocked by the two swallows, who had long since retired and were reluctant to fly out into the deepening gloom. They firmly held their ground, uttering the harsh note they emitted only when disturbed or alarmed, while the bat protested with a sharp, rapid chittering. My light revealed the birds and the bat almost in contact. When its rays fell upon them, the feathered creatures withdrew to the outer end of the beam, beyond the wall, while the furry one moved inward toward the center of the house. Later, it must have found another mode of egress, for at the night's end the swallows were sleeping in their usual place and the bat had vanished. Although the birds were good tenants, keeping their quarters clean and always conducting themselves with propriety, the bats fouled their diurnal dormitory, making their presence most objectionable. Moreover, in the afternoon, or after they retired before dawn, they would sometimes engage in noisy disputes, accompanied by a volley of sharp, irritating notes that dispelled sleep.

Other Blue-and-White Swallows in the neighborhood be-haved much as did those who nested on the ridgeplate. A pair who built in a burrow that they found ready-made in a bank slept together on the nest, one in the cup and the other on the rim, before eggs were laid, during the incubation period, and while their single nestling was growing up. They continued to lodge in the burrow after the disappearance of their newly emerged fledg-ling. Another pair, who raised three fledglings in a natural cavity in a decaying trunk in a pasture, led their newly departed young back to sleep in the hollow with them. Two of these soon van-ished; but the third continued to pass the night in the hole with its parents, even after it had become otherwise independent of them. One of the trio would fly off alone in the morning, and two, doubtless the mated pair, together. Sometimes the pair, sometimes the young bird, would emerge first and fly away with-out waiting for the others. The first might leave eight or ten min-utes before the last.

Soon after my house at Los Cusingos was built, a pair of Blue-and-White Swallows arrived and remained my guests for the next two years, trying in vain in three consecutive breeding seasons to raise a brood here. Appearing first about the end of March 1942, they slept together in various of the many nooks that the roof of rustic, unglazed tiles offered them. About the first of May, they started to build in a site difficult for me to reach, and I did not try to examine their nest. Although they failed to raise a brood, the two swallows continued to sleep together under the tiles through the remainder of the year and the early months of 1943. After their morning exit, they always flew swiftly out of view, to remain away all day. By mid-February they were spend-ing more time near the house; and on February 27 I saw one pick a straw from the roadway and carry it up to the place beneath the tiles where they slept, revealing a growing interest in a nest site, although they still did little building.

Early in April, before the nest was finished, one of the pair vanished. The other remained a few days longer, but on the morning of April 8 I failed to see it emerge from its usual place beneath a tile. That same evening two swallows arrived together. Without hesitation, one of them darted up under the lowest tile of the end row, the usual point of entry. The other flew around and around, clinging to the walls of the house or beneath the eaves here and there, unable to find its way in. Meanwhile the first, unseen beneath the tiles, sang again and again. Finally, he shot out to join the other. After flying around the house, both returned to the sleeping place together, the first entering easily, the second after a moment's confusion.

On previous evenings, the swallows had gone to rest with less confusion. Apparently, the male of the pair who had already slept in my roof for over a year had lost his mate, stayed alone for a few nights, was absent for a night or two while he sought a new partner, then returned with a bride—much as had happened when the swallow at Montaña Azul lost its mate to the Bat Falcon. Since the bride was not familiar with her mate's home, with its many doorways leading into as many narrow passageways, which did not communicate one with another, he first sang to guide her to him; then, voice proving a poor guide in so bewildering a situation, he came out to show her where to enter.

Next morning, April 9, the pair flew about the eaves trying to select a nest site among the scores of crannies available to them. By April 15 they were actively building under a tile of the marginal row at the rear of the house, where they slept, and in early May the female laid two eggs. As at Montaña Azul, the two partners incubated by turns. Four of their sessions on the eggs lasted 34, 59, 48, and 81 minutes. During four hours while I watched, they left the nest unattended only twice, for intervals of 1 and 14 minutes. Probably this pair took longer sessions than the pair at

Montaña Azul because they usually foraged beyond view, and the incubating partner was not disturbed by its mate flitting around near the nest and calling. Since this nest was beneath a tile instead of metal sheets, it did not become so heated at midday, and the swallows could incubate in greater comfort.

These eggs turned out to be infertile, and the swallows continued to incubate them for eleven days beyond the usual fifteen, until in June I found them on the ground. One was broken, but the shell of the other was merely perforated by a tiny hole, which had apparently been made by the bill of the small bird who removed it. At the end of a week, the swallows had relined their nest with dark-colored downy feathers and laid two more eggs. Before another week had passed, these also lay broken on the ground beneath the eaves. They seemed to contain no yolk. I was not sure what had removed these eggs, but I suspected the Southern House-Wrens, who, at the ridge of the roof, were bringing forth their prolific broods in regular sequence without mishaps.

Although when the second set of eggs was lost it was only June 12, and many other birds were still nesting, the swallows apparently made no further attempt to rear a brood that year. The unusually small size of both sets of eggs, and the failure of the first set to hatch, indicated that the female of the pair had low fertility. Despite their failures, the two swallows continued to sleep on or near their nest for more than four months.

Again in early November, first one and then the other swallow disappeared. For two weeks I failed to see a swallow fly up beneath the tiles in the evening or dart out in the morning. Then, late on the rainy afternoon of November 26, while I was removing some boards stored above the rafters at the back of the house, I became aware of a pair of swallows flying around in the gloom outside. After I descended to the floor, they soon entered the nook beneath the tiles where swallows had slept for so long. The fact that the pair went to roost in this particular spot, instead of in one of the many other spaces available beneath the tiles, convinced me that at least one of them had slept there before. The following afternoon this one entered its dormitory without difficulty, but the other was confused and continued to fly up to neighboring parts of the eaves, unable to find its mate until the latter emerged and led it back to the proper row of tiles. Since the first to enter sang while awaiting the other, I believe that it was again the male who had lost his mate, and I witnessed a repetition of the act that I had seen the preceding April, when the male led home a new mate who needed to be guided to his customary sleeping place.

While I watched from a window on subsequent evenings, the female swallow repeatedly entered channels beneath the tiles one, two, three, or even four rows removed from that where her mate had gone to rest. Then sometimes she would complain in clear, mournful notes, while her partner answered with his fine trill from beneath the marginal row of tiles. Since no passageway connected the channels beneath the different longitudinal rows of tiles, she had no recourse except to fly out and try again. The male would continue to sing and she to call until the two were united in their dormitory, when both fell silent. A week passed before the female was able to enter without mistakes.

During the long interval between nesting seasons, I gave much attention to the swallows' times of leaving the roof in the morning and returning in the evening. At daybreak the two would linger in their nook until smoke began to rise from the open fire in the neighboring kitchen. Long after nearly all their feathered neighbors had become active, only ten or fifteen minutes before the sun flamed up above the crest of the forest on the eastern ridge, they would fly out from beneath the tiles. Usually they emerged almost together, but on some mornings, especially as the following nesting season approached, one would delay for a minute or two, rarely as much as five minutes, after its mate had flown out of view. On clear, cool mornings they would sometimes become visible beneath the edge of a certain misshapen tile that did not lie flat, and stand there, gazing out, for several minutes before they flew forth. Usually, as soon as they emerged, they turned their courses up the valley of the Río Peñas Blancas, which flowed in front of the house, and flew toward the high craggy summits of the Chirripó massif until lost to view. Then they would be absent all day. How far they went I could never learn.

The hour of the swallows' return to the roof depended largely upon the weather, but at latest it was earlier than that of most other birds in the vicinity, including both their relatives, the Rough-winged Swallows, who roosted in a nearby canefield, and their neighbors, the house-wrens, who also slept beneath the tiles. On clear evenings they might on rare occasions remain out until half-past five, but usually, especially about the time of the winter solstice, they went to roost at five o'clock or even earlier. On the rainy afternoons so frequent during the second half of the year, they sought shelter far earlier. On some dark, wet afternoons they entered their nook soon after three o'clock. If the rain abated before sunset, they might come out again and fly around catching insects for a while, before their early and final return for the night. If rain continued to fall hard until nightfall, they would stay beneath the tiles, preferring dryness to supper. In this valley, where rain in the forenoon is infrequent and almost never hard, I did not see the swallows take shelter from a morning shower. However, a slow rain at daybreak might delay their departure for ten or fifteen minutes beyond their usual time for emerging.

In mid-February of 1944, this pair began to carry straws into their niche beneath the tiles. Now they stayed near the house during the day instead of remaining out of sight; they might sit together in their nook or in other spaces in the roof for many minutes while the sun was high. The male often sang while the pair rested side by side under a tile. By the end of February, they were building actively; by mid-March, nearly a month after they started, they had practically completed their nest; and on March 19 the female laid the first of three eggs. This year the swallows got farther than in the two preceding years, hatched three nestlings, and attended them until they were a week old, when they mysteriously vanished. After three seasons of failure to rear offspring, the adults then deserted my roof.

From time to time in the next two years, a pair of Blue-and-White Swallows came to investigate the spaces beneath the tiles, and even slept there for a few nights; but three years passed before another nest was built beneath my roof. On May 25, 1947, a newly arrived pair took shelter from an afternoon downpour under a tile at the front of the house. Next day they started to carry up straws; but, as frequently happens when birds build in a man-made structure, the number of closely adjacent, similar sites confused them, and they deposited their material in at least three places. In the evenings, they had the same difficulty. The male often entered first and sang, while his mate flew around outside, vainly trying to find him. Sometimes he emerged and returned repeatedly until she succeeded in following him in, to sleep in closest contact with him, as I could see by shining a flashlight up into the space beneath a row of tiles. On other nights, when she failed to join him, their white breasts were visible in different rows. After three weeks, they abandoned my house without nesting.

Not until fourteen years later did a pair of Blue-and-White Swallows nest again at Los Cusingos, this time not in my roof but in that of my farmhand's cabin nearby, where they raised three young. The last nesting at Los Cusingos was in 1965, once more in my roof. During the past fifteen years, Blue-and-White Swallows have not only remained away from us, but have avoided the neighborhood, while Rough-winged Swallows continue to be abundant. Blue-and-White Swallows prefer higher altitudes.

# 6. A Favorite Food of Birds

MANY years ago, a bird dropped a seed on the high bank in front of our house. It grew into a tree of medium size, with a shapely, rounded crown of twice-pinnate leaves, each composed of many small, dentate leaflets. Its richly branched, drooping panicles of small white flowers were hardly ornamental, but its fruits attracted many birds. I identified the tree as *Dipterodendron elegans*, of the soapberry family.

This umbrageous tree thrived until an afternoon in July, twenty years past, when one of the brief, violent windstorms that at long intervals smite this generally calm valley snapped off half its crown. Two weeks later, a most unexpected repetition of the miniature tornado demolished the remainder of the tree, which was cut up for firewood. It left a descendant in the richer soil at the foot of the bank where the river once flowed, which shot up straight and slender before it spread its crown above the orange and guava trees amid which it stood. On great, round, blackish, earthen nests that tiny *Azteca* ants built on the *Dipterodendron* tree's high limbs, upright, clustered stems of the orchid *Epidendrum imatophyllum* bore abundant pink blossoms, visible from our front windows in the dry season. Rooted in one of the ants' nests with the orchids grew a small fig tree, *Ficus paraensis*, which sent cablelike roots down along the host tree's trunk to the ground. Long, limber stems of a thick-leaved *Peperomia* draped around the ants' nest. I have found the orchid and the fig grow-ing nowhere except on this one kind of ants' nest.

The *Dipterodendron* tree does not flower and fruit with equal profusion every year. It bore an unusually abundant crop of fruit in April 1975, while it was nearly leafless. Attached to hanging panicles, the greenish, brown-tinged pods were irregular globes, about three quarters of an inch long by nearly as broad. Only rarely did these pods contain seeds in each of their two cells. Usually one seed had aborted, and its cell remained smaller than the other, making the pod lopsided. When ripe, the pod split into two valves, exposing the usually solitary seed, ellipsoidal in shape and about three eights of an inch long. The basal two-thirds of each shiny black seed was covered, as by a thimble, with a soft, thin white tissue, making a pretty contrast. This covering, known as an aril, tasted slightly bitter. Rich in oil and probably also in proteins, but lacking starch, it was the only part of the hard-shelled seed digestible by small birds.

The function of this white thimble was to entice birds to swallow the seed, which, after digesting off the aril, they would regurgitate or void unharmed, often at a distance from the parent tree, thereby spreading its progeny far and wide. In this en-deavor, the arillate seeds of *Dipterodendron* were highly success-ful. Rarely have I seen so many birds of so many kinds wait so eagerly for a tree's bounty to become available to them. I passed many hours watching the birds that flocked to the tree at day-break and remained there until past the middle of the morning, noticing their different ways of removing seeds from opening pods and their relations with their competitors. Before the sup-ply of seeds was exhausted in early May, I had counted thirty-one species taking them. One morning, from daybreak to seven o'clock, twenty kinds came to eat the arils. I could not count the individuals who constantly joined and left the shifting, many-colored throng of visitors.

Best equipped to procure seeds were the largest visitors,

White-crowned Parrots and Fiery-billed Araçaris. Although nearly all the other visitors had to wait for the pods to at least begin to open, these middle-sized toucans could bite them open with the tips of their great, vivid beaks. One that I watched carefully was at first unsuccessful, but with a little practice he learned to split the pods, and removed seed after seed, throwing each back into his throat with an upward toss of his head. No other bird obtained so many seeds in so short a time. The araçari demonstrated convincingly the advantage of having such a long bill. Unlike the smaller birds, he could neither cling to the thin, hanging inflorescence stalks nor pluck seeds in flight; but, while perching on a fairly stout twig, he could reach far out and down to seize a pod in the end of his bill and force it open. Later, Fiery-billed Araçaris came in flocks of four or five and satisfied their hunger so quickly that they never remained long. Although the araçaris ignored the smaller birds, the latter never ventured near those great, colorful beaks.

A pair of White-crowned Parrots came frequently and spent more time in the tree than the araçaris did. Unlike all the other birds, they held up a closed pod with one foot while they bit it open with a short, powerful bill. Probably they were more interested in the embryos than in the arils. Primarily seed-eaters rather than fruit-eaters, these and many other parrots are poor disseminators, as they digest the embryos instead of regurgitating the seeds unharmed, as toucans do. Of all the tree's guests, these parrots were of least service to it. Brown-headed Parrots and Orange-chinned Parakeets occasionally alighted in the *Dipterodendron* tree, but I did not see them try to reach the seeds. The parakeets preferred seeds from a neighboring Barrigon tree, which they extracted from amid the soft, fluffy down that filled pods bigger than themselves. Another large visitor was a Blue-diademed Motmot, who came occasionally, plucked an unopened pod, could not extract the seed, and dropped it. After halfhearted attempts to obtain a seed, he flew away. Clearly, he was not equipped to compete either with birds with bigger or thicker bills, like araçaris and parrots, or with smaller, more agile birds with sharper bills.

Golden-naped and Red-crowned woodpeckers came repeatedly to the *Dipterodendron* tree. Sometimes they clung back downward beneath a pod while they tried to open it with their sharp bills. Often they failed; but if they made a small gap, or found a pod just starting to open, they extracted the seed and swallowed it whole. Other birds had to wait for pods to open; but, if they found one just beginning to split, they could insert their bills through the chink and peck out bits of aril. This was true of four very different attendants—Blue, or Red-legged, Honeycreepers, Garden Thrushes (also known as Clay-colored Robins), Red-eyed Vireos passing through the valley on their way northward from their winter home in South America, and Yellow-green Vireos, who earlier in the year had come from South America to nest with us. When the thrushes and vireos could obtain a whole seed, they swallowed it entire, to regurgitate it after digesting off the aril. Tiny Blue Honeycreepers clung beside a pod to remove fragments of aril with their long bills. Green Honeycreepers, Shining Honeycreepers, and Blue Dacnises came seldom. They preferred the red arils of a neighboring *Clusia* tree.

Buff-throated and Streaked saltators, frequent visitors, had a special way of treating the seeds. If one of these finches could procure a whole seed, the bird rested it on a horizontal branch while it removed and swallowed the aril, then dropped the black seed. Since the saltators rarely carried a seed far, they were poor disseminators. Wintering Rose-breasted Grosbeaks of both sexes carried seeds in their bills into neighboring woods, where, beyond view, they may have treated them as the saltators did. However, grosbeaks are seed-eaters, whereas saltators are fruit-eaters, so they may have consumed embryos in addition to the arils. The abundant tanagers sometimes alighted in the *Dipterodendron* tree, but mostly ignored its seeds. Although they, too, eagerly eat arils when they can reach them readily, their short, thick bills put them at a disadvantage in the competition for *Dipterodendron* seeds. A pair of Speckled Tanagers arrived occasionally to swallow whole seeds, one of which the male presented to his mate. A brilliant male Scarlet Tanager, on his way northward from South America, came on several mornings to eat the seeds.

Among the most numerous and active of the birds that sought the arils were nine species of flycatchers: resident Tropical Kingbirds, Gray-capped Flycatchers, Vermilion-crowned Flycatchers, Boat-billed Flycatchers, and Bright-rumped Attilas; Piratic Flycatchers, who had come from South America to breed in stolen nests; Eastern Kingbirds and Sulphur-bellied Flycatchers migrating through the valley; and a vagrant Brown-crested Flycatcher. These flycatchers plucked arillate seeds while flying past a pod, hovering in front of it, or perching beside it; they swallowed them whole and later regurgitated the indigestible seeds divested of their arils. Masked Tityras were fairly frequent visitors and, like the flycatchers, seized seeds either in flight or while perching, and swallowed them entire. Black-crowned Tityras came less frequently. A male White-winged Becard arrived occasionally, plucked seeds on the wing, and promptly swallowed them.

The *Dipterodendron* arils strongly attracted migratory birds, including, in addition to those already mentioned, Baltimore Orioles and Swainson's, or Olive-backed, Thrushes. A female Rose-breasted Grosbeak continued to come for them until the exceptionally late date of April 29. Sulphur-bellied Flycatchers, usually rare spring transients on their way to nest at higher altitudes in Costa Rica or perhaps as far away as Arizona, were never more abundant than when the tree fruited profusely in 1975. They became exceptionally adept at snatching seeds from pods as they darted past. Sometimes five or six of these large flycatchers were present together, and some remained until May 5, when the supply of fruits was almost exhausted. Like some other tropical trees, *Dipterodendron* tends to flower and fruit in alternate years;

and in 1976, when the tree in front of the house, the only one available for watching, failed to produce seeds, I saw not a single Sulphur-bellied Flycatcher at Los Cusingos. In 1977, when the tree fruited but the diseased arils were shriveled and blackish, I noticed very few of these flycatchers, as likewise in 1978, when again the tree failed to flower.

At trees and shrubs laden with ripe berries, many birds may gather them simultaneously without competing; but the *Diptero-dendron* tree's deliberate way of dispensing its seeds caused its visitors to vie keenly for them. Frequently one bird supplanted another struggling to remove fragments of aril or a whole seed from a barely open pod. However, I saw no fighting, and no bird tried to exclude another from the whole tree. During the days when these birds spent so much energy trying to obtain seeds from the limited supply available at one time, they mostly neglected the ripe, easily gathered berries of several species of woody melastomes that fruited profusely a short distance away; and they could also have eaten freely of bananas on the neighboring feeder. Clearly these arils, to me so insipid, were compellingly attractive to the birds, who probably found in them certain nutrients that were rare elsewhere.

The ways that plants disperse their seeds are as fascinating as they are diverse. Some, depending on no external agency, scatter their seeds by the explosion of a turgid or a woody pod, as in jewelweeds and many legumes. Others employ wind to waft afar fruits or seeds equipped with wings or downy tufts; or else, as in the tumbleweeds of open, windswept plains, the whole plant breaks away from the soil and scatters its seeds as it rolls along in a gale. The fruits or seeds of many aquatic plants float in the water that bears them away. Fairly large, roundish fruits, like walnuts and wild avocados, roll downhill. The small seeds of many plants that lack obvious means of dispersal nevertheless travel far, perhaps on the muddy feet of quadrupeds, men, and birds, or lurking among the products of cultivated fields, as is true of many weeds. Larger seeds are often buried in the ground, at a distance from the parent tree, by birds or mammals, notably rodents, who may fail to retrieve them before they germinate.

The great number of plants that depend upon animals to disperse their seeds fall into two main categories, those that reward the animals for their services, and those that surreptitiously attach their fruits or seeds to unsuspecting creatures. We might designate these the liberal plants and the stingy plants. The latter include all those with fruits, seeds, or involucres that by means of hooks, barbs, or gummy secretions stick, often annoyingly, to fur, feathers, clothing, or skin. Familiar examples are tick trefoil (a species of *Desmodium*), bur marigold (a species of *Bidens*), and burdock (a species of *Arctium*). Birds appear to be poor vectors for such propagules, as they would soon remove adhering objects by preening. Far from using small birds as carriers, plants that ripen their seeds in bristly heads or spikes may catch and hold those who carelessly brush against them, as occasionally happens with fatal consequences to such diminutive birds as hummingbirds, chickadees, warblers, and siskins. Clothed man is an excellent vector, as some of these bodies stick tenaciously to fabrics.

Of the liberal plants, which are of greatest present interest, we may again recognize two main divisions. The first includes all those trees, shrubs, vines, and herbs that produce berries, drupes, or similar fruits, in which a thin, easily penetrated skin surrounds the edible tissue in which the seed or seeds are imbedded, as in the grape, tomato, and peach; the animal does not need to wait until a pod or capsule splits open before it can eat the fruit, often with some or all of the seeds that it contains. The second division includes those capsular fruits in which tough or woody walls enclose the seed or seeds, each of which has a hard, or at least not readily digestible, coat partly or wholly covered by soft, nutritious tissue. Usually such tissue grows from the base of the seed and is called an aril. In berries and similar fruits, the ovary or receptacle supplies the food that attracts animals; in arillate fruits, the seeds themselves do so.

An advantage of arils enclosed in pods appears to be that they give the plant greater control over its seeds; until they mature and the enclosing capsule splits open, they are unavailable to all except strong-billed birds, as I saw at the *Dipterodendron* tree. When food is scarce, birds and mammals may devour berrylike fruits before they ripen. The thick capsule also makes it difficult for insects and fungi to attack the nutritious tissue within. On the other hand, to form such a capsule requires much material, sometimes more than goes into the capsule's contents, although perhaps not of such valuable nutrients, such as proteins and fats. Instead of producing relatively few pods with arillate seeds, a plant might yield a much greater number of berries to attract disseminators. Apparently, the kind of fruit that a plant produces depends largely upon its evolutionary history and the vagaries of mutation. Possibly, too, it is related to the chemistry of the edible tissues.

Arils are usually rich in oils or other lipids and in proteins, as are the seeds from which they grow, but poor in starch and sugars. They are rarely sweetish, a notable exception being the arils of granadillas, fruits of certain passionflowers, which within a thin, parchmentlike shell contain a gelatinous mass of arillate seeds. They are sold in tropical markets, and are agreeable to eat if one has no objection to swallowing many seeds. Berries are often sweetish, but usually poor in oils and proteins; many are so watery that one wonders that plants can entice birds to disperse their seeds for such paltry rewards.

Many tropical trees, shrubs, vines, and herbs bear arillate seeds; within a hundred yards of our house, I have found twenty species that do so. They are rare in the temperate zones, for which reason their ecological importance was, until quite recently, largely unrecognized. Probably most familiar in northern lands are the bright red arils that enclose the seeds of *Euonymus*

and *Celastrus*, of the staff-tree family, and the red "berries" of the yew, which are actually arillate seeds not enclosed in pods, for the yew is a gymnosperm. The mace of commerce is derived from the arils that embrace nutmeg seeds. In addition to granadillas, arils eaten by man include the delightful Mangosteen, the vile-smelling but delicious Durian, and the treacherous Akee, le-thally poisonous if not gathered at just the proper stage and cooked with all precautions. It is probably not without signifi-cance that, with the exception of granadillas, these arils valued by man come from the Old World, where large primates have been present much longer than in the Western Hemisphere.

Arils usually have a bright color that contrasts not only with the surrounding foliage but also with the capsule that bears them. The aril may be white and the pod red or yellow; it may be red between yellow valves; or yellow in a brownish pod; or black in a green or reddish pod. If the seed is partly exposed, as in *Dip-terodendron*, it may be of a color that contrasts both with its aril and the pod. A pod exposing arillate seeds is often a beautiful, conspicuous object.

Much more abundant at Los Cusingos than *Dipterodendron* trees are trees and shrubs of the genus *Clusia*, of which six species grow near the house. Most are epiphytes, growing on trees or rocks, although they may stand on the ground after the decay of the trunk that originally supported them. They have opposite, glossy, simple leaves and waxy white, rose-tinted, or yellow flowers, some of which attract pollinating, stingless bees by offer-ing them very sticky gum that they use in their hives. Their fruits range in size from that of an olive to that of an orange. Accord-ing to the species, these capsules split into from four to eleven thick valves, which spread out like the petals of a flower. Along the inner side of each valve of the species with smaller fruits is an elongated mass of lobed, coherent arils, bright red or orange in color, in which the tiny seeds are embedded. These fringelike arils contain a large oil globule in many of their cells, but have

◄ *Clusia*: Closed Pods and Open Pod Exposing Arillate Seeds

little or no starch. To me they are tasteless or slightly bitter. In contrast to many arillate seeds, those of the clusias that I have examined have thin, soft seed coats; yet they must resist digestion during the brief interval when they remain in birds, who spread them from tree to tree through forest and clearings.

A tree of *Clusia rosea* grew on a calabash tree in front of our dining-room window. Of all our clusias, it has the largest pods, but bears relatively few of them, with the result that competition for their contents was even keener than in the case of the *Dipterodendron* tree. *Clusia rosea* differs from the species with smaller fruits in that the seeds, each completely enclosed in an entire aril, rather than a lobed one, do not cling together in a mass, and are held in deep embayments in the fruit's central axis rather than exposed on the inner surface of the valves. As soon as a capsule of this *Clusia rosea* tree opened the merest chink, hungry birds began to extract the arils. First to procure them were sharp-billed woodpeckers, who could cling back-downward beneath a pod and remove part of the contents through a tiny cleft. Slender-billed honeycreepers also clung inverted, or hovered beneath a fruit long enough to extract seeds. Thick-billed tanagers and finches were so handicapped that they rarely tried to compete.

A family of Golden-naped Woodpeckers spent much time in this clusia tree. Dominant over all the other visitors, they could displace the almost equally big Red-crowned Woodpeckers from a pod. Both kinds of woodpeckers took precedence over the honeycreepers, of which the Green could displace the Shining and the latter could supplant the Blue. Although, as at the *Dipterodendron* tree, Blue Honeycreepers were among the most numerous visitors, they were clearly subordinate to all the others. To compensate for their frequent exclusion from opening clusia pods, they repeatedly tried to intercept arils that a parent Golden-naped Woodpecker was passing to its young, but always without success, as far as I saw. Sometimes a bird drove another of its own kind from an opening pod; even members of the same closely knit Golden-nape family supplanted one another with mild pecks. However, no bird tried to drive another from the small tree, and I saw only one brief, inconsequential clash, between a female Shining Honeycreeper and a female Blue Honeycreeper. These birds so eager for arils were certainly not starving, for on the feeder nearby were enough bananas for all.

One morning while I watched this *Clusia rosea* tree, excited cries from its guests announced the arrival of by far the biggest of all its visitors, a male Lineated Woodpecker with a flaming red crest. When I first glimpsed him, he appeared to be carrying a long, curved twig. Closer scrutiny revealed that this was his lower mandible, three or four times normal length and bent slightly to one side, projecting far beyond his upper mandible. Clinging for many minutes beneath a single opening pod, this poor woodpecker with a grotesquely deformed bill laboriously extracted the red arils, whether with his upper mandible or with his tongue, I could not tell. Even after he had removed a few seeds, he had trouble eating them; sometimes he supported them on his foreneck until he somehow worked them back into his mouth.

For five weeks, this unfortunate woodpecker continued to visit the clusia tree. Since such a deformity does not develop in a day, it was evident that he had managed to survive with it for a considerably longer interval, even if he could not peck into wood. Doubtless the nourishing clusia arils helped greatly to sustain him. He appeared to be in good condition, except the last time I saw him, when, after twenty-four hours of rain, he looked bedraggled. At first perturbed by his presence, the other visitors to the clusia tree soon became reconciled to his almost daily visits and ate close by him.

At clusias with smaller but more numerous fruits, from which seeds were more readily removed by short-billed birds, the attendants were more diverse. In addition to those that also came to the *Clusia rosea* tree (except the Lineated Woodpecker), they included Orange-collared Manakins, Vermilion-crowned Flycatchers, Gray-capped Flycatchers, Ochre-bellied Flycatchers, Garden Thrushes, Orange-billed Nightingale-Thrushes, Red-eyed Vireos, Yellow-green Vireos, Scrub Greenlets, Baltimore Orioles, Blue Dacnises, Golden-masked Tanagers, Bay-headed Tanagers, Speckled Tanagers, Silver-throated Tanagers, Blue Tanagers, Palm Tanagers, Scarlet-rumped Tanagers, Buff-throated Saltators, and Streaked Saltators—twenty-five species in all. At these small-fruited clusias, as at most trees and shrubs with abundant crops of arillate seeds or berries, the birds ate with little mutual interference.

Although arils of one kind or another are available to birds through much of the year, they are most abundant early in the rainy season, from March to June, when migrants are passing northward and resident birds are nesting. They help the latter to nourish their young. Above all, the four species of honeycreepers that visit the clusia trees fly to their nests with many conspicuous billfuls of the orange or red arils. I have seen Golden-naped Woodpeckers so stuff their nestlings with these arils that they could take no more. The oil-rich arils abundant during the spring migration help the small travelers to accumulate fat to fuel their long journeys. No birds are more eager for them than Philadelphia Vireos preparing to leave after wintering in El General, and Red-eyed Vireos, Swainson's Thrushes, and Sulphur-bellied Flycatchers passing through the valley after wintering in more southerly lands.

Doubtless it was no accident that the only Gray Catbird that I have seen in the valley of El General in over forty years was plucking the soft, waxy white, slightly sweetish arils from between the two red valves of the globose pods of the liana *Doliocarpus dentatus*. The dense tangles that this woody vine of the dillenia family forms high in trees conceal its visitors so well that I would not have noticed the silent, secretive catbird, who was doubtless migrating, if I had not been watching intently for birds coming to eat the seeds. Of those that I detected in the vine tangles, migrating Swainson's Thrushes were the most frequent. Others were Orange-collared Manakins, Orange-billed Night-

*Davilla kunthii*: Open Pod Exposing Seed Enclosed in White Aril ▶

ingale-Thrushes, Scarlet-rumped Tanagers, and Buff-throated Saltators.

Another vine that attracts many birds is *Souroubea guianensis*, a vigorous, glossy-leaved epiphyte of the marcgravia family that burdens trees in forest and clearings. Each of its green flowers is subtended by a large, spurlike nectar cup, from which humming-birds sip nectar without touching the anthers or stigma; pollen-gathering bumblebees are the usual pollinators at Los Cusingos. Its fruits, slightly flattened globes up to nearly an inch in diame-ter, are pale green, sprinkled with minute brown scales. When the pods ripen in June and July, each splits into five thick, fleshy valves, which fall away at the touch of a bird's bill, exposing many small seeds all tangled together by their arils into a bright red mass, as accessible to blunt-billed as to sharp-billed birds. The eighteen species that I saw eat them ranged in size from Fiery-billed Araçaris to tiny Blue-crowned Manakins and in-cluded all the honeycreepers, finches, and tanagers that took the clusia seeds, with the addition of Tawny-bellied Euphonias.

Among the tall forest trees with arillate seeds is *Alchornea la-tifolia* of the spurge family. The small green pods of this broad-leaved tree are borne in richly branched panicles, over a foot long, that hang below the smaller branches. When they ripen, usually in April, but sometimes in November, each pod splits into four valves, conspicuously exposing twin seeds, a quarter of an inch in diameter, in bright red arils. One April, when an *Al-chornea* tree that sprang up in a pasture fruited profusely, it at-tracted many migrants in addition to resident birds, including Swainson's Thrushes, Yellow-throated, Red-eyed, and Phila-delphia vireos, Chestnut-sided and Tennessee warblers, Summer Tanagers, and Rose-breasted Grosbeaks. The Chestnut-sided Warblers nibbled into the arils without swallowing the seeds, and the grosbeaks broke the seeds in their thick bills, but most of the other birds swallowed seed and aril. The latter might have car-ried some of the indigestible seeds on their northward flights and dropped them far from the parent tree, whose wide distribution over tropical America probably owes much to migrants indebted to it for energy that helps them on their long journeys.

Another tree whose wide distribution through tropical America probably owes much to migratory birds is *Lacistema aggregatum*, formerly placed in a family of its own but now considered to be a member of the flacourtia family, with minute, petalless flowers reduced to a single stamen and pistil. This small, glossy-leaved tree, rarely fifty feet high, springs up in second-growth woods and hedgerows. Between April and June of alternate years, it bears abundant crops of glossy red capsules, each of which splits into two valves, exposing a thin, white aril that covers the single hard, smooth, brown seed. Migrating Red-eyed Vireos and Swainson's Thrushes swallow many of them, and Mourning Warblers take them occasionally. The resident birds who eat whole seeds range in size from Fiery-billed Araçaris to Yellow-bellied and Lesser elaenias and Orange-collared and Yellow-thighed manakins. Scarlet-rumped Tanagers, Bay-headed Tanagers, Buff-throated Saltators, and Streaked Saltators pluck a seed, mandibulate it, evidently pressing out juice and detaching part of the aril, then drop the seed still covered by enough of the aril to make it appear white. These are among the few arils that attract Bananaquits, who, without removing the seed from its pod, suck out some juice, or at most eat very small fragments. The aril sticks so tightly to the seed that it is difficult to remove all of it in my mouth. Domestic chickens eagerly eat fallen seeds; and I saw White-fronted Doves and Ruddy Quail-Doves beneath *Lacistema* trees so frequently that I could hardly doubt that they were gathering seeds from the ground, although they would not permit me to approach near enough to see this. Including the chickens and the two doves, twenty kinds of birds ate the arils of *Lacistema*; but the tanagers, the saltators, and the Bananaquit did not earn them by dispersing its seeds, and these were probably digested by the chickens and doves.

Another small tree of the flacourtia family, *Casearia sylvestris*, attracted more birds than any other species with arils that I have watched. Only three-sixteenths of an inch in diameter, the pods open by three valves, exposing from one to seven minute, hard, shiny, brown seeds, each covered by a thin orange aril, rich in oil. Although each of the pods offers little food, they are numerous on the slender branches. At only two of these trees, growing in tall second-growth woods, I watched thirty-nine species of birds eat the arils. In addition to most of those that I saw at other trees, the visitors to *Casearia sylvestris* included Dusky-capped and Yellow-bellied flycatchers, Greenish Elaenias, and Eye-ringed Flatbills—all members of the flycatcher family—White-throated Thrushes, Gray-headed Greenlets, Scarlet-thighed Dacnises, White-shouldered Tanagers, and Gray-headed Tanagers. Even Bananaquits, who rarely take fruits, ate many of these tiny arillate seeds. A related tree, *Casearia arborea*, which in September opened its little three-valved pods to expose masses of yellow arils, drew some of the fall migrants, especially Blackburnian Warblers and Yellow-bellied Flycatchers.

A short distance within the forest at Los Cusingos stands a tall *Virola koschnyi*, a tree of the nutmeg family locally called *candela*, because its oily seeds, threaded on a stick, were used as torches in the days when every kind of manufactured article was difficult to procure amid the forests of this isolated valley. From late May to August, each of its brown pods splits into two woody valves, between which hangs a single inch-long seed, embraced by a bright red aril, which divides near the base into either narrow or broad, strap-shaped branches that form an irregular network over the shiny brown seed coat. Pleasantly spicy when ripe, these arils are painfully hot and peppery when not quite mature. Among the fairly big birds that I watched swallow them entire were Blue-diademed Motmots, Rufous Pihas, Masked Tityras, Garden Thrushes, and White-throated Thrushes. It was amusing to watch the thrushes try strenuously to force down a whole, aril-covered seed and sometimes fail. I wondered why they did not peck off pieces of aril while the seed hung between its separated

*Compsoneura sprucei*: Open Pod Exposing Seed Enclosed in Red Aril;
Seed Removed from Aril ▶

valves. In other regions, several kinds of large trogons, toucans, and cotingas take the seeds of related species of *Virola*; but small birds that cannot swallow them entire appear to avoid them— which is to the tree's advantage, for without ingesting the seeds they would not disperse them. *Virola* is related to the nutmeg trees of Indonesia and other islands of the southwestern Pacific, whose seeds are swallowed by several species of imperial pigeons known as "nutmeg pigeons." After digesting off the mace, they cast up the seed uninjured, as Alfred Russel Wallace recorded long ago.

The largest arillate seeds at Los Cusingos are those of *Compsoneura sprucei*, a slender tree of the understory, also of the nutmeg family, widely scattered through the forest. In April and May each of its pale yellow pods separates into two valves, exposing a bright red aril, entire rather than branching as in *Virola*, which covers like a loosely fitting sleeve the pale brown seed, which is attractively mottled with deep brown. The open capsules, hanging like little red lanterns beneath slender, leafy twigs, are as beautiful as they are conspicuous. Of all the arils that I have examined, these are the only ones that, in addition to oil, contain much starch. At first almost tasteless, they left a slightly stinging sensation in my mouth. They appear to be sufficiently nutritious to attract birds, who certainly could not fail to notice them. Nevertheless, I have watched in vain to see a bird eat one, perhaps because each tree bears too few to draw frequent visitors. A tiny female Blue-crowned Manakin, who flew up to an aril several times, might have detached a few fragments or plucked off an insect. Blue-diademed Motmots carried many of these red seeds to their nestlings, who left some lying uneaten in their long burrow. Placed on the feeder, these arils were neglected by the birds, who were nearly all too small to swallow the seeds whole, but might have pecked into them. Domestic chickens likewise disdained them; but a horse ate them eagerly, suggesting that mammals rather than birds might be the chief disseminators of *Compsoneura*.

At Los Cusingos and elsewhere in Costa Rica, I have watched ninety-two species of birds take the arillate seeds of twenty-four species of plants. None of these birds nourishes itself with arils alone; all eat berries and capture insects, especially for their young. Trees laden with berries are as well attended by a great variety of colorful birds, constantly flitting around, coming and going, as those that offer an abundance of arillate seeds. The juicy, sweetish, deep purple or black berries, about a quarter of an inch in diameter, of only two trees of the Scorpioid Miconia of the melastome family, one in the forest and the other in a clearing, were eaten by forty-one species of birds, nearly all of which also take arils.

Serious conflict among the avian visitors of trees and shrubs with many berries is as rare as at trees with arillate seeds. Even at the *Dipterodendron* tree and the *Clusia* with the biggest pods, where competition for arils that only gradually became available was keenest, the meekest of the attendants, Blue Honeycreepers, appeared to obtain a satisfying amount, for they spent much time in these trees when other foods were readily available nearby. Birds that are largely frugivorous would gain little by maintaining feeding territories, for they wander widely as, now here, now there, a tree or shrub offers many berries or arillate seeds. They appear often to find these trees by traveling in loose, mixed flocks, or by watching the activities of other attendants. Species whose diets overlap widely, although perhaps they are never exactly the same, occupy the same area and eat in the same trees, as is true of the four kinds of small tanagers of the genus *Tangara*—Silver-throated, Bay-headed, Speckled, and Golden-masked—that I have often watched take the same berries and arillate seeds. Although these lovely tanagers wear very different colors, they are much the same in size and habits. The rarity or absence of hostile behavior or competitive exclusiveness among the frugivorous birds of tropical America favors the great diversity of colorful feathered creatures that delights the bird watcher.

# 7. Bananaquits

WHILE I sat at early breakfast, a tiny bird, barely four inches long, sipped nectar from the pink flowers of the green-and-red-leaved Caña de India shrubs outside the open window. It had a blackish head with a long white stripe above each eye. Its upper plumage, wings, and tail were largely dark grayish olive, with a yellowish rump and a small white patch at the edge of each wing. Its throat was pale gray, and the remaining underparts yellow, becoming paler beneath the tail. Its color pattern was surprisingly similar to that of several much larger flycatchers with white brows and yellow breasts, including the Vermilion-crowned and Boat-billed flycatchers and the Great Kiskadee. Clinging in all positions to the spreading panicles of the Caña de India, the little bird probed flower after flower with its short, sharp, prominently downcurved black bill. I could not tell whether it was a male or female, as both sexes wear the same colors.

This bird, known as the Bananaquit, is among the most widely distributed of all the small land birds of tropical America. From the Caribbean lowlands of southern Mexico it spreads over the continents to Bolivia, Paraguay, and northeastern Argentina, avoiding only some of the more arid regions, cold highlands, and vast unbroken forests. In Costa Rica, it nests upward to about 4,000 feet, and in southern Venezuela it has been reported as high as 6,600 feet on the slopes and summits of the isolated, tablelike mountains called *tepuis*. On the island of Hispaniola, it

Bananaquit ▶

has been found on mountaintops 8,800 feet high. With the curious exception of Cuba, it occurs throughout the West Indies and Bahamas; it resides on many other small islands near the continents; and it occasionally reaches Florida. Although everywhere readily recognizable by its form, habits, and distinctive bill, over so great and varied a range it has evolved no less than thirty-five named subspecies, including the wholly black race of the Antillean islands of Grenada and St. Vincent.

On Trinidad, Tobago, Puerto Rico, and other Caribbean islands, it is by far the most common, widespread bird. On Tobago it is so numerous that in six weeks, Gross (1958) found fifty-four breeding and dormitory nests within a radius of half a mile of his hotel. Amid the more varied bird life of the continents, it is not so outstandingly abundant; yet in many localities, including Los Cusingos, it is among those most often noticed, especially in gardens with a wealth of flowering shrubs and trees. In this valley it frequents coffee plantations, shady pastures, scrubby growth, and light, open woods—indeed, it is found wherever nectar-yielding trees and shrubs bloom in sunshine. Although it avoids the deep shade of the rain forests, it enters them, at least for short distances, attracted by the flowers that adorn the crown of some lofty tree. In other regions, this amazingly adaptable bird thrives in habitats as diverse as arid scrub, dense mossy cloud forests, and mangroves, as well as in suburban gardens.

Restlessly active and far from shy, the Bananaquit nourishes itself chiefly with the nectar it sucks from flowers with its forked, fringed, protrusile tongue. Unlike the hummingbirds that share the blooms with it, it does not hover, but clings to the stalks of flowers with its head up or down while it inserts its bill into one after another in rapid succession, usually an instant in each. It visits small flowers, like those of the Caña de India shrubs that grow along the northern side of our house, in the "legitimate" manner, pushing its bill into their throats and evidently pollinating them. To reach the nectar of the great red hibiscus blossoms on the opposite side of the house, it inserts its bill between the bases of the petals, or pierces them, and it regularly perforates great tubular blossoms, such as the golden cups of the Allamanda, the violet corollas of the Thunbergia that grows in front of the house, and the red trumpets of the Flame-of-the-Forest tree in the pasture behind it. Hummingbirds of many kinds vary their procedures in the same way, according to the size and form of the flower.

Bananaquits enter the banana plantation to cling beside a great, dangling, red flower bud while they probe the tubular white flowers clustered beneath the latest upturned bract. They push their heads between the long, clustered stamens of *Inga*, *Calliandra*, and other acacialike flowers. In the sunny early months of the year, the small white flowers of the Copalchí tree and the vine *Serjania mexicana* provide much nectar for Bananaquits. In rainy August and September, the cherrylike red blossoms of tall Cerillo trees draw them into the forest to share the tree's bounty with a variety of hummingbirds and other species of honeycreepers. On the island of Trinidad, the Snows (1971) listed fifty species of trees, vines, shrubs, herbs, and epiphytes that supplied nectar to Bananaquits.

Although the nectar of flowers is primarily a source of sweet carbohydrates, recent studies have demonstrated that, in many plants, it is not devoid of vitamins, amino acids, proteins, lipids, and other essential nutrients (Baker and Baker 1975). Nevertheless, it fails to provide a complete diet for birds, and, like hummingbirds, Bananaquits supplement it with many small insects, spiders, other tiny invertebrates, and the eggs of these creatures, which they glean from twigs, foliage, and webs, while they cling in the most diverse attitudes, erect or inverted. Rarely they catch insects in flight, and even more seldom they rummage amid fallen leaves on the ground. One morning in August, I watched a Bananaquit hunting over the rough bark of a Spanish Plum tree in such a way that at the first glimpse I mistook it for a Black-and-White Warbler newly arrived from the north, the white superciliary stripes on its black head supporting the illusion suggested by its posture. It clung with head, tail, or side up-permost while it extracted insects or spiders from crevices. An inch or two seemed to be the limit of its ability to creep over the rough bark on one of the few occasions when I have seen any member of the honeycreeper family engage in the activity sug-gested by the name.

Fruits seldom attract Bananaquits. In recently burned clear-ings in the forest, where Pokeweed grows rankly, they puncture the berries to suck out the purple juice, getting their bills glisten-ing wet. In an intensive study of the feeding habits of tanagers and honeycreepers in Trinidad, the Snows saw Bananaquits take fifteen kinds of fruits, from most of which they extracted juice by piercing or chewing the berries, although they swallowed others whole. Yet fruits were a minor component of their diet. Among the less frequent visitors to our feeder, Bananaquits drink the juice of halved oranges. They appear to lick moisture from the surfaces of bananas and plantains, or to swallow scarcely visible fragments, rather than to eat freely, like all the other visitors.

Although many honeycreepers, tanagers, and a great variety of other birds eagerly seek the oil-rich arils of various kinds of trees and vines, Bananaquits mostly neglect them. I have watched them swallow many of the tiny seeds, enveloped by thin orange-colored arils, of *Casearia sylvestris*, and nibble at the white arils ex-posed by the opening of the red pods of *Lacistema aggregatum*, another small tree. From the furry brown bases of the big leaves of Cecropia trees, I have more frequently seen them gather many of the tiny white protein corpuscles that are the principal food of the Azteca ants that nearly always inhabit the trees' hollow trunks and branches—dainty tidbits for tiny birds. Strangely, Biaggi (1955) found particles of stone in the stomachs of Ba-nanaquits in Puerto Rico.

In Central America, I have never known a Bananaquit to en-ter a house for food, but while dining one Sunday in Giradot, Colombia, I watched one or more repeatedly enter the crowded restaurant to eat sugar from a bowl set on a high sill inside the glass window. On Caribbean islands, where Bananaquits abound amid flowering trees and colorful gardens, they live far more intimately with man than on the continent. Gross (1958) gives a charming account of their behavior on Tobago, where hotels welcome their presence because they amuse guests. There they fearlessly enter open dining rooms to take sugar from bowls or from the bottoms of teacups where it remains undissolved, sometimes within inches of human diners. After such a feast, their black bills are often coated with white granules of sugar, which the birds dislodge by briskly shaking their heads. Sometimes, while one Bananaquit freely dipped into the sugar bowl, another advanced along the spoon, while a third awaited its turn nearby. Or a parent, perching on the rim of a bowl, placed sugar into the gaping mouth of a fledgling who stood with fluttering wings on the opposite side. At open bars these birds sipped liqueur from the corks of bottles and from glasses that had not been emptied by the human drinkers, apparently without becoming tipsy. Neither bread crumbs nor other kinds of solid food attracted them. Wetmore (1927) found Bananaquits equally familiar with man in Puerto Rico, where they flew into houses through open windows and doors to search for insects and spiders, removed sugar from bowls in front of guests dining in country hotels, and entered rural shops to drink syrup set on the counters for them.

Like many other birds of the rainy tropics, Bananaquits sometimes bathe high above the ground. I have repeatedly watched them splashing in the water that collects in tank bromeliads growing on trees.

As a songster, the Bananaquit is far from brilliant. He pours forth a rapid, undulating sequence of thin, high-pitched notes, which by courtesy might be called a trill, although it seems more worthy of an insect than of a bird. Although the Bananaquit has little melody to offer, he gives freely of what he has; few birds sing more persistently or continuously through the year. Here in the valley of El General, Bananaquits sing in every month, but by no means with equal fervor in all of them. Song becomes profuse in June and continues with moderate or high intensity through the remainder of the long wet season and into the sunny months of January and February, to wane as drought becomes severe in March, just as other birds are becoming songful. During the wet, and often gloomy, months from September to November, and at the beginning of the drier weather in December, when few other feathered creatures sing, Bananaquits are the most songful birds of the region. In April and May, when most birds sing most profusely, Bananaquits are rarely heard. The months in which they sing freely are those in which they nest. In both of these activities, they join the hummingbirds, whose diet closely resembles theirs, and part company with the majority of passerines, who take different foods.

In their season of full song, Bananaquits perform indomitably, continuing to pour forth their wheezy little trill when the sun shines hotly at high noon and many birds fall silent, and not infrequently singing while rain pours down. In contrast to the situation here in El General, in the West Indies, Trinidad and Tobago, Bananaquits sing, as they nest, throughout the year. They are reported to sing as soon as they are fully feathered, before they have acquired adult plumage, but I have not noticed such precocity in Central American Bananaquits. Here, as on Puerto Rico and Tobago, only males sing (Biaggi 1955; Gross 1958).

The Bananaquit's call is a slight monosyllable, sometimes wiry sharp, sometimes lisping. It is especially sharp and tirelessly repeated when two of these little birds quarrel. Their disputes are mostly settled by posturing, flitting around each other, and voicing sharp notes. On the single occasion when I saw two of them come to grips, they rolled together on the lawn for less than a minute, then separated, apparently uninjured.

On a morning in early May, I watched an adult male hold a fairly large, yellowing leaf in his bill while, with profuse song and vibrating wings, he addressed another Bananaquit in immature plumage. As the latter flitted around in a shrub, the former followed, faced it, and, still holding the leaf, continued his high-pitched song. After the immature bird flew away, the songster dropped his leaf and fell silent. Although he appeared to be courting the one in transitional plumage, a leaf such as he held would not ordinarily be placed in a nest. Similarly, courting Blue-diademed Motmots often hold leaves or other pieces of vegetation in their bills, although they never take such materials into their unlined nesting burrows.

Last November, in a hibiscus shrub just outside my window, I watched a different display. Two Bananaquits in adult plumage were a foot or two apart. The bird on the left bowed rapidly up and down through a wide arc, while fluttering its wings. It continued this for a minute or two, always facing the other, who moved from spot to spot within a radius of a few inches and also fluttered its wings, but bowed less continuously and deeply. At the end of the display, the chief performer flew away, and the other soon followed. Both were silent. I could not tell whether the Bananaquit who bowed most vigorously was courting or defending territory.

### Nesting

Of all the birds I know, the Bananaquit is the most indefatigable builder. Certain other birds construct more elaborate nests, but none, as far as I can learn, makes so many, or spends so large a share of its time building. To build appears to be the great purpose of its life, its favorite activity.

This absorption in nest construction becomes understandable when we learn that Bananaquits not only have an exceptionally long breeding season, even for a tropical bird, but also sleep in nests throughout the year. To their sleeping habits we shall presently return. In the valley of El General, laying begins about the middle of May, after the rainy season has become well established. From May until March, I found forty-four nests holding eggs, as follows: May, five; June, six; July, four; August, six; September, two; October, four; November, one; December, five; January, seven; February, three; March, one. The single case re-

corded for March was in a year when vegetation remained unusually fresh because several heavy showers fell in the usually dry
month of February. Bananaquits thus continue to nest throughout the wet season, even during the torrential rains of October
and November, and into the early part of the dry season, when
the combination of sunny skies and soil still moist after months
of soaking rain favors the year's greatest profusion of flowering
herbs and shrubs in open places. As the dry season continues and
the ground loses its moisture, the abundance of flowers decreases
greatly, although some of the most spectacular trees come into
bloom. With a reduced supply of nectar, Bananaquits have few
nests with eggs or young in March, and I have found none in
April, when returning showers refresh vegetation that has not
yet had time to flower freely. Not until May's lush growth covers
the land do Bananaquits resume nesting. Yet April is the month
when I have found most nests of the bird population as a whole.
It is of no little interest that Flower-piercers, which likewise subsist upon nectar and tiny insects, but in cool highlands instead of
warm lowlands, also breed in months when scarcely any other
passerine birds nest. In both highlands and lowlands, I have
found hummingbirds of a number of species breeding most freely
when Flower-piercers or Bananaquits had eggs or young.

In other regions, the Bananaquits' breeding season is somewhat different. On Barro Colorado Island in Gatún Lake on the
Caribbean side of the Isthmus of Panama, I found nests in which
eggs were laid in December and January; and one pair was almost
continuously engaged in reproduction from January to June, in
which interval they raised two broods and were attending their
third when I left the island in June. In Trinidad, Bananaquits are
said to breed throughout the year, although actual records for all
months appear to be lacking. The seventy-nine nests reported by
ffrench (1973) show a peak of nesting in January, when twenty-
four were recorded, with a gradual decline until June, when four
were found. July had none; August, one; September and October, none; November, one; and December, five. If these records

reflect the true distribution of nests throughout the year, rather than the amount of time devoted to searching for them, it is evident that in Trinidad the Bananaquit's breeding is much more strongly concentrated in the first six months than in the valley of El General at about the same latitude.

While searching for nests of other birds, I have sometimes wished that Bananaquits built less assiduously, for I have too often spent much time and energy examining nests well above my head, only to find that they were empty ones of this industrious bird. At close range, however, the Bananaquit's nest is unmistakable, readily distinguishable from those of wrens, who likewise build roofed structures. A closed, usually thick-walled nest, roughly globular or ovoid in shape, it is entered through a narrow, round, downwardly facing doorway in one side. Nests used only for sleeping and those in which broods are raised are similar in shape. Those that serve only as dormitories may be slighter, with thinner walls and roof, but they grade into breeding nests and no sharp line can be drawn between the two kinds. The male's dormitory may be as substantial as a brood nest, and after he has slept in it for weeks, the female may choose it for her eggs.

Bananaquits build their nests in trees and shrubs in gardens, pastures, and thickets, in vine tangles at the forest's edge, in boughs overhanging rivers, or among the broad bases of the fronds of a spiny palm tree, never, in my experience, in dense woods. Around our house, their nests are frequently placed in thorny orange or lemon trees, usually among the lower boughs. The fifty-six nests that I have recorded, mostly in El General, but a few in Panama and Venezuela, ranged in height from fifty-one inches to fifty or sixty feet; thirty-seven of them were from five to ten feet above the ground. The highest was a male's dormitory; but one pair built a nest fifty feet up and another thirty-five feet up. Since low nests are more readily found and examined than high ones, the average height may be greater than my records indicate, but it is certain that both dormitory and breeding nests are very often situated within hand reach, usually rather conspicuously near the ends of leafy branches rather than toward the center of a tree.

Occasionally, a Bananaquit builds upon the abandoned nest of some other small bird—once I found this in the case of a Variable Seedeater's nest and once with an Orange-collared Manakin's—converting an open cup into a closed structure, much as Vermilion-crowned and Gray-capped flycatchers sometimes do. Although I have never heard of Bananaquits building on, or in, a human construction on the continent, on Tobago they frequently do so. Gross noticed a nest on a glass chandelier beneath which guests constantly passed in a hotel hallway, and another in a large Christmas tree in the main reception hall of the same hotel. Composed chiefly of glittering tinsel and small ornaments that the Bananaquits had pilfered from the lavishly adorned tree, it was a fantastic structure.

Nests that will soon receive eggs are usually built by a male and female together. Males build their dormitories alone, often to the accompaniment of profuse song. Although I have watched the construction of many nests, none remains more vividly in memory than the first, which I found just fifty years ago. I had pushed my *cayuca* far into one of the smaller of the many coves that indent Barro Colorado Island's wooded shore, until boughs interlocked above me and shut out the sky. At the cove's head stood a small palm, its columnar trunk bristling with formidable black spines, which extended up the stalks of the fronds that arched gracefully over the water. In the axil of one of these fronds, I noticed a small accumulation of fibers and strips of vegetation. On a neighboring twig, a Bananaquit hesitated with a billful of similar materials. Tying my vessel to a tree, I stepped ashore to watch from amid dense undergrowth; but the birds refused to approach the nest while I stood there. Accordingly, I reembarked and pushed the *cayuca* a little farther out into the cove, where, gently swayed by wavelets that found their way into the nook from the broad lake, I watched the pair at work.

The male and female appeared to take equal shares in building. They flitted briskly among the trees, tugging at bits of slender vines and palm-leaf fibers until they returned to the nest with full bills. Often they gathered materials so rapidly that before one had finished arranging his or her contribution, the other was perching nearby with a billful, ready to enter the moment its partner flew out. Whenever they met at the doorway, I heard high-pitched, rapidly repeated twitters. I could not see what they did inside the covered structure that opened on the landward side, but when I went ashore again and stood beneath the great heliconia leaves, they would not continue to build. So I returned to watch from my vessel until late in the morning, so absorbed in the charming scene that I might have forgotten the busy world of man if the *cayuca* had not at intervals been more violently rocked by waves stirred up by a great ship passing unseen through the canal.

One pair took four or five days to finish a nest for breeding; but a juvenile Bananaquit, working alone, finished its dormitory in three or four days. The cozy covered nest is usually four or five inches in diameter. An old, but still occupied, nest that has been beaten down by heavy rains may be considerably less high than broad. The round doorway that faces obliquely downward is slightly more than an inch and a half in diameter. The interior of a breeding nest is about three inches in diameter; that of a dormitory, two and a quarter inches. The materials of these nests vary according to what the immediate vicinity affords, and include coarse vegetable fibers, grass blades, whole small bamboo leaves, strips from the great leaves of the banana and related plants, pieces of vines and weed stems, tendrils, fibrous rootlets chiefly of epiphytic plants, shreds of papery bark, string, cotton, and more or less green moss or stems of an epiphytic *Lycopodium*. The interior may be unlined or, in breeding nests, softly lined with fine fibers, seed down, and sometimes downy feathers.

The first egg may be laid four or five days after a nest is finished, or the female may sleep in it for a month or more before an egg appears. Sometimes she lays in a nest in which her mate has long been lodging, much as occasionally happens among woodpeckers. The eggs are deposited early in the mornings of consecutive days. In thirty-nine nests in Costa Rica and Panama, I found two eggs or nestlings, never more. A few nests with a single egg or nestling may have lost another. Three eggs are not infrequently laid on the islands of Trinidad, Tobago, and Puerto Rico, and sometimes also in Venezuela. Since the eggs are difficult to remove without injuring them or the nest, I have always examined them by inserting a small mirror and electric bulb through the doorway. Viewed by reflection with artificial illumination, they are dull white, speckled with brown. Others who have taken the eggs in hand describe them as creamy or buffy, with brownish or drab spots and blotches concentrated on the thicker end, where they may almost obscure the ground color. Ten eggs from Trinidad averaged 17.2 by 12.8 millimeters; twenty-three from Puerto Rico, 17.5 by 12.6 millimeters.

Because the nest's doorway opens obliquely downward, it is often difficult to see the incubating parent without coming so close beneath it that the Bananaquit leaves and will not return. A nest exceptionally favorable for study faced down a steep slope where, sitting in my blind well downhill, I could look upward and see the head of the occupant. Here I watched from 1:25 P.M. until nightfall on February 27, and from daybreak of the next day until 1:02 P.M., a total of twelve and a quarter hours. I could not distinguish the parents except by voice; but since I saw no changeover and never heard the incubating partner sing, I concluded that only the female incubated, as with all honeycreepers and tanagers that I have studied. She sat with steadfastness unexpected in so small a bird. Her seven sessions that I timed ranged from 47 to 82 minutes and averaged 60.7 minutes. Her seven recesses varied from 12 to 29 minutes, with an average of 17 minutes. She covered her eggs for 78 percent of the daylight hours.

Returning from an outing, the female would pause in a neighboring tree and repeat a lisping *tsip* many times over before, with

admirable skill, she flew upward directly into the narrow aperture, seeming scarcely to touch the rim as she shot through it.
After entering, she always turned to sit with her head in the
doorway, looking out. Once, while she incubated, a female Blue
Honeycreeper pulled some loose fibers from the back of her nest,
where the Bananaquit could not see the thief. Apprised by the
shaking of her nest, the Bananaquit darted out and chased the
honeycreeper into a nearby avocado tree. Here the two con-
fronted each other, the Blue Honeycreeper answering the Bananaquit's *tsip* with a nasal *mew*. Soon, without having touched,
the two little birds flew off in opposite directions, the honeycreeper with her plunder. In the morning, the male Bananaquit
sometimes accompanied his mate when she returned to her nest,
but he never came closer to it than the next tree, where he sang
for a few minutes before he disappeared. In the afternoon, I
failed to see him.

A few days later, I gave this female Bananaquit some "intelligence tests." First, while she was absent, I closed her doorway
with a big, loose fluff of white cotton. Returning to find her en-
tranceway blocked, she climbed over and around her nest, then
seized the cotton in her bill and pulled it out, only two minutes
after her arrival. When she tried to carry the cotton away, it
caught on a big thorn beside the doorway and resisted all her
efforts to remove it. Accordingly, she climbed around the obsta-
cle to sit in her nest with the mass of cotton, bigger than herself,
hanging in front. After her next departure, I closed the doorway
with a green leaf, which, only one minute after her return, she
seized by the edge and carried away. The excitement brought her
mate into the nest tree, where I had not seen him while I made
the record of incubation. After the female removed the leaf, he
went three times to look into the nest. Then, satisfied that all
was well, he flew away, singing.

On the day when I watched her, this female Bananaquit incubated with greater constancy than one studied by Biaggi in
Puerto Rico for a total of 102 hours and 27 minutes during

eleven days. The 100 sessions of his female ranged from 1 to 161 minutes and averaged 41.8 minutes. She warmed her eggs most constantly on the fourth day of incubation, when she sat for 74 percent of 559 minutes. On the eighth day, her constancy was lowest, only 52 percent of 645 minutes. During the eleven days of observation, this Bananaquit's absences from her nest ranged from 1 to 51 minutes and averaged 26 minutes.

At two of my nests, the last nestling hatched twelve days after the second egg was laid, and at two others this interval was thirteen days. In Trinidad, Tobago, and Puerto Rico, the Bananaquit's incubation period was often twelve days, but occasionally as long as fourteen or fifteen days, probably due to disturbance of the incubating female. The tiny hatchlings' bright pink skins bear no trace of down. Their eyes are tightly closed. The interior of their mouths is red and the flanges at the corners are white, as in tanagers. After they have been fed, a pouch or swelling appears on the right side of each neck and looks blackish through the skin, probably from the small insects that it contains—much as in flower-piercers, hummingbirds, and other nestlings into whose throats substantial quantities of food are poured rapidly by regurgitating parents. When the Bananaquits are four or five days old, their eyes begin to open and the dark rudiments of feathers appear beneath their pink skins. The pinfeathers grow out until, when the nestlings are about ten days old, the plumage begins to expand at their tips. At twelve days of age, the open-eyed nestlings are fairly well feathered on their back and wings, although their heads are still largely naked. If touched, or even closely looked at, they may dart from the nest when only fourteen or fifteen days old and fly too well to be caught. Often, however, the young remain in their snug nursery for seventeen or eighteen days, and one that I watched did not fly until nineteen days of age. Newly emerged fledglings resemble their parents, but their tails are shorter, their colors are generally paler, and the long stripe above each eye is buffy instead of pure white.

Both parents, but chiefly the female, feed the nestlings, with food carried in their throats or perhaps in deeper regions. Only rarely can one detect an insect's legs or wings projecting from the bill of a parent Bananaquit approaching its nest with food. The closed nest makes it difficult to watch feeding until the nestlings are older, when they stretch their necks through the doorway, below which the parent clings while it produces food from its throat and, with rapid movements, passes it to both of them, alternately. The parents bring up the food without the muscular strain so evident in regurgitating hummingbirds. As the day of its departure approaches, a hungry nestling may emerge and cling below its doorway to take its meal, then turn around and reenter headfirst.

Like hummingbirds and others fed by regurgitation, young Bananaquits are fed much less frequently than are small birds whose parents bring food in their bills. Two nestlings, five to twelve days old, were watched by Biaggi for fifty-five and a quarter hours on eight days, during which their mother fed them one hundred and thirty-seven times and their father twenty times. Accordingly, they were fed at the average rate of 2.8 times per hour, or only 1.4 feedings per hour for each of them. The parents apparently swallow the droppings of very small nestlings, but carry away in their bills the white fecal sacs of older ones, keeping the nest clean.

By day the mother broods her nestlings for decreasing periods until they are about a week old. Sometimes she ceases to cover them at night when they are only ten days old, but often she continues to accompany them until they fly. When sleeping alone, or upon eggs or tiny nestlings, she turns back her head among her outfluffed plumage, and only her yellow breast is visible in the doorway. After two young are well grown and feathered, they occupy so much of the nest that their parent is forced forward and sleeps with her head exposed in the doorway.

After their departure at seventeen to nineteen days of age, the fledglings are rarely seen. They flit from twig to twig, and often perch side by side amid concealing foliage, at regular intervals tirelessly repeating sharp, squeaky notes that guide their parents to them with food. In contrast to many other birds who rear their young in roofed nests, Bananaquits do not lead their newly emerged fledglings to sleep in the brood nest or some other dormitory, but leave them outside until they can find or build nests in which to sleep—a matter to which we shall presently return. A female who has accompanied her nestlings every night until their departure often continues to sleep alone in her nest. If she has gone elsewhere during their last nights in the nest, she may return to lodge in it after they have flown. The same individual may behave differently in different nestings. The parent who ceased to brood her nestlings after their tenth day left her nest unoccupied for several nights after they had flown; but in less than a week she resumed her old habit of sleeping in this nest, in which she laid the first egg for a second brood two weeks after the departure of the first. Another female brooded her nestlings every night except their last in the nest, then returned on the evening of their exit, to sleep there alone. When she raised a later brood in a new nest, this same female brooded her young by night as long as they remained in it, and slept in it on the evening after they departed.

In their long breeding season, Bananaquits have time to raise several broods. On February 25, 1935, two young, hatched from eggs that had been laid in late January, left a nest beside the main building on Barro Colorado Island, and fourteen days later, on March 11, the female laid again in the same nest, in which she had been sleeping. The young of this second brood flew out, somewhat prematurely, on April 9. Six days afterward, I noticed their mother building a new nest, already far advanced, about twenty-five feet from the first, and when it was finished she lodged in it. A few days later, a Streaked Flycatcher, gathering materials for her own nest, tugged at the Bananaquit's nest until it fell. Thereupon, the Bananaquit returned to sleep in her first nest until she and her mate completed a third nest, again twenty-five feet from the first. On May 2 she started to sleep in this nest and continued to lodge there until, on May 11, she laid the first egg of her third brood, thirty-two days after the young of her second brood had left the nest. Between late January and early June, this female thus raised three sets of young.

## Sleeping

Although other honeycreepers, especially the Blue, wander widely in flocks, Bananaquits are sedentary birds, never forming flocks of their own kind and only exceptionally joining mixed companies of small birds. They do not remain in a restricted territory, but roam about seeking flowers. However, they appear never to wander far, for every night throughout the year each returns to sleep in a nest. Although pair bonds seem to persist throughout the year, each partner invariably sleeps in its own nest; I have never known two individuals past the nestling stage to lodge together. While the male, as we have seen, helps the female to build the nest in which she will sleep and lay her eggs, I doubt that she often reciprocates the favor. The many males that I have watched build their dormitories have worked alone, often singing profusely while they added piece after piece in rapid succession.

On many a night I have peeped into a Bananaquit's dormitory with a flashlight and seen only a fluff of yellow feathers plugging the doorway. If the sleeper awakes in the beam, the feather plug is suddenly replaced by a white-striped black head with dark shining eyes and a sharp, strongly curved bill. Unless the nest is shaken, or his visitor noisy, the diminutive bird maintains this attitude of alertness until the intruder extinguishes the light and steals away.

Bananaquits go to rest much earlier than many of their feathered neighbors who roost amid foliage, and this is especially true on rainy evenings. I have not known them to seek shelter in their nests earlier in the day. Usually the male retires later in the evening than his mate, even when she has neither eggs nor nestlings to brood in her nest. Sometimes he escorts her to her dormitory before flying to his own. Often, as he prepares to enter for the night, he sings among the branches near his nest, at times continuing for many minutes; but the moment he flits through the doorway, he becomes silent until morning.

In Puerto Rico, Biaggi proved by banding birds captured in their dormitories that four or five different individuals might successively sleep in the same nest in the course of a week or ten days, and he doubted that this was because each abandoned its dormitory after being caught in it. In Costa Rica, where populations of Bananaquits are much less dense, I have found no indication of such opportunism in the selection of dormitories. Although the birds that I watched were not banded, I believe that I would more often have seen Bananaquits inspecting nests already occupied in the evening if they were searching for lodgings that they had not made.

While I dwelt beside the Río Buena Vista, I followed the activities of a pair of Bananaquits who slept and nested around my thatched cabin for over a year. In early April of the first year, the male, singing profusely, built his dormitory A, nine feet up in a small guava tree beside the kitchen. This sheltered him nightly for more than three months, during which I failed to discover his mate, if he already had one. In mid-July, when this nest had become dilapidated, he started nest B, only five feet above the ground, on one of the lowest boughs of the orange tree in front of my window. He built so slowly that after eight days he had hardly more than the bare outline of a nest.

On the morning of July 22, while a fine rain fell, this Bananaquit set about completing his task with a will. The dark and gloomy heavens failed to depress his spirits, nor the drizzle to impede his work; he sang incessantly as in quick succession he brought innumerable billfuls of material to the nest. He was not obliged to travel far, for he found two convenient quarries close at hand. The first, of which he made most use, was the thatch of my roof, to which he flew scores of times to pull away long, slender shreds of weathered sugarcane leaf, softened by the rain. He tugged valiantly until he had torn off a strip that met his approval, and made up a load of several pieces before setting forth on the short flight to his nest. The second quarry was a nest with an interesting history, in the top of the orange tree where he was building. A pair of Blue Tanagers had built this nest earlier in the year and raised a family in it. Then a Gray-capped Flycatcher had claimed the empty bowl and roofed it over, converting it into a domed structure with the doorway in the side—a transformation much the same, on a larger scale, as Bananaquits sometimes effect with a small open nest. Before the Gray-capped Flycatchers could use the remodeled nest, a pair of Piratic Flycatchers wrested it away from them and raised a brood in it. Now the Bananaquit was pulling well-weathered weed stems and grass blades from the abandoned structure and taking them down to his own nest lower in the orange tree. In the intervals of gathering heavier materials, he picked up downy chicken feathers from the yard. The little bird worked and sang with tremendous energy until the middle of the morning, then seemed to tire.

That evening, the builder slept for the last time in nest A in the guava tree that had sheltered him for three months. The following day, he continued to build, until his new dormitory was ready for occupancy. The nest in the guava tree remained empty.

The Bananaquit did not long enjoy the use of his new shelter. Before the middle of August, his mate, who now at last appeared, claimed it and laid two eggs in it. Why she did not have a nest of her own, built in the customary manner by both together, I do not know. Possibly one had been constructed and lost at a greater distance from my cabin, and, pressed for time, the female had requisitioned this sleeping nest for her eggs. The transfer of possession was effected so quietly that I was amazed to find the eggs, already well advanced in incubation, in the nest where I had believed that the male still slept. He had, however, gone back to his earlier dilapidated lodging in the guava tree behind the kitchen. He slept here only a few nights, then took up his abode in a nest, C, apparently newly finished, across the roadway that passed in front of the cabin. This was also in a guava tree, eleven feet above the ground, and seventy-five yards from his first dormitory. The nest he had relinquished to his mate was about midway between these two guava-tree nests. This latest lodging was to serve him until January, a period of nearly five months, the longest occupancy of a Bananaquit's nest of which I know.

The female Bananaquit prospered in the low nest in the orange tree, hatched both eggs, and with her mate's assistance brought forth two healthy fledglings. These she left to roost in the open, beneath heavy September rains, while she continued to sleep in the nest where they had been raised. In early October I found an empty Bananaquit's nest and, in an experimental mood, tied it among the lower branches of the orange tree. The female's sleeping nest falling to the ground soon after this, she found a convenient substitute in the one that I had attached close beside it. After I had returned the fallen structure, nowise injured, to its original site, a young Bananaquit, possibly one of the two hatched in that same nest a little more than a month earlier, came to sleep in it. Frightened by my early morning visit, it did not return a second night.

In the evening, just before retiring, the male and female Bananaquits often foraged in the orange trees in front of my cabin. They hopped nervously around each other, continually fluttering their wings and revealing the small white patch on the outer edge of each, while every few seconds they repeated their sharp, metallic monosyllable. They searched for tiny insects among the dark orange foliage, often hanging upside down to pluck something from beneath a leaf. Presently the female would dart into the low nest that I had given her, continuing her sharp calls until she vanished inside. Then the male flew to his nest in the guava tree across the roadway.

In mid-October, this pair built a new nest, D, eight feet up in the guava tree at the southwestern corner of the cabin. Because the two partners worked together, I was certain that the female, not the male, would occupy it. By the evening of October 18, it was nearly finished, and she entered it for the night. The nest I had tied in the orange tree was now deserted. Even after the new nest had been used as a dormitory for several nights, the birds continued to add bits of material to it. The female slept here for a full month before, in mid-November, she laid her second set of eggs in it. These hatched in early December. She brooded the nestlings every night until their departure on December 24, and on Christmas Eve she retired alone into the nest that they had just abandoned.

Meanwhile, the male's nest C in the guava tree across the road was becoming old and weather-beaten. After the year's end I no longer found him there, and several weeks passed before I located his new nest, E, in a Red-flowered Poró tree beside my neighbor's house. One evening in mid-February, I found him clinging below the doorway of his mate's nest, D, in the guava tree at the corner of my cabin, singing loudly, which at this season he rarely did. She had already entered for the night and would not permit him to join her. After a while, he desisted from his attempt to push inside and retreated to a perch nearby, where he devoted much attention to his feet. His mate had evidently been pecking them to make him release his hold on her doorsill. Then he flew over and entered his own nest, E, which was already deteriorating. Although much older, the nest he had helped the female to build in October was in far better repair; probably for this reason he wanted to sleep in it with her. However, she preferred to be alone. I have seen a Streaked-headed Woodcreeper, a Southern House-Wren, and a Rufous-browed Wren repulsed in much the same way when they tried to join their mates in the dormitory.

At the end of February, the female Bananaquit's second nest, D, fell from the guava tree, after sheltering her for more than four months. Thereafter, the pair changed dormitories so often that, occupied as I was with the activities of many other kinds of birds that now began to breed, I found it difficult to follow their movements. Birds of many kinds extract materials from their neighbors' unguarded nests to use in their own, which probably explains the frequent loss of the Bananaquits' dormitories, unwatched by day at this season when many birds were nesting but not the Bananaquits. Then, in mid-April, I discovered the female sleeping in a new nest, F, in a Red-flowered Poró tree near the kitchen. A flimsy, hastily built structure, its roof was hardly more than an open meshwork, through which much sky could be seen. It must have been quite pervious to the rain, which now fell hard almost every afternoon. After it had been occupied for a few nights, the pair resumed work and made it as snug as any.

In early May, the female Bananaquit's nest in the Poró tree, after only three weeks of use, met the fate of several of its immediate predecessors, doubtless pulled apart by a bird gathering material for its own nest. Two days later, the male Bananaquit, who preferred low nests, was found sleeping in a half-finished structure in a lemon tree in the front yard, only five feet above the ground. During the two following mornings, he worked at making his roof thicker with thatch from my roof and materials pilfered from a Gray-capped Flycatcher who was tearing pieces from her old nest to build a new one. With the Bananaquit's assistance, the demolition of the abandoned structure proceeded rapidly. The female Bananaquit lost her dormitory, nest F, and her mate promptly built a new one for himself! A reasonable inference was that he had again surrendered his own bedroom to her. Unfortunately, I did not know the location of his previous dormitory and could not prove this; but, in view of the known history of this pair, the circumstantial evidence is strong.

Again the female Bananaquit did not help her mate with his nest, even if he were building it for her ultimate use. Nevertheless, on the evening after the new dormitory was finished, she entered, as though to try it out and see whether she liked it better than the one that he had apparently already relinquished to her. Meanwhile, the male hopped excitedly around the doorway of his new nest, fearful, no doubt, of again losing his lodging. But after a minute she emerged, and both flew off together. Later, the male returned, and sang a good deal before he darted into his neat new dormitory for the night.

On a rainy evening two weeks later, the male Bananaquit retired early into his low nest in the lemon tree. Soon his mate arrived and tried to force herself in beside him, or perhaps even to push him out and occupy this tight new shelter alone. But a male Bananaquit's endurance has limits; he had helped to build her nests, relinquished two of his own to her, and now this attempt to push him out-of-doors on a cold, wet night! Valiantly he strove to keep her outside, singing in the nest in his tense excitement, a most unusual occurrence. Before long, both contestants fell to the ground, clinched together. Immediately separating, the male promptly returned to his nest, while his partner flew off through the rain, calling sharply. I proved that it was the male who had returned to the nest by putting him out; he revealed his identity by singing a few notes before reentering, despite all the rain and gloom. As far as I have seen, two grown Bananaquits will not in any circumstances sleep together. Indeed, the nest is hardly large enough for two.

The next evening, the female Bananaquit did not come near her mate's nest. Probably she had learned her lesson. Soon after this I moved away from the valley, terminating my year-long acquaintance with these engaging birds.

### A Young Bananaquit's Efforts to Establish a Dormitory

Nearly seven years later, on March 22, 1944, when I lived in my present abode at Los Cusingos, I for the first time found a juvenile Bananaquit building a nest. With a dingy yellow breast and buffy superciliary stripes, it did not appear to have started to molt into adult plumage. Nevertheless, it worked with energy worthy of a building adult, carrying billful after billful of fibrous materials, grass inflorescences, and moss to its nest ten feet up on a leafy twig of an *Inga* tree in front of the house. Three days later,

it had finished a nest like those of adult Bananaquits. That evening I was surprised to see, not the builder, but an adult Bananaquit retire into the nest that the juvenile had made for itself.
Apparently, this usurper was a bird who had recently lost two
neighboring dormitories, used as sources of building material by
flycatchers, and it solved its housing problem by dispossessing
the youngster who had intruded into its territory.

By April 1, this nest had vanished, doubtless having gone to
swell the structures flycatchers, tanagers, and other birds were
making for their broods on all sides. Three days later, a juvenile
Bananaquit, evidently the same one, was building in a guava tree
behind the house. It labored with tremendous zeal, bringing dry
grass picked up from the lawn, orchid roots, sometimes whole
plants of the miniature orchid *Oncidium titania*, and bits of
papery guava bark pulled from neighboring trees. In forty-five
minutes, it carried sixty-three billfuls to its nest. Then it took a
well-earned rest for fifteen minutes. Such intense activity, too
exhausting to be continued through the day, was relaxed after
the middle of the morning. But in three days the nest appeared
to be completed. The evening after it was finished was dark and
wet. As I approached the nest, a bird who had retired early fled
from it and did not return for the night.

Next morning, sharp little notes, many times repeated, drew
my attention to the Bananaquits in the garden. Two mature individuals were sipping nectar from the violet flowers of the Stachytarpheta hedge, while the young bird made occasional visits to its
nest. Several times one of the adults chased the juvenile, and
twice one or the other of them entered the newly made nest in
the guava tree. In the evening, these pursuits were repeated. An
adult male, easily recognized by his bright plumage and song,
drove the young one around the corner of the house. Then he
entered the young bird's nest, which he had inspected earlier in
the day. After he was comfortably ensconced within, the builder
of the nest approached and rested hesitantly upon a nieghboring
bough, making no attempt to force an entry. While it lingered

nearby, calling, the old bird emerged from the nest to drive it away. Soon the mature male returned to his lodging. The young builder appeared once more, fluttered before the doorway, saw the intruder within, then silently flew toward the neighboring forest. Again it had toiled only to provide a home for another!

Undiscouraged by the loss of two nests, the young Bananaquit continued to build one after another in the trees around my house, until in the course of two months it had made seven. The facts that I have so rarely seen juvenile Bananaquits building, and that the nests were always constructed in sequence rather than simultaneously, made me confident that the builder was always the same individual. In none of its nests, except possibly the last, was it permitted to sleep for over a week. Most were wrested from it by adults of its kind; one was torn apart by a Vermilion-crowned Flycatcher gathering materials for her own nest. In late May, the young bird was acquiring adult plumage. By the month's end, it had either been displaced from its seventh nest by an adult or, becoming itself an adult in appearance, could no longer be distinguished from its persecutors. Probably, by dint of indomitable persistence and tireless building, it had won the right to live and sleep on territory originally claimed by an adult pair.

Lacking a nest, young Bananaquits roost amid foliage, like other honeycreepers. In November I discovered one in dull juvenile plumage carrying material into a calabash tree in front of the house, but, disturbed by an adult, it did not complete its nest. A few nights later, I found it sleeping in a crotch in the top of this calabash tree, in an open nest built earlier in the year by a finch or tanager, possibly somewhat renovated by the Bananaquit. Although this nest lacked a roof of its own, it was well covered by the foliage of the calabash tree. The young Bananaquit slept here for only a few nights, after which a Southern House-Wren roosted in the open nest canopied by foliage. As the birds went to roost in the evening, angry notes came from the top of this tree, suggesting that the slightly larger wren drove away the young Bananaquit. When they attempt to establish homes for themselves, immature Bananaquits must often compete not only with their own but with other species.

In March of a later year, I watched another Bananaquit in immature plumage build in one of the calabash trees in front of the house. By evening it had only a slight structure, too small to hold it, precariously attached to the side of a mossy bough. After sunset, I watched the little bird trying to settle down for the night. It hunted over the mossy limbs of the tree in which it had built and of a neighboring calabash tree, apparently searching for its skimpy nest. Failing to find it, the Bananaquit flew to a different calabash tree, where a Paltry Tyranniscus was incubating two eggs in a covered nest of mosses and plant down, suspended beneath a mossy branch. Twice the Bananaquit approached this cozy nest with a side entrance, as though to enter; but each time the pair of tiny flycatchers, uttering excited cries, dashed at it so vigorously that it fled. Finally, the Bananaquit flew into a dense cluster of foliage at the top of a guava tree beside the house, where it settled down for the night. From the ground I could detect only its head amid the clustered leaves.

### Lodging in Nests of Other Species

In the same calabash tree where I had watched the preceding episode, an adult Bananaquit attempted, one evening in June of a later year, to enter a nest in which a female tyranniscus was incubating two eggs, and it was not so easily repulsed as the juvenile had been. The mournful complaints of the tyranniscus drew my attention to the Bananaquit advancing along the liverwort-draped branch toward her mossy nest. She attacked, and for several seconds the two small birds seemed to grapple amid the liverworts, where I could not see them well. When they separated, the Bananaquit had some downy gray feathers in its bill. It stayed near the nest until the mate of the tyranniscus arrived, and the spirited attacks of both flycatchers drove the intruder from their nest. Alone, a tyranniscus was no match for a Bananaquit, with its sharper bill.

Later that evening, when the sun was setting, the pertina-
cious Bananaquit returned and, despite the parents' attacks, entered their nest beneath the mossy bough, repeating the slight,
sharp notes that seemed to be its battle cry. A tyranniscus went
to the doorway, and the two clutched together and fell straight
downward, but separated before they touched the ground. Not
easily dissuaded from its design to steal a lodging for the night,
the Bananaquit again entered the nest; again a defender grappled
with it and they fell without reaching the ground. After this, the
intruder departed, leaving the female tyranniscus to warm her
unharmed eggs through the night.

Among the great variety of pensile nests made by American
flycatchers, that of the Sulphury Flatbill, or Yellow-olive Flycatcher, is outstanding. A structure shaped much like a chemist's
retort, with a round chamber entered through a downwardly directed spout, it is composed of blackish rootlets and fibers. Attached to a slender twig or vine, it hangs conspicuously over a
clear space in a shady garden or pasture, or at the roadside. The
plainly attired flatbill who builds it sleeps in it before she lays her
eggs and often for weeks or months after her young have flown,
never to return. Other small birds sometimes occupy this well-
enclosed nest, difficult of access. In flatbills' nests that the builders had abandoned, I once found a juvenile Bananaquit lodging,
and twice adults, one of whom slept in the hanging retort for at
least two weeks.

For years, male and female Tawny-bellied, or Spotted-
crowned, Euphonias slept in snug pockets amid the liverworts and
mosses that grew densely on the calabash trees in front of the
house, or amid the clustered stems of orchids perched upon these
trees, each euphonia in its separate niche. These euphonias, who
build covered nests with a side entrance, are the only members of
the tanager family that I have found roosting elsewhere than
amid foliage. One day I noticed fresh straws around the edges
of the pocket in the brown liverworts where a female euphonia
had been lodging for many months. I suspected that they had
been placed there by a Bananaquit. In the evening, when the eu-

phonia came to enter her dormitory, she paused outside, repeating her peculiar *churr*. When she flew to the doorway, she was greeted by pecks from a small bird inside. She persisted in trying to enter until she and an adult Bananaquit fell out, clutched together, and tumbled to the ground. After separating, both flew up to the pocket at about the same time, and again they grappled and fell. Finally, the euphonia returned alone, and, after hesitating in front for a while, she entered, to remain for the night with her tawny belly filling the doorway, as she always did.

After a pair of Yellow-faced Grassquits raised a brood in a thick-walled, roofed nest with a doorway in the side, built amid the clustered red-and-yellow foliage of a *Codiaeum* shrub in the garden, an adult Bananaquit slept there for at least two weeks.

One evening, while I watched the dormitory of a Riverside Wren above the rocky shore of a mountain torrent, a Bananaquit in adult plumage flew across the channel and cautiously approached the moss-covered globe. If it expected to find shelter for the night, it was disappointed. The wren, who had retired five minutes earlier, emerged when the smaller visitor reached the doorway. The Bananaquit vanished; and the wren returned at its leisure to its dormitory.

Like other species of the genus *Thryothorus*, Rufous-breasted Wrens are skillful builders, who construct covered nests high in trees and vine tangles or within a few inches of the ground. Yet, strangely, they often sleep in nests built by other birds, or at the bases of broad leaves of tank bromeliads. On three separate occasions, I have found Rufous-breasted Wrens and Bananaquits sleeping alternately in the same flimsy nests in view of our windows. I had watched a Bananaquit build one of these nests, and the other two also appeared to be the work of these birds rather than of wrens. On several evenings, I saw one of these Bananaquits come to its nest before the wren arrived and flit around nervously, uttering slight notes while it hesitated to enter. Once it went in but promptly emerged, as though it feared being caught inside by the sharp-billed wren. After the wren had retired, the Bananaquit flew to the entrance; the wren seized it; and I heard low squeaks that seemed to come from the smaller Bananaquit. The latter flew away. The wren left the nest, but soon returned and stayed. On subsequent nights, I sometimes found the wren, sometimes the Bananaquit sleeping in this flimsy nest. The wren would not even permit its mate to join it in the dormitory. Recently I found a Bananaquit passing nights in a well-built, mossy nest, apparently made by a Riverside Wren, in which a Rufous-breasted Wren had long been lodging.

A Bananaquit's nest, abandoned by its builder, was occupied for a few nights by a Chinchirigüí, or Plain, Wren. Other intruders into Bananaquits' nests include small marsupials of the genus *Marmosa*. Once, when I was about to stick a finger into a Bananaquit's nest to learn whether it held eggs, the snarling, sharp-toothed jaws of this tiny opossum made me withdraw my hand quickly. Possibly the furry animal had devoured eggs or nestlings before installing itself in the nest. Ants sometimes occupy the nests; and, on Tobago, Gross found a six-inch lizard in one on three successive days. The small, round hole sometimes found in the top of a nest appears to be the work of a nocturnal predator, possibly a bat. I have never seen any animal attack a nest by day; but the large, black-and-yellow snake called the Mica would have eaten two nestlings if I had not arrived in the nick of time.

On Tobago, Puerto Rico, and doubtless other Caribbean islands, Bananaquits are trapped and kept in cages for their songs, but this deplorable practice appears to be rare on the continent, where many superior songsters are available. Harming nothing, useful as pollinators, delighting us by their fearlessness and tireless activity, Bananaquits are a welcome addition to a garden, but they hardly win admiration for their songs.

# 8. *The Gentler Side of Nature*

A s every conscientious biographer must know, to reach a just estimate of a complex personality involved in intricate historical events— a Themistocles, say, or a Cromwell—is far from easy. How much more difficult, then, must it be to form a fair and balanced judgment of the character of the natural world, so infinitely vaster and more complex than any individual, with such immense creativity mixed with such great capacity for destruction. How insidiously easy it is to exaggerate one aspect of nature at the expense of the contrary!

When we survey the planet that bears us, we may concentrate attention on the violence that periodically harasses it, the earthquakes, volcanic eruptions, hurricanes, and floods, or the vast glaciers that scrape all life from millions of square miles; or we may remember that enormous expanses have remained relatively tranquil for the long ages needed to cover them with luxuriant forests teeming with the most varied life. When we turn our attention to vegetation, we may reflect how plants everywhere spread their foliage in sunshine, peacefully performing the beneficent labor of photosynthesis; or we may be impressed by the intensity of their silent competition for living space, and the multitudes of seedlings that succumb in the conflict. Surveying the animal kingdom, we may be horrified by its vast carnage; or our hearts may be warmed by its many modes of cooperation, by

Frugivorous Birds at Feeder. Left to Right: Scarlet-rumped Tanager (male); Blue Honeycreeper (female); Speckled Tanager (sexes similar) ▶

the tender solicitude of parents for their young. And when we view man—oh, man!—what an utterly bewildering array of incongruous attributes he presents!

We live in an age of growing violence. The two major powers have accumulated great stocks of bombs, each powerful enough to destroy a city, and ready for instantaneous use. To walk city streets at night is to invite assault and theft; housebreakings and bank robberies are shockingly frequent. Wars and civil disorders continue to afflict a world that tries ineffectively to preserve peace. Although people profess to prefer order and security, they often seem to thirst for violence—so long as it does not hurt themselves. They flock to movies displaying violence, spend countless hours watching similar episodes on television, and buy countless books filled with tales of murder and horror. Millions take pleasure in hunting and slaughtering inoffensive animals. I suspect that in a world devoid of violence many would be unbearably bored.

In such an atmosphere, the harsher aspects of nature receive great publicity. Books on aggression and the fiercer predators are eagerly read. In a few hours of watching televised nature films, I have seen more fighting and acts of violent predation (doubtless artificially staged) than I have witnessed in many years amid tropical forests. Popular accounts, no less than strictly scientific writings, focus attention upon the grimmer aspects of the living world. The genes that control development and behavior are held to be programmed to promote their own multiplication with relentless selfishness, even to the extent of pitting parents against offspring and siblings against siblings. According to the widely accepted principle of "competitive exclusion," two related species with the same vital needs cannot continue to coexist, for the more efficient will eliminate its competitor. Anthropologists, undervaluing all that we owe to the fairly innocent arboreal stage of the primate lineage that became human, emphasize the contribution to the making of man of a later stage, when our ancestors hunted large prey in packs, like wolves and wild dogs. Scientists and laymen alike appear to delight in presenting the harsher, more violent aspects of the living world, because they provide the excitement that people crave. Just as historians often devote more pages to wars than to the more peaceful pursuits that occupy a larger share of people's time, so those who write about animals often give disproportionate attention to their more violent activities.

The living world is so vast and many-faceted that no one can grasp it whole. Although prolonged study yields many surprises, on the whole we find there what we seek. If we look for its fiercer aspects, we have no difficulty convincing ourselves that nature is "red in tooth and claw." Many of us, however, prefer to contemplate its gentler side, its constructive activities, and the peace, cooperativeness, and altruism we find there. This is what attracts us to nature, while the harsher side repels. It is, above all, in the world of plants that we enjoy quiet beauty, unmarred by rampant strife; although, if it were not so prolonged and silent, the struggle for life between a strangling fig and the tree that it slowly chokes to death in a network of inexorably constricting roots, or that between a tropical liana and the trunk encircled by its coils, would appear no less violent than a lion's attack upon an antelope. Nevertheless, to discover peaceable coexistence among animals delights us more than to witness it among plants, because it is less widespread and expected, and animals are more like ourselves in their capacity for aggression and destruction, among other things. Happily, from my windows, as farther afield, I have seen much more of the milder than of the harsher aspects of animal life, as doubtless has already become evident to my readers. In the present chapter, I shall deal with the subject more pointedly, in the hope that it will help to correct the unbalanced views that are all too readily formed.

One of the most delightful spectacles that nature affords is a tropical tree profusely laden with fruits that brightly colored birds are eating in the sunshine. In a few hours of watching, I have counted two or three dozen species visiting such a tree, with more individuals than I could number in the constantly shifting crowd. They continually come and go, so that not all the species that visit a tree are simultaneously present, but eight or ten species, some of which are represented by several individuals, may be there at one time. Most of the visitors are small, colorful tanagers, honeycreepers, orioles, manakins, and woodpeckers, with a number of more soberly clad finches, vireos, thrushes, and flycatchers. More rarely larger birds, such as parrots, trogons, toucans, and oropéndolas, join the feasting crowd.

Nearly always, these so diverse feathered creatures, including both residents and migrants, eat together harmoniously. Fights scarcely ever occur, and I cannot recall having seen one individual try to exclude another, of its own or a different species, from a tree. At most, one bird displaces another from the cluster of berries or the opening pod where it is eating, without actual contact—which seems a breach of good manners rather than hostile action.

A multitude of lovely birds peacefully sharing the bounty of a generously fruiting tree provides a slight foretaste of the messianic concord that might pervade the living world if all animals could nourish themselves with fruits instead of preying upon one another. While watching birds at such a tree, I have sometimes wished that men of different nationalities and races, all classified in the same species, could live as amicably together as do these birds of diverse species, families, and orders. They offer us an example of tolerance that we might well copy. And they assure me that nature is neither so harsh nor competition between individuals and species so relentlessly sharp as certain theoretical biologists would have us believe.

A tree covered with bright blossoms rich in nectar or a flowering hedge presents a spectacle hardly less enchanting than a lavishly fruiting tree. Here the visitors, chiefly nectar-sipping hummingbirds, with an admixture of honeycreepers, are mostly smaller than those at fruiting trees and in more rapid agitation, so that their colors are not so easily seen as those of the fruit-eaters. But now and then a hummingbird, poising before a flower with his head toward the watcher, presents a dazzling vision of glittering metallic hues that change as the hovering bird shifts his orientation. Sometimes a hummingbird, claiming exclusive possession of a flowering shrub or tree, tries to drive away every other nectar-drinker, including not only birds but also large butterflies and bees. Nevertheless, a profuse floral display draws too many visitors for a territory-holder to exclude, and defense becomes a futile waste of time; hummingbirds dart about and often chase one another but rarely clash. Nature's bounty overcomes competition. As at the fruiting tree, the spectacle of so many different species coexisting without serious conflict is no less pleasing to the thoughtful watcher than the glittering visual display.

Competition for nest sites need not involve violence. Among the many birds that nest in holes in trees, but cannot carve them, are the tityras—stout, thick-billed, starling-sized members of the cotinga family, which appear almost wholly white as they fly high overhead or rest in a treetop, uttering low, unbirdlike grunts and other dry notes. A cavity carved by small woodpeckers, high in a dead tree standing in a clearing near rain forest, is their preferred nest site. Often a pair of tityras chooses a hole in which the woodpeckers sleep, or even one that the industrious carvers have newly completed for nesting, although never, as far as I have seen, a hole that contains the woodpeckers' eggs or young. The tityras, chiefly the female, carry in dry leaves, petioles, flower stalks, and similar materials to form a deep, loose litter on the bottom. They may continue this activity even in plain view of the woodpeckers, who peck over the trunk or work at a new hole without trying to drive the intruders away. In the evening, when the woodpeckers retire to sleep in their dormitory, often four or five members of a family together, they may throw out some of the trash that the tityras have taken in during the day. Tiring of this housecleaning when they are ready to rest, they hasten to finish a new hole nearby, and as soon as it is spacious enough, they move into it, leaving their former residence

in undisputed possession of the usurpers. In every case that I have watched, the change of ownership has been effected peacefully, with at most a few feints of attack by the tityras, never a clash. In this manner, I have repeatedly seen Masked Tityras take occupied holes from Golden-naped Woodpeckers and Black-cheeked Woodpeckers in Costa Rica; and in eastern Peru I watched Black-crowned Tityras steal a cavity from Yellow-tufted Woodpeckers.

In much the same manner, a female Masked Tityra gained possession of a larger cavity in which three Fiery-billed Araçaris roosted. Although the tityra feared these toucans with huge, brilliant bills, she industriously carried leaves into their chamber during the day, when they were absent. Before long, the araçaris had difficulty fitting themselves into the reduced space, even by laying their long tails over their backs, as they habitually do when they sleep. Finally, they abandoned the hole to the persistent tityra without any fighting. I have read of fierce, sometimes mortal, conflicts between different species of cavity-nesting birds in both the North and South Temperate Zones, but in the tropics I have never seen fights for nest sites. Mild-mannered tropical birds win their cavities by gentler methods.

Sometimes two pairs of Masked Tityras contend for the same hole, or perhaps for exclusive possession of a big dead tree that contains several apparently suitable cavities, as they prefer not to nest close together. The contestants perch among the leafless limbs, often not far apart. Presently one of either sex flies at a member of the other pair, who moves to avoid contact. Then all four flit around confusedly, apparently greatly agitated, uttering grunty notes and twitching their short tails as they rest between movements. After a while, the four fly toward the neighboring forest, as though to forage in company. Soon they return to continue their dispute until evening, when they again fly away together. For nearly a month, two pairs disputed mildly, day after day, without, as far as I saw, the loss of a single feather, and with-

◀ Masked Tityras, Male at Left

out reaching a conclusion before the nesting season ended and they lost interest.

Like the tityras, Buff-throated Saltators are territorial birds that space their nests rather widely. These large, thick-billed finches have olive-green upper plumage and grayish underparts, with a pale buffy throat framed in black. In thickets and dooryard shrubbery they build bulky open nests, in which they lay two bright blue eggs, irregularly scrawled with black. In April, long ago, I was surprised to find two saltators' nests in coffee shrubs only eight feet apart, by far the closest I have seen. Each of the two females had her own mate. One was clearly dominant over her neighbor, who had somehow lost her tail; and she neglected no opportunity to chase her rival from the latter's nest.

Although incubation was often interrupted by these chases, the subordinate female managed to hatch one of her eggs, in sixteen instead of the usual thirteen or fourteen days. The dominant saltator still tried to keep her unwanted neighbor away from nest and nestling, but the sight of the baby bird had an unexpected effect upon her. Looking into the subordinate's nest, to make sure that she was absent, the dominant saltator was greeted by the uplifted, gaping mouth of the nestling, hungry because its parents were so often driven away. Repeatedly, the dominant female gave the nestling food that she was taking to her own young, and she even brooded it briefly. Antagonistic to the parent, she treated the nestling tenderly, when by killing it she might have effectively rid herself of an unwanted neighbor. The opposition between her territorial instinct, which impelled her to drive away the other female, and her strong parental impulses, which prompted her to feed and brood that female's offspring, made her a strange mixture of hostility and gentleness.

While studying the courtship assemblies, or "leks," of manakins, I have sometimes wondered at the curious mixture of cooperation and competition, of rivalry and friendliness, that the living world presents. Many of these diminutive, largely frugivorous birds of tropical America are so elegantly attired that the Germans call them *Schmuckvögel*—jewel birds. In none of the dozen species that have been somewhat adequately studied does the male take the slightest interest in the tiny, cuplike nest, where the plainly attired female alone incubates two eggs and raises the nestlings with berries and insects. A number of males gather each year in the same traditional spot in forest or thicket. Here, in the less social species, each male establishes his own courtship station, which may be a branch high in a tree or a small patch of ground from which he carefully removes all fallen leaves and other litter, until it appears to have been swept clean with a broom.

At his chosen post, each manakin performs his courtship antics within hearing, and often also within view, of at least some of his neighbors. These performances vary greatly from species to species. In *Manacus*, they consist chiefly in jumping back and forth across the bare court, between slender upright saplings. In *Pipra*, they include circular flights, about-faces, and sliding backward along a high, horizontal branch. The visual displays are accompanied by vocal calls and, in some species of *Manacus* and *Pipra*, by sharp notes, like the sound of snapping a dry twig, made by their wings, some of whose feathers have thickened shafts. When a female appears, each male intensifies his displays at his own station, trying to attract her to himself—he cannot compel her. Approaching the male of her choice, she may passively await his attention, or she may join him in a "dance." A male and a female *Manacus* leap simultaneously across the bare court, the two repeatedly passing each other as they jump in opposite directions between the upright stems. If the female approves of the male, she invites him to mount her; if not, she may approach another. After her eggs have been fertilized, she nearly always goes to a distance to lay and hatch them.

For many modern evolutionists, the supreme genetically controlled endeavor of every organism is the transmission of its genes to posterity. These male manakins are engaged in the most momentous of all competitions—that of contributing the maximum number of each individual's own genes to the ongoing stream of life, to the exclusion of those of his rivals. One might expect these little birds who play for such high stakes to be implacable enemies, yet it is hard for the patient watcher to resist the con-clusion that they are friendly cooperators. In the first place, by gathering year after year in the same locality, made conspicuous by all their noise and bustle, they help the females to find them. Moreover, they create a situation in which a female can readily compare potential mates and freely choose the one who, by the perfection of his plumage or the energy of his displays, appears likely to father the most vigorous offspring. As though all this were not enough, in the long intervals when no female ap-proaches an assembly, two males often perch close together on a twig between their separate stations, where, in a subdued man-ner, they direct their courtship antics to each other, seeming by such friendly intercourse to relieve the tedium of waiting.

Although I have never seen manakins fight, their hostility can be aroused by flagrant violation of the "rules" of the court-ship assembly. When Chapman (1935) placed a mounted mu-seum specimen of a male Golden-collared Manakin on an active court, it was strenuously attacked by the outraged owner. It is significant that, to provoke the manakins to violence, the fa-mous ornithologist had to create a highly artificial situation. Among Black-and-White Manakins, who crowd scores of courts into a small area, conflicts appear to be more frequent than in species whose display stations are more widely spaced. Neverthe-less, Snow (1962), who studied these birds in Trinidad, found them more friendly than aggressive.

Other manakins are still more social. In the genus *Chiroxi-phia*, two or three males display on the same perch, where they join in highly coordinated dances. In wet mountain forests, three or four male White-ruffed Manakins choose the same prostrate mossy log for their charming display, which consists in flying down to it with a slow, bouncing motion that makes each look like a tiny black balloon with a white patch in front (Skutch 1967).

Like manakins, hummingbirds gather in courtship assemblies. In the treetops of tropical American woodlands, or in the deep shade of forest or thicket, a number of males gather, year after year, in the same place to attract females by their voices. Some sing chiefly at dawn, others morning and evening, while the most persistent songsters continue all day long throughout a breeding season that lasts several months. Some of these hummingbirds have charming little songs, but the voices of others are dry or squeaky. The approach of one hummingbird to the courtship station of another usually sets off a pursuit that carries both rapidly out of view. The tiny birds fly so swiftly that it is not easy to learn either the sexes of the participants or the outcome of these chases. Although often a male pursues one of his neighbors in the assembly, both soon return to proclaim their presence on their usual stations, apparently none the worse for the encounter. The very persistence of these assemblies from day to day proves that their members rarely, if ever, injure one another. Solitary rather than social, hummingbirds are not the most pacific of feathered creatures; nevertheless, they are capable of fairly peaceful cooperation in an enterprise that is essentially competition for the multiplication of their genes.

Among tropical American birds that form no lasting pair bonds are certain members of the troupial, or oriole, family, including oropéndolas, caciques, and grackles that nest in crowded colonies. The females alone build the nests, incubate the eggs, and feed the young. The bigger, less numerous males do not have separate posts in the colony or, as far as one can tell, particular females attached to them, but move at random among the nests, idle except for occasional calls and courtship displays. One might expect that, mingling together indiscriminately with little to occupy them, they would often quarrel, yet they seldom do. One male frequently flies toward another, who relinquishes his perch to the first and moves to a neighboring branch, thereby avoiding contact. If a chase develops, it does not end in a battle. I have passed many hours watching trees laden with the long woven pouches of Montezuma Oropéndolas and Yellow-rumped Caciques without seeing a fight, and I lived a whole season amid a busy colony of Great-tailed Grackles without noticing any quarrels among the glossy, yellow-eyed males. Female oropéndolas pilfer loosely attached strands from neighbors' nests and even try to snatch fibers from their bills, all without inciting a tiff. Strangely, the only fight between Great-tailed Grackles that I ever saw occurred as I was passing through southern Mexico by train. From the window, I watched two males grappling and rolling over on the ground, continuing until I lost sight of them.

In many species of birds, the young separate from their parents as soon as they can feed themselves more or less adequately; sometimes the parents drive them away. Among permanently resident birds of tropical and subtropical lands, however, ornithologists are discovering a growing number of species in which the young remain with their parents for a year or two, and occasionally longer, forming closely knit family groups. Usually each family has a single nest, in which the oldest female lays; more rarely, two females lay in the same nest, or the group builds several nests. Occasionally the young, nonbreeding members of the family help to build the nest or incubate the eggs, but they assist chiefly by taking a large and important share in feeding and protecting the nestlings and fledglings, who are usually their younger brothers and sisters. More seldom, a nonbreeding bird joins some other pair and helps to raise nestlings who are not its siblings. Such cooperative breeding has been found among gallinules, kingfishers, todies, bee-eaters, puffbirds, woodpeckers, jays, bushtits, wrens, babblers, wood-swallows, wren-warblers, mudnest-builders, and other families. Among the lank black anis of tropical America, cooperative breeding takes a somewhat different form. Several females lay full sets of eggs in the same nest, where they are incubated by turns by all the parent birds, male and female; and all help to feed and brood the nestlings, some-times assisted by juveniles of an earlier brood (Skutch 1976).

These groups of cooperative breeders, which are nearly al-ways expanded families, represent the highest development of social life among birds. One of their most pleasing features is the almost total absence of friction among their members. Although each family defends its territory against neighboring families, among the parents and their helpers almost perfect amity pre-vails. I have spent long hours watching jays, wrens, bushtits, puffbirds, woodpeckers, and other cooperative breeders without witnessing antagonism, and other ornithologists, studying differ-ent species in different parts of the world, have reported the rare-ness of aggressive encounters. It is as though the older members of a human family, including grown children, could cooperate in keeping house and raising the little ones without sometimes dis-agreeing and exchanging harsh words.

Although in at least some of these families of cooperative breeders a social hierarchy exists—the older members usually being dominant over the younger members, and males over fe-males—encounters that reveal social status are so rare that the hierarchy may not be evident. Just as Chapman found it neces-sary to create an unusual situation to reveal the Golden-collared Manakin's capacity for aggressive action, Woolfenden and Fitz-patrick (1977) resorted to artifice to disclose the social hierarchy of the Florida Scrub Jay, one of the most thoroughly studied of cooperative breeders. At a feeder which offered coveted peanuts to one jay at a time, dominant individuals often supplanted their subordinates, or prevented their approach until the former were satisfied.

Since I have watched mammals more casually than birds, I have become familiar with fewer that are gentle and peaceable. Outstanding in this respect are the Howler Monkeys, who live in clans or family groups of males, females, and young, at peace with all nonpredatory animals. Wholly vegetarian, they eat the fruits, buds, leaves, and flowers of a large variety of trees. Each clan claims a territory that it defends against adjoining groups, not by fighting but by voice. Mature males have large, bony larynges that produce deep bass roars, audible for a mile, and so powerful that they may terrify a timid newcomer to the forests where they dwell. When two clans meet at their common boundary, they may shout at each other in a sort of arboreal peace conference that, unlike many human peace conferences, averts violence and bloodshed. The deafening logomachy over, each troop peaceably goes its own way (Carpenter 1934). The social system of Howler Monkeys resembles that of cooperative breeders among birds about as closely as the contrasting methods of reproduction of mammals and birds permit, with the difference that some of the male Howlers leave their clans and join others, thereby avoiding continuous close inbreeding, whereas among birds the females more often do so.

The greatest of existing primates is also an exceptionally peaceable vegetarian, as Schaller (1965) found while living intimately with Mountain Gorillas in central Africa. They are much more gentle than Chimpanzees, who suddenly attack, kill, and eat baby baboons, and even occasionally snatch a human baby from its mother for the same purpose. That the staid Gorilla is no less intelligent than the more excitable Chimpanzee is suggested by Patterson's (1978) outstanding success with Koko, a captive female, who by the age of seven had learned to use about 375 signs of the hand language of the deaf regularly and appropriately. She could ask questions, tell how she felt, refer to past and future events, be insulting, and even lie!

The quadruped grazers and browsers, including antelopes, gazelles, zebras, and deer are, on the whole, pacific animals, which often live in large herds. The tallest of them, the Giraffe, has been called, by one who knew it well on the African plains, a "gentle giant" (Foster 1977). Periodically, however, the peaceful tenor of their lives is interrupted by the sex hormones, which, coursing like some inflaming poison through the veins of adult males, causes erstwhile companions to struggle desperately for possession of the females. Next to the carnivorous habit, sexual rivalry is chiefly responsible for the strife that afflicts the animal kingdom.

Since competition for food is the principal source of conflict, it is fitting that food may also help to diminish hostility and fear among animals. By consistently offering food, we can often overcome the shyness of free animals and even, with patience, entice timid birds and quadrupeds to take it directly from the hand of the biped that it instinctively avoids. The birds of many kinds that frequent a fruiting tree, follow a swarm of army ants to snatch up the small invertebrates that the ants drive from concealment, or roam through the woodland in a mixed flock whose members forage in diverse ways are all drawn together by the quest of food.

One of the most curious, and mutually beneficial, of all these associations of disparate creatures is that between cleaner animals and their clients. In tropical America, Giant Cowbirds, Bronzed Cowbirds, and Great-tailed Grackles pluck ticks, flies, or other parasites from cattle that patiently accept this service, although these birds derive most of their nourishment from other sources. Africa, with a far greater variety of large herbivores, has specialist cleaner birds in the two species of oxpeckers of the genus *Buphagus*. With sharp claws and stiff tails that enable them to cling, woodpeckerlike, to vertical surfaces, these plainly attired starlings climb over the bodies of antelopes, buffaloes, giraffes, zebras, rhinoceroses, warthogs, and domestic cattle (but apparently not of elephants) picking off ticks and blood-sucking flies, along with loose skin and oozing blood of the large animals themselves. In this manner, the oxpeckers procure the whole of their food.

The herbivores that benefit from the attentions of these cleaner birds would not eat them even if they could catch them. Similarly, Marine Iguanas, which subsist upon seaweeds, are not likely to desire the flesh of the Small Ground Finch that on Fernandina Island, in the Galápagos, industriously picks ticks from the rough skin of these reptiles as they lie inactive on the shore, as Amadon (1967) discovered. The foregoing examples involve little or no modification of the behavior of the animals that are cleaned, but other cleaners follow an occupation that would be extremely dangerous without reciprocal adaptations between them and carnivorous clients. Among these are the "crocodile birds," including the Egyptian Plover and the Spur-winged Plover, which feed close to basking crocodiles along the Nile and pluck tsetse flies and other parasites from them, perhaps occasionally entering their open jaws to remove particles of food, as Herodotus and Pliny reported long ago (Howell 1979).

Most surprising of all are the cleaner fishes, of which at least forty-two species in fourteen families inhabit warm seas, while others live in fresh water. These little fishes remove from the bodies of larger fishes external parasites of all sorts, bacteria, diseased tissues, and the remains of food. The clients benefit by this hygienic treatment, while the cleaner is nourished by the particles it gathers from them. So great is the disparity in size between the diminutive cleaner and some of its clients that the former can swim into the open mouths of the latter, pick off particles of food or parasites, and emerge through the gill slits. So many fishes desire the services of the cleaners that they queue up at regular stations in the coral reefs, patiently awaiting their turns. While the cleaner works over its body, the client often sinks into a sort of lethargy, neglecting its respiratory and balancing movements, even falling on its side. Although some of these clients prey upon other fishes, they seldom harm the cleaners (Wickler 1968). The relation between cleaner fishes and their clients is one of our most striking examples of how, by the reciprocal exchange of benefits, hostility may be overcome and creatures of the most diverse kinds dwell in concord.

Finally, let us consider what makes animals gentle and tolerant of others, whether of the same or a different species, and what, on the contrary, makes them fierce. On the whole, the vegetarians of all kinds are milder and more social than the carnivores, especially than those carnivores that prey upon other creatures most like themselves, as do certain warm-blooded vertebrates upon other warm-blooded vertebrates. Although many herbivorous mammals graze or browse in large herds, often composed of several species, the carnivores hunt alone, or at most in small, savagely predatory bands, such as those of lions, wild dogs, and hyenas. Raptorial birds are typically solitary, and often so truculent that the females have become much larger than the males, the better to protect themselves when they mate.

Among the mildest of all birds, and the least inclined to quarrel, are the fruit-eaters, including tanagers, honeycreepers, and manakins. A generously fruiting tree spreads a feast adequate for all that come to enjoy it, making it unnecessary to struggle for places at the banquet. Such trees fruit at different seasons, now here, now there, over a wide area, thereby making fruit-eating incompatible with the strict maintenance of territories, which is one of the causes of conflict among animals. A Deity who wished to create a planet devoid of strife would cover it with a greater variety of plants that yield edible fruits than we find on ours, make these fruits more nutritious, and ensure that animals did not become too numerous for the plants to support. Such a world, devoid of the horror of predation, would be pervaded by a delightful harmony, for, as Aristotle declared long ago, if there were no lack of food, those animals that are now afraid of man or are wild by nature would be tame and familiar with him, as likewise with one another.[1] Predation has engendered fear, which makes many of the gentlest animals dangerous when too closely approached by man; but fear should be absent in a world of peaceful vegetarians.

The second great source of conflict among animals is competition for mates, which is most violent in species that practice simultaneous, or harem, polygyny, like some seals and ungulates, and is least intense in those that remain throughout the year, or

---

1 Aristotle *History of Animals* 608b. 30.

for life, in monogamous pairs, like many tropical birds. Among the latter, pair formation often occurs at an early age, long before breeding begins, and so unobtrusively that it escapes even the careful watcher. Animals that remain faithful to their partners from year to year avoid the annually renewed competition for mates. Next to being permanently paired, the courtship assembly, or lek, is the most harmonious mating system. The males who compose these assemblies do not contend directly for females so much as for favored stations, and typically they do so by formal contests rather than by fierce battles that may cause injury or death. After the assembly has been established, the females freely choose their temporary partners, as in manakins and Ruffs.

Permanent residence promotes concord among birds, and possibly among other animals, whereas migration or wide wandering increases discord. With the notable exception of geese and swans, migratory birds do not remain permanently paired, as so many sedentary birds do. Moreover, for most small birds migration is incompatible with the cohesion of families from year to year, which is indispensable for cooperative breeding and all the advantages thence arising. Arrangements permanent residents can afford to make in a leisurely manner, such as the acquisition of territories and mates and the adjustment of relations with neighbors, must be more hurriedly and brusquely made among birds who begin a short breeding season after a long journey. Just as a pioneer community tends to be more disorderly than one long established and well governed, so a population of migratory birds is likely to be less peaceful than one of permanent residents.

From the foregoing survey we may conclude that the factors that promote gentleness and concord among animals are: (1) a vegetarian and, especially, a frugivorous diet; (2) permanent residence, which permits animals to adjust their relations with their neighbors without haste and violence and favors (3) enduring monogamous pair bonds or persisting family ties leading to cooperative breeding; (4) the reciprocal exchange of benefits between individuals of the same or different species; and, not the least important, (5) a restrained rate of reproduction that does not over-burden the resources of the habitat. Among birds that are not monogamous, courtship assemblies, with free choice of partners by females, are more conducive to harmony than harem polyg-yny by dominant males who compel the females. The contrary factors that increase discord, violence, and fear are: (1) preda-tion and the carnivorous habit; (2) wanderings or migrations that disrupt pairs and families and cause the abandonment of ter-ritories; (3) harem polygyny; and, above all, (4) excessive repro-duction that throws animals into severe conflict for food and liv-ing space.

Nature is so vast and complex that to judge it fairly is far from easy. Some writers emphasize too strongly the strife and suffering among animals; others, ignoring or glossing over unpleasant facts, paint too rosy a picture. It is incumbent upon all who write or teach about nature or portray it in the visual media to en-deavor to present a fair and balanced view, difficult as this may be to achieve.

# 9. *Little Hermit Hummingbirds*

ONE morning recently, a Little Hermit flew into the bathroom through the open window. The tiny brownish hummingbird had dusky cheeks and ear coverts, margined above and below by pale buffy stripes. Its rump was chestnut, its breast cinnamon. Much of its length of less than four inches was occupied by its long, conspicuously downcurved bill and its two white-tipped central tail feathers. The hermit began its inspection by hovering around my head, its sharp bill so near my eyes that I closed them. Then it examined the sheets, pillowcases, and towels on the shelves of the open cupboard. Several times it poised in front of the mirror on the wall, as though viewing itself, but without trying to chase or fight its image, as other birds sometimes do. When it had satisfied its curiosity, the tiny sprite flew out the way it had come. Little Hermits frequently enter our rooms. It was probably the same one that had hovered in front of the lighted television screen my son was watching the preceding day.

When birds of other kinds, including certain other species of hummingbirds, blunder into a room, they often try to escape upward, flying around and around just below the ceiling, alighting at the tops of the walls, while neglecting wide-open doors and windows. Frequently they must be helped to find their way out, lest they become exhausted by long-continued, futile fluttering. Neither the Little Hermit nor its larger relative, the Long-tailed Hermit, wastes precious energy in this fashion; accustomed to flying by narrow passageways through thickets and the under-growth of woodland, they seek a low exit and are never trapped in a room with an open door.

Some years ago, when I dwelt for several months in a house situated at the edge of Costa Rica's Caribbean rain forest, a Little Hermit occasionally searched for insects in the large dining room. This room had a long row of glass windows along the riverward side, whence the rains came, and screened windows and a door on two other sides. If it could not promptly find its way out, the little visitor did not become panic-stricken and dash itself against obstructions, as some birds would have done. On the contrary, it floated slowly back and forth along the windows, searching for a gap through which it could escape. When we opened a window, the hermit soon found it and passed through, without having buffeted itself, perhaps fatally, against unyielding, deceptive glass or treacherous metal cloth. Similarly, when the Little Hermit searched for insects, or perhaps recently hatched spiderlings, in the huge, unsightly webs that fat *Nephila* spiders spun beneath the broad eaves of this house, it was careful not to become en-tangled. Had it done so, it might have provided much nourish-ment for the spiders.

It is not only inside the house that I have been the object of a Little Hermit's close scrutiny. More often such inspections have been made while, machete in hand, I cut my way laboriously through the densely entangled second-growth thickets in which the hermit dwells in warm lowlands. Of a sudden, a low hum-ming close to my ears would make me desist from the struggle to move forward through the stubbornly resisting tangle and look around me. There, half an arm's length from my face, would be the inquisitive hummer, hovering motionless on beating wings, gazing intently at this strange intruder into its domain. By swift darts it would change its point of motionless hovering to view me from various angles, sometimes making the circuit of my body, and often venturing so near that its wings sent a refreshing breeze against my heated cheeks. Then, its tour of inspection over, with a sharp *cheep* it would dart off and vanish into the depths of the thicket, where I could follow only with great difficulty.

Reflecting upon such experiences, often repeated with various species of dull-colored, long-billed hummingbirds of the forest undergrowth and thickets called "hermits," but seldom with the glittering hummingbirds of sunnier places, it has occurred to me that they are probably near-sighted. Since they must work with their eyes close to the flowers they probe, the tiny insects they catch, or the nests they build, it would not be surprising if hummingbirds are myopic.

If the Little Hermit scrutinizes a person in a manner that, if practiced by another human, would be offensive or embarrassing, it sometimes permits an equally close inspection of itself. Many years ago, when I was beginning to learn the names of tropical American birds, one of these hermits was cooperative as few birds are. Although I had already watched many individuals hovering before flowers, they rarely remained in one spot long enough for me to distinguish the finer details of their color pattern. One evening, however, a Little Hermit rested on a low twig in a scrubby pasture while I advanced to within four or five feet and, taking notebook and pencil, described what I could see of him while his back was toward me. Then I moved cautiously nearer, and still he did not budge. Approaching to within a foot, I leaned forward until I could clearly see his dusky chin and throat and the orange-buff of his foreneck. Becoming more confident, I was about to reach forward to pick up the bird, who I suspected was injured or perhaps stuck to the twig by a gummy secretion, for a more minute examination; but, before I could touch him, he spread his wings and shot away.

The Little Hermit ranges through the rainier parts of continental America from southeastern Mexico to western Ecuador, eastern Peru, Amazonian Brazil, Venezuela, and the Guianas. It is abundant on the island of Trinidad. From the lowlands, where it is most numerous, it extends upward to about 4,500 feet, and in Guatemala it has been reported 1,000 feet higher. In some parts of its range, it inhabits the dense undergrowth of humid forest. In the regions where I know it best, including the Caribbean lowlands of Central America and the southern half of Costa Rica's Pacific slope, the Little Hermit prefers forest edges, open woods, and tall thickets that spring up where rain forest has been felled, and it is not often seen in the depths of heavy forest. From these shady abodes, it frequently enters sunny openings, banana and coffee plantations, flower gardens, and even buildings to search for flowers and insects, and it sometimes nests in a clearing with scattered trees and shrubs. Most at home in dim undergrowth, Little Hermits fly and seek food within a few yards of the ground, occasionally rising higher.

Like nearly all hummingbirds, the Little Hermit sucks nectar from a great variety of flowers, before which it poises on wings vibrating so rapidly that they are invisible to the human eye, which detects only a vague haze, in the midst of which the slender brownish figure seems to float. The hermit inserts its bill from the front, and appears to pollinate small flowers, such as the violet florets of *Stachytarpheta*; fragrant white orange blossoms; lavender pineapple florets; and the deep pink-and-purple flowers of the orchid *Elleanthus capitatus* emerging from the glistening jelly that surrounds them.

Flowers with long, slender corolla tubes are treated quite differently. One morning in May, I watched a hermit visit the bright red blossoms of the Costa Rican Skullcap, whose two-inch-long tubes are only an eighth of an inch in diameter at the top. To avoid pushing her curved bill down the narrow, nearly straight tube, the hummingbird pierced the red tissue near its base and stuck her bill through the perforation to reach the nectar. This operation seemed simple enough, yet required great precision. Hovering on vibrating wings, she set the point of her bill against the outside of the tube and then apparently flew forward until it broke through. The bill's tip had to be placed exactly in the middle of the narrow tube; otherwise, it slipped off instead of penetrating the tissue, as I saw happen more than once. After she had pierced the near side of the tube, the hummer had to elevate her body and bend down her bill so that it would slip along the passageway to the nectar, and not jab through the far side of the tube into the outer air—a mishap I did not see occur. Several times the hummingbird pierced each of the open corollas in the brilliant inflorescence of the tall mint, as I saw while standing close beside her.

After the hermit's departure, I plucked the head of red flowers for more minute scrutiny. The bird returned and hovered two or three inches from the fingers that held them, fanning my face with her wings. I stood immobile, hoping that she would continue to perforate the corollas in my hand, but after a moment she vanished.

In September I watched hummingbirds visit the lavender flowers of *Poikilacanthus macranthus*, which flourished in the rich, rocky soil beneath the dying *Goethalsia* trees, as told in the next chapter. The slender corollas of this shrub of the acanthus family are slightly over three inches long; the closed, tubular basal part one and three quarters inches long. The chief visitors were Rufous-tailed Hummingbirds, who inserted their bills down the tubes in the "legitimate" manner, and Little Hermits, whose more strongly curved bills consistently pierced the corollas. Hovering beside a flower, its bill inclined obliquely downward with the tip against the base of the corolla, the hummingbird interrupted the steady wingbeat of hovering flight to raise its wings well above its back and give them one or a few strong, rearward strokes. This imparted a jerky movement to its body; its tail swung up and down, as the forward thrust of this maneuver forced the bill through the delicate tissue of a flower on its thin, yielding branch. In quick succession, the little thief stole nectar from many flowers without pollinating any of them.

Little Hermits often visit the great, six-inch-wide blossoms of the Scarlet Passionflower, displayed during the dry season near the ground from the basal shoots of vines that clamber high into the trees to spread their leaves in the sunshine. Apparently un-

Little Hermit Piercing Corolla of *Poikilacanthus macranthus* ▶

able to reach the nectar richly secreted at the bottom of the deep central well, protected by an elaborate collar surrounding the stalk that holds pistil and stamens aloft, the hermit gleans secretions from accessory nectaries on the bracts, or else gathers insects attracted to these sweets, leaving the contents of the well at the center of the flower to its larger, longer-billed relatives, the Long-tailed Hermit and the Green Hermit. The Little Hermit also plucks insects from twigs and foliage, or deftly extracts them from spiders' webs, but it seldom, if ever, catches them by darting back and forth in the air, as many hummingbirds do.

### Courtship

With two well-authenticated exceptions (the Bronzy and Rufous hermits) the sexes of hummingbirds form no lasting attachments; the female builds her nest and raises her young without a male's attendance. In the breeding season, male hummingbirds of a number of tropical species join in assemblies, which may be high in trees or near the ground. Here, each on his own perch, within hearing if not within view of some of his neighbors, each tirelessly repeats utterances that are often thin and squeaky, but in some species charming. Whatever their quality, these vocalizations may be called songs, for their function is the same as that of the most brilliant performances of songbirds.

In light, second-growth woodland with tangled undergrowth, I wandered into the midst of a singing assembly of Little Hermits. All around me, small voices came from unseen sources. More than their voices, the constantly wagging, white-tipped tails of the tiny brown songsters helped me to detect them in the dim light against the brown litter that carpeted the ground, amidst dead leaves caught up on bushes and vines, of much the same color as the birds' plumage and usually bigger than they were. By careful scrutiny, I picked out a number of the hermits. Each rested on a thin dead twig or horizontal vine, usually from a few inches to two feet above the ground. With his long, slender, curved black bill held obliquely upward, his throat swelling with his voice, his tail beating up and down to keep time—now rapidly through a wide arc, now slowly with slight amplitude— the hummingbird poured forth his little ditty. Not very shy while singing, he often remained at his post while I moved around at no great distance, severing vines and branches with my machete and snapping dead twigs underfoot—noises that I could not avoid as I advanced through the undergrowth. When I approached within two or three yards of a songster, he rose on invisible wings, slowly, like a toy balloon released from the hand, and lightly settled on a nearby perch, to resume his interrupted chant and tail-wagging. This tail movement is so ingrained in the species that females and even fledglings perform it while they perch.

Although hardly brilliant, the Little Hermit's song is more lively and complex than the monotonous squeaking, all in much the same key, of his larger relatives, including his neighbor, the Long-tailed Hermit, and the Green Hermit, who lives at higher altitudes. One version of the Little Hermit's song began with a measured *chip chip chip chip*, followed by a rapid, lilting *do da do a da* in a higher pitch. Sometimes the whole refrain consisted of five notes, the first two uttered deliberately, the final three more hurriedly. Now and then, the song shrank to a whisper. The vivacious little ditty had a pleasant swing and cadence, but the voice was too high and thin to satisfy human ears. Snow (1968) and later Wiley (1971), who tape-recorded the hermits' songs in Trinidad, showed that close neighbors had similar songs, different from the songs of other groups in the same expanded assembly. This variation, which was surprisingly great in the assemblies of White-eared Hummingbirds that I long ago studied in the Guatemalan highlands (Bent 1942), along with other evidence, points to the conclusion that the songs of hummingbirds are learned rather than innate. Apparently, young males who join an established group learn the song that prevails there.

At the height of the breeding season, each Little Hermit

repeats his song throughout a long day, in bright or gloomy weather. In a day-long watch, David and Barbara Snow found that one male sat on his perch for 444 minutes, or 70 percent of the ten and a half hours recorded. Performing at the rate of about thirty songs per minute nearly all the time he was on his perch, this bird delivered about 12,000 songs in a day.

At Los Cusingos, the assemblies of Little Hermits are situated in lush, humid thickets, in second-growth woods with thick undergrowth, or, more rarely, in old forest, especially near the edge, where shrubs and vines grow most densely. An assembly may spread over fifty yards or more. Because of the difficulty of seeing the hermits amidst dimly lighted undergrowth, and their habit of shifting to sing on another perch if disturbed, I have not learned the exact number of participants, which is probably several dozen, for, standing in the midst of an assembly, I have heard voices arising from unseen throats on every side.

These assemblies are active through most of the year. At Los Cusingos, the hermits fall silent at the height of a severe dry season, when flowers become scarce. In two very dry years, I failed to hear them for about two months, from about mid-February to mid-April. In a wetter year, singing was resumed in early April, when renewed rainfall had refreshed the vegetation and flowers were increasing. In addition to this dispersal of the assembly during the driest and leanest months, I have noticed a decrease in vocal activity in the midst of the rainy season, from late August or early September through October, which is often our wettest month, with twenty or more inches of rain. On some days in this interval, the hermits sing chiefly in the early morning; on others, especially in September, I failed to hear them. Otherwise, their chorus of scattered voices may be heard in any month, and at almost any hour of the day.

The periods when the singing assemblies are most active correspond only roughly with the months when eggs are laid. In August, September, and October, when the assemblies are only slightly active, I have found no newly laid eggs in El General, but neither have I found any in January and February, when the hermits sing a great deal in their assemblies. In January, females incubate eggs laid in December, or attend nestlings. If they continued to lay after the weather turns dry in January, their young might not be independent when food becomes scarce in February and March. If the habitat remains favorable, an assembly persists in the same spot year after year; I know of one that did so for at least eighteen years. Snow found a hermit, recognizable by his peculiar song, performing on the same perch after an interval of three years.

The Little Hermits' singing assemblies, like those of other hummingbirds, are often situated where flowers are rare or lacking. Accordingly, it is not likely that they sing to proclaim possession of a feeding territory. The only convincing explanation of these gatherings is that they provide a traditional, easily found locality where the solitary female can come when her eggs need fertilization, and perhaps assess the qualifications of the males who compete for her attention while they cooperate to attract her. Nevertheless, as in other species of hummingbirds—and in contrast to what occurs at the courtship assemblies or leks of manakins and other birds with comparable mating systems—it is exceedingly difficult to learn exactly what happens when a female arrives, and in what circumstances coition occurs. The difficulty arises from the virtual impossibility of distinguishing the sexes under the actual conditions of observation and of keeping the birds in view after they begin to move.

While I watched one hermit singing on his habitual perch not more than six inches above the ground, another, possibly a female, flew up and poised on wing in front of and a little above him. The songster rose above his perch and floated in the air, facing the other. After a moment of this, the two darted away and were promptly lost to view amid the dark foliage. Such has been the invariable outcome of the pursuits of this nature that I have witnessed, among hermits and other hummingbirds with singing assemblies. Possibly the participants in some, or even

most, of these chases are both males, of which one has intruded into the other's domain. But that the males do not seriously fight with or injure one another we may be certain from the
fact that they are soon back again, singing as tirelessly as ever on
the same perches.

All of an August morning, I sat in a blind in a grove of tall
second-growth trees in view of the perches of two members of a
hermits' singing assembly. On several occasions, I saw one of
these birds and another of unknown sex and provenance hover
face to face in the air and, hanging on vibrating wings, float
slowly upward, one sometimes slightly above the other. Then
they would break this formation and dart away so swiftly that I
could not tell which was pursuer and which pursued. At another
time, one rested on a low twig, about a foot from the ground,
while another hovered in front of and above it. The first performer floated nearly upright in the air, a little above the stationary one, while it swung from side to side through an arc of not
over one foot. Then it altered its posture, bringing its body into a
horizontal position, with its head and spread tail bent strongly
upward, giving the whole hummingbird a crescent form, the
horns pointing skyward. In this curious posture, it wafted from
side to side, at the same time rotating back and forth through
180 degrees to change the direction it faced. Or it might rotate
thus while scarcely changing its place in the air. Suddenly, performer and spectator darted away. The stationary member of this
couple occupied a perch often used by the more assiduous of the
two songsters in sight of my blind; but whether the songster was
displayed to by another hermit, or whether he displayed before
one who had come to occupy his perch, I could not learn.

In the forest at Los Cusingos, one morning at the end of
March, I watched a more marvelous display. One hermit, whom
I took to be a female, rested upon a slender dead twig about a
foot above the ground, while another, apparently a male, floated
a few inches above her upturned head, on wings beating so rapidly that they were invisible. With his head and tail held strongly

upward, he reminded me of a tiny boat with sharply upcurved bow and stern, floating upon an invisible liquid. Making a sharp humming sound as of a bumblebee, he oscillated gently back and forth over a distance of a few inches, and at the same time more slowly up and down. Every few seconds, he turned an about-face, and at longer intervals he revolved rapidly through a complete circle, or even made a turn and a half. He varied the performance by shooting rapidly and wildly back and forth for a foot or two, while his wings buzzed more loudly and insistently. After each of these interludes of more vigorous display, he resumed the quieter floating above the female, with gentle oscillations back and forth and up and down, and frequent rotations in the air.

After I had watched this spectacular performance for several minutes, it occurred to me to time it. The hummingbird continued to display for five minutes or more by my watch. He must have performed in my presence for nearly ten minutes, and I do not know how long he had been displaying before I arrived. What wonderful endurance of wing he had!

To me, looking down from above, the hermit's most conspicuous color was the chestnut of his rump and upper tail coverts. To the supposed female, viewing him from below, his cinnamon breast and whitish thighs, the feathers of which stood out in prominent tufts, must have been his outstanding features. During the whole display, she kept her long bill pointed straight up toward him; when he dashed back and forth in longer arcs, she moved her head to follow. She appeared to be intensely interested in what he did.

At last, the tiny acrobat darted away through the underwood; then she to whom he displayed promptly vanished, too. This appeared to be a courtship ceremony; yet in this locality there had never, to my knowledge, been a singing assembly, and now, at the end of a severe dry season, the assemblies were inactive.

In October, while cutting a trail through heavy lowland forest near the Pacific coast of Costa Rica, I witnessed a similar performance. In a patch of great-leaved *Heliconia* in an opening amid the forest, a female hermit rested on a low twig, while a male hovered above and a little in front of her, his body curved in the usual crescent form. He oscillated from side to side and also rotated about a vertical axis, while the perching female elevated her head toward him. I do not know how long the hermit had been performing before I found him so engaged; but a minute or so after my arrival, he alighted upon the female's back, whereupon she moved to avoid him and came to rest a short distance away. The male resumed his display above her, then again tried to settle on her back. Again she flew, this time beyond my sight; and the male also vanished. Here, too, there was no courtship assembly, at least at this season.

Nearly always spectacular in their small way, the hermits' displays vary greatly in detail and perplex the observer who tries to interpret their significance without being sure of the participants' sexes. In April I found one of these small birds resting about eight inches up on a long, slender, arching dead leaf stalk of *Cyclanthus bipartitus*. It was swinging its tail rapidly up and down, and pointing its bill toward another, who floated above it, moving slowly from side to side, rotating on a vertical axis, and dashing more swiftly back and forth with sharp sounds, much as already described. After a while, the spectator rose into the air and the performer settled on the perch that the other had just left. The roles of the two hummingbirds were now reversed, the displaying one becoming the passive watcher, the original spectator becoming the performer. I clearly saw this reversal repeated several times and detected no differences in the aerial performances of the two individuals. Sometimes the hovering bird held both head and tail upward, in the characteristic crescent shape, but at other times its tail was bent strongly downward. This mutual display continued for perhaps a minute, although it seemed much more prolonged. Then one hermit chased the other, or perhaps they again reversed roles and chased alternately, back and forth above their perch. Finally, they flew off through the woods together. This also occurred at a distance from an assembly.

Rarely, hermits display well above the ground. On an afternoon in April, while I watched a Blue-throated Goldentail Hummingbird incubate in a mossy nest in the big bamboo at a corner of our garden, a Little Hermit alighted on a spray thirty or forty feet above the ground. While it perched there, with head tilted up and tail swinging rapidly through a wide vertical arc, a second hermit arrived and began to display by floating back and forth above the first, its head and tail bent upward to form the horns of a crescent. Soon both rose into the air; then one settled on a neighboring twig of the bamboo and the performance was repeated, whether by the same bird or the one who had been a spectator, I could not tell. This bamboo was several hundred feet from the nearest singing assembly. Although manakins, Ruffs, and other birds perform their more or less elaborate courtship rites in their assemblies, I suspect that hummingbirds usually do so at a distance. The singing assembly may be primarily an arrangement for bringing together a male and female, who fly off together to consummate their nuptials.

### Nesting

Of the twenty-five occupied hermits' nests that I have seen, all but two were fastened beneath fronds of small palms, often species of *Bactris*, forbiddingly armed on stem and leaf with long, sharp, black spines. Usually the nest was attached to the tapering end of one of the terminal divisions of the palm frond, but one was bound to the apex of a lateral pinna, and another to the tips of two lateral pinnae that had been fastened together. The lowest of these nests was twenty-three inches up; the highest, seven feet; most were between three and five feet above the ground. Nearly all were in light second-growth woods; a few were in more open parts of ancient forest. One was in a clump of palms left in a narrow clearing newly made in the heavy forest near the Pacific coast of southern Costa Rica.

Of the two nests not attached to palm fronds, one was suspended five feet up beneath a coffee leaf in a small plantation at an altitude of 2,800 feet above sea level—the most elevated point where I have found a Little Hermit nesting. The nest highest above the ground was twelve feet up in a small banana plantation between the old forest and second-growth thickets at Los Cusingos. Instead of being attached to a ribbonlike strip of banana leaf, in the manner of all the nests of the Bronzy Hermits and Band-tailed Barbthroats who built in this plantation, the Little Hermit's nest was fastened below the right-angled, downturned corner of a large sheet of leaf, like the nests that Long-tailed Hermits sometimes built in this same banana grove.

A typical hermit's nest matches in shape the tapering apex of the leaf beneath which it is fastened. It is roughly a cone, not entirely hollow but with a pocket in its base, which is uppermost. The materials of the nest are varied. One was composed of light-colored vegetable down; tawny pappi; long, chestnut-colored scales from the fronds of tree-ferns; some shreds of inner bark; some long, slender fragments of fern fronds and monocotyledonous leaves; a few tufts of green moss; and cobweb for binding. Another was made chiefly of brown, fibrous materials, fine coiled tendrils, bits of moss, and dry flowers of the *Inga* trees that shaded the coffee plantation where it was situated. Cobweb in liberal quantities is an indispensable ingredient of all nests. Not only does it bind together the materials, it is the only thing used to attach the structure to the leaf, over the back of which it forms a close, light-colored network that contrasts strongly with the dark green leaf. It is constantly renewed during the period of incubation.

These nests measure about one and three-quarters inches in diameter at the top in the direction parallel to the surface of the leaf, and one and one-half inches in diameter perpendicular to this. In height they are more variable, measuring from two and one-half to four inches, without including the peculiar "tail." The inside diameter is about one inch; inside depth, one and one-eighth inches. The "tail" may be a loose, slender, downward prolongation of the apex of the inverted cone, composed of fern

Little Hermit Incubating ▶

scales and other materials such as form the outer layer of the nest itself, all bound together with cobweb; if so constructed it is not remarkably long. Or it may consist chiefly of a single long, narrow, dry grass blade, or some other bit of dry vegetation resembling a straw, in which case it may be nearly a foot long and hang far below the body of the nest. Some nests have almost no "tail." Some have no lining on the side of attachment, so that the breast of the incubating bird touches the green tissue of the supporting leaf.

One morning in July, in light second-growth woods on a knoll beside the creek where most of my nests were found, I watched a hermit who appeared to be selecting a site. She flew rapidly from tip to tip of the fronds of the small, spiny palms, clinging for a moment beneath each tapering apex, until she had visited five or six. Sometimes the similarity of the two divisions of the frond's terminal segment confuses a building hermit, who attaches material to both tips before completing her nest on one of them. Many birds are similarly confused when they try to build on one of several almost identical sites, like the rungs of a ladder.

Probably only a hummingbird could attach a nest beneath the smooth, slippery tip of a living palm leaf. At first the hermit has no place to rest and must work wholly on the wing. She begins by attaching fragments of plants to the leaf with cobweb. Arriving with strands of spider's silk, she hovers facing the underside of the leaf tip, where her nest will be. Then, always with her bill toward the leaf, she floats around it on vibrating wings, making one, two, or three complete revolutions, clockwise or counterclockwise, often on a spirally descending course, while she wraps the cobweb around the back of the leaf-tip. Sometimes she reverses her course to make a turn in the opposite direction. After she has fastened a small mass of materials to the leaf in this manner, she may cling to this mass, still sustaining much of her weight on her beating wings rather than on the delicate structure, while she inserts another fragment into the accumulation.

After the mass has acquired a conical shape and approaches the size of a completed nest, the builder may rest on it with folded wings while she hollows out the top to form the nest cavity, probably largely with her hidden feet, or with her bill wipes cobweb on the rim and exterior. Even at this stage, she continues to circle around the leaf-tip with cobweb, reinforcing the nest's attachment. One Little Hermit brought material to her nest twenty-one times in one hour early in the morning—the most rapid building that I have watched. In the next half-hour, when the sun beat down hotly into the narrow clearing in lowland forest, she came only five times. After she had worked four days, her nest appeared to be finished. At no time did another hermit accompany her.

Two days after a different nest was completed, an egg was laid in it. After another interval of two days, the second egg was laid. At other hermits' nests, too, the interval between the appearance of the first and second eggs was approximately forty-eight hours, as with other hummingbirds. At one hermit's nest, however, the eggs were laid on consecutive days. The eggs are regularly deposited around sunrise, between 5:30 and 6:30 A.M. Each of twenty-three nests held two eggs or nestlings. Two nests had a single nestling, the second having probably been lost. The minute, pure white eggs are long and slender, with little difference between the two ends—oblong rather than ovate. Those of one set measured 11.5 by 7.1 millimeters; in another set, both were 11.9 by 7.9 millimeters.

In the valley of El General, Little Hermits, like certain pigeons and seedeaters, have two annual breeding periods. The first starts with the return of rain in April and continues into August. The second starts toward the end of the long wet season in November and terminates at the beginning of the dry season in January. In August and January, I have found no newly laid eggs, but the young of late broods are still in their nests. In twenty-four nests, eggs were laid as follows: April, five; May, five; June, five; July, four; November, one; December, four. The months in which

I have seen no nests with either eggs or young are those when singing by males is either quite suspended, as in usually dry February and March, or when their song is greatly reduced, as in very wet September and October.

Only the female hermit incubates. The leaf that forms a green roof above her head shelters her and her offspring from rain and does much to conceal them from hostile eyes, but also imposes severe restrictions on the posture she may assume while sitting. Many birds like to vary their orientation in the nest, sitting now facing in one direction and now in another, apparently easing their long hours of incubation by these shifts in position. The hermit beneath her green canopy is limited to just one way of sitting, and that in a posture that appears so strained and uncomfortable that we wonder how she can maintain it as long as she does. She invariably sits with her breast toward the leaf where her nest is attached, her head thrown far back, and her bill tilted sharply, almost vertically, upward. This is the only way she can find room for her long bill without poking it through a perforation in the green tissue in front of her—an expedient that seems never to have occurred to her kind. Her tail is also tilted obliquely upward at the side of the nest away from the leaf, where the rim is lowest. Ensconced in the deep, downy pocket, she seems bent almost double, the back of her head almost touching the upper surface of her tail. The tips of her wings project above the nest's rim slightly forward of her tail, almost filling the narrow space between this and the back of her head. Although this looks like a tortured posture, the hermit doubtless does not find it so, for she may sit almost immobile for an hour or more by day, and probably continuously through the night. Her larger relatives, the Long-tailed Hermit and the Green Hermit, always sit in the same fashion in their nests fastened beneath leaves. Their longer bills cause them to bend their heads even farther back, and their posture appears still more strained.

How does the Little Hermit manage to extricate herself from this confined space, where she seems to fit so tightly? Although it hardly seems possible and I cannot explain all the details, she somehow starts her wings beating in this space, which appears too narrow to permit such movement. Slowly rising higher, she increases the amplitude of her wing-beats and floats off the nest obliquely upward and *backward*. As soon as she is clear of the leaf, she reverses the direction of her flight and darts forward and away. Her return is as neat as her departure. She flies directly and unhesitatingly down into her cozy pouch, never alighting on the rim in the manner of heavier birds less skillful on the wing. When she folds her wings, she is already incubating her eggs! The pensile nest rises slightly as she flies from it, and sinks a little when it again feels her weight of only three grams.

During the night, one hermit slept with her head drawn down into the nest, but not turned back or buried in her feathers. Her exposed bill, rising obliquely, touched the left margin of the supporting leaf with its tip. As far as I know, whether on or off the nest, all hummingbirds sleep with their heads exposed and bills forward, as doves also do.

Although male hummingbirds of many species congregate to sing, the more solitary females rarely build their nests in view of one another—the chief exception known to me being the Violet-headed Hummingbird, whose nests were found close together along a forest stream, as I told in A *Naturalist in Costa Rica* (1971). Accordingly, when I found two hermits' nests only twelve feet apart in April 1955, the discovery called for careful study. These nests were in a more open part of the forest, beside a little-used road near its edge. They were in the usual situation, beneath fronds of spiny palms, one three feet up and the other seven feet up—the highest of all the Little Hermits' nests that I have seen, except that attached to a leaf of a banana plant.

After each of these nests held two eggs, I passed all of one morning and all of the following afternoon watching the two females incubate. I sat unconcealed, since they paid as little attention to me as they did to each other. In slightly more than twelve hours, the hummingbird at the low nest, who had been incubating for eight days, sat for nine intervals, ranging from 16 to 92 minutes and averaging 60.7 minutes. Her nine absences lasted from 10 to 25 minutes and averaged 18.3 minutes. She covered her eggs for 77 percent of the twelve hours. In the same period, the hermit at the high nest, who had completed her set of eggs only three days earlier, took fourteen sessions, varying from 9 to 59 minutes and averaging 27.9 minutes. Her fifteen recesses ranged from 9 to 29 minutes and averaged 15.1 minutes. She incubated with a constancy of 65 percent.

When the low nest had nestlings and the eggs in the high nest were about to hatch, I watched again through six hours of the morning. The hermit with eggs took nine sessions, ranging from 17 to 36 minutes and averaging 27.1 minutes. Her nine recesses ranged from 9 to 15 minutes and averaged 12.6 minutes. Now she incubated with a constancy of 68 percent, little more than ten days earlier. Another hermit that I watched through six hours of the morning took nine sessions of 13 to 67 minutes, averaging 27.2 minutes. Her ten recesses varied from 5 to 22 minutes and averaged 10.4 minutes. She devoted 72 percent of the six hours to incubation. Another Little Hermit was in her nest for 62 percent of four hours. Evidently the Little Hermit's constancy in incubation ranges from 60 to 80 percent of the active day, which is the range of constancy that I have most frequently found in tropical passerine birds of which only the female incubates.

During the course of incubation, the hermit continues to add materials to her nest, just as many other kinds of hummingbirds do. Usually, when she returns with something in her bill, she first settles in the nest, then tucks the bit of down or cobweb into the rim in front of or beside her. But at times, coming with a skein of cobweb in the tip of her long bill, she only half-settles in the nest, or merely hovers close in front of it, then circles on wing around the back of the leaf, once, twice, or even thrice, ending her revolutions by dropping into the nest in the usual manner, then perhaps wiping her bill against the rim. Thereby she continually extends fresh strands of cobweb from the nest to the leaf and keeps the attachment firm. One hermit brought material nine times in six hours, and thrice passed cobweb around the back of the leaf. The hermit in the higher of the two neighboring nests added to it five times in twelve hours; her neighbor in the low nest only twice in the same interval. As with other incubating hummingbirds, nest reinforcement was largely confined to the forenoon; the latest hour at which a contribution was brought was 12:12 P.M. I did not see any of these birds turn or adjust her eggs with her bill.

Little Hermits are not shy at their nests. While I stood beside one nest measuring the eggs, the owner suddenly arrived with a piece of moss in her bill and dropped into the nest ten inches from my face. After sitting so close beside me for a minute or two, she rose from her nest and hovered all around me, scrutinizing me from a distance of less than one foot. Then she disappeared. Another hermit with nestlings examined me almost as closely while I stood beside her nest.

The exceptionally high nest in the banana plantation was puzzling. One day a Little Hermit hovered beside it. Two days later, a Long-tailed Hermit flew up to it, then poised in front of the mirror, attached to a long stick, which I had raised to view the two eggs. Later, the Long-tailed Hermit took a fiber to it. To learn which of these birds owned the nest, I watched for the first five hours of a July morning of sunshine and a little rain. The nest clearly belonged to a Little Hermit; but it was visited four times by a Band-tailed Barbthroat, probably the individual whose nest hung beneath a narrow strip of another banana leaf, eight feet away. Once a Rufous-tailed Hummingbird flew up to examine the Little Hermit's nest; and three inspections were made by one or more hummingbirds who left so promptly that I could not identify them. Thus, before eleven o'clock in the morning, the Little Hermit was visited eight times, by at least three other species of hummingbirds. All the hummingbirds' nests that hung so conspicuously beneath banana leaves, belonging to four species, seemed to excite the curiosity of other hummingbirds of the same or different species, and were visited more or less frequently by them. Sometimes the Little Hermit continued to sit while another hummingbird poised close beside her, and sometimes she left. Despite interruptions, she covered her eggs with a constancy of 71 percent, and she brought material to her nest four times.

At one nest, the second egg hatched between fifteen days and one hour and fifteen days and twelve hours after it was laid. At another nest, the incubation period was between fifteen days and fifteen days and six hours. At five other nests, it was approximately sixteen days. Since the first egg receives a good deal of incubation before the second is laid, the female sometimes passing the night on the single egg, it frequently hatches more than twelve hours before the second, and at one nest it did so more than twenty-six hours before the second egg. Only the second egg can be used for an accurate determination of the incubation period.

Newly hatched hermits are minute, pink-skinned creatures, naked except for a double row of tiny tufts of tawny down along the center of the back. Little black swellings reveal the position of their tightly closed eyes. Their rudimentary bills are whitish. The empty shells from which they have escaped are not intentionally removed by their mother, but are sometimes brushed from the nest as she rises from it. If they remain, they are gradually broken into fragments, which work down into the nest's soft lining and are found there after the young birds' departure.

Soon after they hatch, the sightless nestlings orient themselves with their heads toward the supporting leaf. This is the position that, with rare deviations, they will maintain until they fly; it was the invariable orientation of their mother while she hatched them, and she will continue to assume it while she broods them. In sitting with head inward, hermit hummingbirds resemble Royal Flycatchers, of which both incubating females and nestlings from a tender age always rest in the shallow niche in their long pensile nest with heads at the back and tails in the doorway.

To feed her nestlings, the mother hermit reaches over their backs. When they have become so big that their heads rise above the nest's rim at mealtime, it can be seen that they bend them far up and back to receive food. To regurgitate a meal, she inserts her long bill into a nestling's throat while she hovers beside the nest on rapidly beating wings, exactly as though she were sucking nectar from a flower. Sometimes, especially while the nestlings are very small, she touches and appears to hold with her feet to the nest's rim while she delivers food, although her wings continue to beat as rapidly as when she hovers free in the air, and she seems to depend chiefly upon them to maintain her position. After her nestlings are bigger, she often feeds them while floating in the air, without touching the nest at all.

Two nestlings, respectively one and three days old, were fed four times in two hours of the early morning. In the first six hours of the day when two nestlings were two and four days old, their mother brought food eight times, or at the rate of 0.66 feeding visits per nestling per hour. A single nestling, thirteen or fourteen days old, was fed fifteen times in six hours. The intervals between its meals ranged from seventeen to thirty-five minutes. On a single visit, the mother of two nestlings often regurgitates twice to each of them alternately, or sometimes twice to one and once to the other. Feeding may last for twenty to twenty-five seconds, and a continuous act of regurgitation from three to twelve seconds. Unlike passerine parents, the hermit does not remove the nestlings' droppings after she has fed them. Their habitual orientation permits them to eject their excreta over the outer side of the nest's rim, at least after they are a few days old.

After the nestlings hatch, their mother, gathering food for them, reduces her time on the nest. On a clear morning, a female brooded two nestlings, aged two and four days, for eleven intervals, ranging from 9 to 27 minutes and averaging 14.7 minutes. She covered them for 45 percent of the six hours. When only ten days old and still largely naked, nestlings were no longer brooded at night. Such early cessation of nocturnal brooding is usual in hummingbirds at low altitudes, where nights are mild.

When the nestlings are about ten days old, their eyes begin to open, their skins have become darker, and their feathers start to unsheathe. At the age of fifteen or sixteen days, they are fairly well clothed. When fully feathered they resemble the adults, with the same blackish facial bands and pointed, whitish-tipped central tail feathers. A little natal down still adheres to the tips of their dorsal feathers. When twenty or twenty-one days old, they spontaneously leave their nests, already flying well. After alighting on a twig, they constantly turn their heads from side to side and wag their tails rhythmically up and down, as adult hermits do. Soon they vanish amid dense vegetation, where it is hardly possible to find them. Probably their mother continues to feed them for a few weeks longer, as other hummingbirds do.

In eighteen nests of which I know the outcome, thirty-six eggs were laid and twenty-four hatched; but only ten nestlings survived to fly from six of these nests. Thus, 33 percent of the nests yielded at least one fledgling, and 27 percent of the eggs produced flying young. The causes of loss were various. Two nests broke away from their leaves. Four nests with eggs were abandoned, probably when the parent had been attacked or killed; one egg was abandoned after the other had vanished. Four nestlings died in three nests; two of them were infested with the larvae of dipterous flies, which made great swellings beneath the skin. From four nests, eggs or nestlings vanished, apparently taken by predators, which may have been responsible for the abandonment of other nests. Although they hang so inconspicuously beneath the leaves of palms covered with forbidding thorns, the nests are very vulnerable. Nevertheless, enough survive to keep Little Hermits abundant over their wide range, wherever suitable habitat remains.

# 10. *Trees*

MANY of the trees over which I look from my windows are well over one hundred feet high, and nearly all bear abundant foliage throughout the year, even in March, our driest month. One of the most beautiful is the Large-leaved Jacaranda, locally called the *gallinazo*. Although it grows in rain forest, it is more abundant and conspicuous in second-growth woods and even in pastures. Its habit of growth is peculiar; it shoots up slender, tall, and straight, frequently reaching a height of forty or fifty feet before it puts forth a single branch. Conspicuous at the edge of a patch of second-growth woods at the bend of the creek in front of our house is the columnar trunk of a jacaranda that surpassed all others in its youthful race to rise above its neighbors before it branched. It was at least a hundred feet high, but barely more than nine inches thick at breast height, before the first limbs grew out, near the top, where they were for months difficult to detect amid the gigantic leaves that clustered at the apex, making the young tree resemble a tall palm surmounted by a thick rosette of fronds, for which it was mistaken by visitors new to the tropics.

The pinnately twice-compound leaves of such vigorous young trees are often six or seven feet long by a yard broad, with up to forty-four primary divisions, arranged in opposite pairs. Along much of the stout rachis, these primary pinnae are about twenty inches long and bear as many as fifteen pairs of opposite leaflets, each three to four inches long by about one and a quarter inches

wide, and strongly oblique at the base. One of these leaves may have over a thousand leaflets, with the photosynthetic capacity of a whole bough. Their work done, these big leaves are cut off and drop in the manner of the small leaves of deciduous trees, leaving a prominent scar where each was attached. The petiole and rachis, from which all the pinnae have fallen, resemble a stout stick, with a large swelling at the base, where the leaf was attached to the trunk. These brown sticks are called *caballitos* (little horses) by children, who ride them, pretending that the basal swelling is the horse's head, although it more closely resembles a hoof.

The jacaranda tree grows so tall before it branches for a good reason. In the neglected clearings where it often starts life, a riotous profusion of scrambling shrubs and woody or herbaceous vines competes with young trees for place in the sun, frequently burdening them so heavily that even stout trunks bend over or break. By developing no branches to which lianas and scramblers can cling, but only leaves that soon become detached, the jacaranda tree gives such plants little support, while it devotes all its resources to rising above them. Other pioneering trees, such as the widespread *guarumos*, or Cecropias, have developed a similar strategy for survival. Instead of compound leaves, the Cecropias bear broad, palmately lobed, simple leaves that fall from the swiftly growing trunk, which rises high, although never as tall as the jacaranda, before it branches. In the wet tropics, the vines and scramblers that so often overwhelm young trees greatly retard and complicate the regeneration of forest.

After a jacaranda tree has won the contest with competing vegetation, it branches rather sparingly to form a low-convex crown, now with twice-pinnate leaves much smaller than it bore in youth. In old forest, where it probably most often springs up in an opening created by tree-fall, it spreads this crown above that of most of its neighbors. In the sunny days of March and early April, mature jacaranda trees cover their lofty heads with generous panicles of lavender trumpet-flowers, a delightful display visi-

◄ Unbranched Young Large-leaved Jacaranda

ble from afar. Like a number of other tropical trees, they tend to bloom profusely in alternate years.

These lovely flowers are followed by flat, elliptical, woody pods, three to four inches long by about two inches broad. After drying and turning brown, they split along their edges into two flat valves, each with a long, narrow row of seeds along its center. This happens while the pods hang in clusters at the treetop, releasing the small, flat, winged seeds, which in the light October breezes waft into our rooms through open windows. Arriving from the north in this month, Rose-breasted Grosbeaks in small flocks pluck the seeds from the pods in the high treetops, bite out the embryos, and drop the membranous wings, which drift slowly downward. One morning I watched a female or young Baltimore Oriole join the grosbeaks and examine the insides of pods, although I did not see it eat a seed. Was it imitating the grosbeaks?

Close beside the jacaranda that grew exceptionally tall before it branched stands a slightly lower tree with a more profusely branching crown covered with small, simple leaves. Called *Goethalsia meiantha* in honor of the engineer who supervised the construction of the Panama Canal, it belongs to the linden family and has no well-known local name. Like the jacaranda, it grows scattered through old forest, but is more abundant in second growth. It became the dominant tree in a tract of dark, rich, very rocky land that ages ago was the bed of the Río Peñas Blancas, which still flows noisily beside it. This land had apparently been planted with maize, about fifty years ago, when scarcely anyone lived in this part of the valley and the surrounding hills were heavily forested. Probably the tract bore only a crop or two before it was abandoned, to become covered with rapidly growing Targuá, Cecropia, *Inga*, and *Goethalsia* trees that were already thirty to forty feet high when I acquired the land forty years ago. In the tops of these trees was a courtship assembly of Blue-throated Goldentail Hummingbirds, who sang breezily, each male on his chosen twigs, through the bright, warm days of January and February. For the next ten years, they performed here, until the *Goethalsia* trees, continuing to flourish after most of the short-lived associated trees had died out, made a heavier, more closed woods than goldentails choose.

When full-grown, at about forty years of age, these *Goethalsia* trees covered the rocky land in an almost pure stand. A fallen tree measured one hundred and twenty feet, but others were higher, possibly up to one hundred and fifty feet. They had slender trunks, rarely as much as eighteen inches thick above their buttresses. At its base, each trunk flared out irregularly into thick planks, which might become two or, rarely, three feet wide and, gradually narrowing, extend two or three yards up. Between them, at ground level, were deep embayments. The crowns of ascending branches were narrow and rather open.

In July and August, *Goethalsia* trees cover themselves with small, pale yellow flowers. By October, their fruits are nearly full grown. When the weather becomes drier in January, these fruits turn brown, but most remain on the trees until the rains become frequent in April and May, when they fall in great numbers. Their structure is unlike that of any other fruit that I know. Each has three double wings and splits into three carpels, each containing a few small seeds in a hard little nodule surrounded by a slightly folded elliptical wing, about an inch and a half long by an inch wide. Carried by breezes, they spread widely through the woods and over adjoining pastures. Despite their great numbers, I look in vain for seedlings; and scarcely any saplings have sprung up beneath the grove of *Goethalsia* trees. To germinate, the seeds evidently require some special condition that I have failed to discover. This can hardly be fire, for *Goethalsia* grows in forests that have not been burned for centuries.

A path through this grove of *Goethalsia* trees was one of my favorite walks. With them stood a few more massive, longer-lived White Mayo trees, and in their shade grew many ferns, clumps of low, thorny *Bactris* palms, and flowering shrubs, including three members of the acanthus family. The tallest was *Razisea spicata*, which from October to December bore masses of bright red flowers, whose long, thin tubes were probed by the long, curved bills of Long-tailed Hermit Hummingbirds. In August and September, slender, brittle-stemmed *Poikilacanthus macranthus* displayed equally long and thin lavender flowers, which Rufous-tailed Hummingbirds visited in the "legitimate" fashion, while Little Hermit Hummingbirds consistently pierced their bases to extract nectar. At the sunnier edges of the grove flourished *Blechum costaricense*, a yard-high half-shrub, which at the beginning of the dry season attracted butterflies and little stingless bees to its pale lavender flowers. On an outcrop of rocks grew begonias and two kinds of ferns with buds on their leaves, a species of *Dryopteris* and *Leptochilus cladorrhizans*, whose fronds terminated in narrow, yard-long ribbons that rooted and produced plantlets at their ends. Delicate fronds of *Selaginella* covered much of the less rocky ground.

In a decaying stub of a *Goethalsia* tree, I found a pair of Rufous-winged Woodpeckers carving the only nest of their species that I have seen, and spent many hours watching it until their two young flew. Entering this second growth from the adjoining old forest, Streaked-chested Antpittas and Thrushlike Manakins built their rarely found nests.

A few years ago, when probably about fifty years old, the *Goethalsia* trees started to die, not from any disease that I could discover, but simply because they had reached the limit of their lifespan and could not grow taller. Soon they began to fall, some breaking off well above the ground, others becoming uprooted. They crashed down during heavy afternoon rains, when I hesitated to enter this wood for fear of being crushed, or on the following night; I never saw one fall in the forenoon. Their descent broke many of the young trees that had sprung up to succeed them, including Cerillos, with yellow latex and flowers that resemble red cherries, and Chonta palms that grow tall on high, thorny stilt roots. With so many dying trees, and shattered trunks littering the ground, the grove lost some of its charm.

As far as I saw, this tract of woods was spared the excessive infestation of scrambling and climbing plants that so retards the reforestation of some clearings in rain forest. This favored the growth of pioneer trees that lacked the special adaptations for outmaneuvering the creepers that jacaranda and Cecropia trees display. But when these short-lived pioneer trees became senile and fell, they broke many of the trees that might have carried the succession a step farther toward mature rain forest. Thus, whatever its course, the reestablishment of tropical rain forest is a slow, hazardous process, probably taking centuries. Yet with what thoughtless haste hungry or avaricious men continue to destroy the shrinking remnants of this most fecund home of terrestrial life!

From my study's southern window I have watched a Milk Tree grow until its compact, full-foliaged crown rises well above every other tree at the forest's edge. This tree of the mulberry family, aptly called *el rey de la selva* (king of the forest) in northwestern Ecuador, once dominated the climax forest that has all but vanished from the Térraba Valley, including El General. Many are growing up amid the falling *Goethalsia* trees, probably carried there from the neighboring old forest chiefly by Agoutis, who eat the large, hard seeds and bury excess food. Sapling Milk Trees are more abundant and flourishing here, where large Milk Trees are absent, than in the old forest, where they stand tall, suggesting that light secondary woods and openings in the forest made by the fall of ancient giants favor the reproduction of some of the major rain forest trees. Unlike other saplings, every slender young Milk Tree is strongly bent over, as though weighed down by its great oblong leaves, which sometimes become thirty inches long by eight inches broad. Until fully grown, these leaves are bronzy or pinkish, and hang limply, like the young leaves of many other tropical trees. As they mature and harden, they rise to stand in two ranks along the main stem, which, by bowing over, enables them to spread out horizontally and increase their exposure to the sunlight that filters through the forest above them.

Not only branchless young Milk Trees up to head high are

bent in this fashion; even on those that have grown several times taller and branched, the topmost limbs are strongly bowed rather than erect. Nevertheless, large Milk Trees nearly always have splendidly upright trunks, which, like massive columns three feet thick, rise clean and straight for sometimes as much as fifty feet to the lowest branch. I was puzzled to account for this transformation of the bent sapling into the upright tree. Examination of many young trees revealed that, near the point where each begins to curve, the sapling produces a nearly upright branch, which in turn bends over. In similar fashion, a third stem grows up from the second, and perhaps a fourth from the third. In trees less than half grown, flexures in the trunk and scars where the bent-over ends of stems have fallen reveal how the tree has grown. But massive old boles have thickened in a way that so completely obliterates these traces of an irregular habit of growth that one would never suspect that each is a sympodium, or series of branches superposed to form a single axis, rather than a simple trunk.

Milk Trees, which often stand one hundred and fifty feet high, are among the few at Los Cusingos that each year shed nearly all their leaves simultaneously. This usually occurs from November to January, as the wet season passes into the dry, but it may happen in June or July, and neighboring trees become leafless at different times. But the period of nudity is brief, and soon their tall crowns are again covered with fresh foliage. They are called Milk Trees because an incision in their smooth brown bark causes a copious flow of white latex, which in pioneer days was used as a substitute for milk. Humboldt (1852–53) recorded that slaves on a plantation he visited in Venezuela grew fat on this liquid. Large sheets of bark are sometimes removed and beaten until they become thick, fibrous mats, which our Negro boatmen along the Río Esmeraldas in Ecuador used as mattresses. Exceptionally long-lived for tropical trees, Milk Trees rarely die unless killed by fire. It is surprising that the massive trunk of a tree so

◄ Milk Tree: Sapling, Trunk of Mature Tree with Aroid; Sapling Viewed from Above (inset)

resistant while alive should be riddled by insects and decay within a year after it has been felled. Accordingly, its timber was neglected, until it came into demand for such temporary uses as forms for concrete, and chemical treatment made it acceptable for plywood.

The Milk Tree's peculiar habit of growth is shared by another tree of quite different affinities. The Achiotillo, of the family Guttiferae, grows in abandoned clearings and light second-growth woods, often on sterile soil, rather than in heavy old forest. Its chief resemblance to the Milk Tree is in the form of the sapling's leaves, which grow almost as long and broad as those of young Milk Trees, but are more pointed, and opposite instead of alternate. As though overburdened by these big leaves, unbranched saplings bend over, just as young Milk Trees do, and spread their foliage in a more or less horizontal plane. Successive shoots, at first upright, bow down in much the same way; but by adding shoot to shoot the tree sometimes attains a height of sixty or seventy feet, with a fairly straight trunk up to eight inches thick, ragged with cinnamon brown bark that peels off in long, stiff flakes. When young, both of these trees have leaves much larger than those of their neighbors of different species and, to take full advantage of their photosynthetic capacity, they have adopted the same growth form.

Although a few Mayo Blanco trees grew amid the *Goethalsia* trees on the dark, rocky riverside land, I found none of the more slender Mayo Colorado or Recino trees there. This rapidly growing tree thrives in abandoned clearings on red-clay hilltops and steep slopes, where it sometimes grows in almost pure stands. Unlike the jacaranda and Cecropia, it branches while a small sapling, but it sheds its dead branches and twigs so freely that in some parts of Costa Rica it is called *bota ramos* (drop branches). We gather them to kindle fires in our kitchen stove. Like the related Mayo Blanco, it blooms chiefly from late March to early June; but odd trees of the Mayo Colorado may flower at any season. Their long, compact panicles of yellow flowers stand conspicuously erect above the foliage, often almost solidly covering the lofty crown. In April and May, when the two mayos are in full bloom, they are the chief adornments of this valley. A steep slope above the river opposite Los Cusingos, where Mayo Colorado trees have sprung up thickly, is at this season ablaze with yellow bloom, deeper in tone than the golden flowers of the glossy-leaved Mayo Blanco. The chief visitors to the spurred flowers of both species are big Black Bumblebees; but smaller bees, a few butterflies, and hummingbirds, mostly the Snowy-breasted but also the White-crested Coquette, Violet-headed, and Rufous-tailed hummingbirds, also come for their nectar and probably help to pollinate them.

As the mayos' small, three-ridged capsules ripen in October, they are torn open by Red-lored and White-crowned parrots, who extract the embryos from the winged seeds, which, if spared by them, germinate abundantly and promptly where the wind wafts them to the ground. One morning, when with difficulty I had counted five or six of the big Red-lored Amazonas in the old, spreading Mayo Colorado on the hilltop behind the house, fifty or more suddenly burst forth with a raucous din. So difficult are green parrots to detect amid green foliage!

At a corner of the house stands an old, spreading tree of the Rose-Apple, which from its original home in southeastern Asia has been widely naturalized in the tropics. Each of its "powder-puff" flowers consists of many long, white stamens, which almost conceal the four green-and-white petals and the single long style at the center of the fluffy, four-inch-wide mass. Their most frequent visitors are Green Honeycreepers, who insert their long bills among the clustered stamens to sip the nectar abundantly secreted into the cupped top of the ovary. Turquoise Dacnises and wintering Baltimore Orioles also drink the nectar, and even thick-billed Scarlet-rumped Tanagers can reach it. Although the Rose-Apple tree blooms throughout the year, it does so most freely in the dry season, and only then does it set more than an occasional fruit.

In late November, we watched a Cinnamon-bellied Squirrel come to the Rose-Apple tree every morning at sunrise. He climbed over and over the same branches, and often hung head-downward from pencil-thick twigs, while he searched for fruits at their tips. When, finally, he found one less than half grown, green and hard, he carried it up to a thicker limb, where he sat to eat it. He must have been very hungry to spend so much energy searching for such hard fare!

In April and May, when the rains return, the Rose-Apple tree is laden with smooth, whitish, globular fruits, an inch to an inch and a half in diameter. Each hollow sphere of thin flesh is crowned by the four persisting sepals and loosely encloses one or two large, brown seeds. The flavor of the slightly sweetish flesh suggests the aroma of roses. Rose-Apples are eaten by wasps, birds, children, and, less frequently, by adults. The seeds are most interesting. Instead of the two cotyledons that one expects in a dicotyledonous plant, a single seed may contain from two to twelve, which are thick and irregular in shape but fit closely together in a compact mass. They belong to the one to five embryos that a single seed produces, each of which may have from one to four cotyledons. Sometimes two embryos are attached to the same cotyledon. Two seedlings may share a single primary root, or one seedling may have two primary roots. The cotyledons remain underground, often where an Agouti has buried the seed, and little clusters of shoots rise above the surface.

Between my study window and the forest an Orange-flowered Poró tree stands tall and slender. Like the Rose-Apple, it is an introduction here, brought from its home in western South America and Panama to shade coffee plantations of the central highlands. In the dry season, in some years as early as January, but in others not until March, it drops its leaves and bears masses of bright orange flowers, conspicuous from afar. Only long-billed hummingbirds can reach the nectar of the Red-flowered Poró without tearing or piercing the thick tissue of the long, slender standard that tightly encloses all the other floral parts except the

◀ Rose-Apple Tree Flowers and Green Honeycreeper (male)

calyx, but the Orange-flowered Poró has a more open flower, with a retracted standard, and offers its nectar freely to the birds, who flock to it in great numbers and variety.

On bright, sunny mornings, the high treetop is full of nectar-sipping birds, including Baltimore Orioles; Green Honeycreepers; Blue, or Red-legged, Honeycreepers; Shining Honeycreepers; Turquoise Dacnises; Bananaquits; Tennessee Warblers; and several kinds of hummingbirds, difficult to identify so far overhead against a brilliant sky. The first Orange-chinned Parakeets I ever saw in the valley of El General were drinking nectar from the orange Poró flowers; and Crimson-fronted Parakeets, seldom seen here, come chiefly to visit them. Sometimes these long-tailed parrots pluck a flower, extract the nectar, then drop it, but mostly they stick their bills into flowers still attached, hanging head downward to reach them. After perhaps half an hour of silent feasting in the tree, they all shout together as they fly up the valley in a compact flock, high above the treetops.

In April, the Orange-flowered Poró sheds its pods. After drying, each brown pod, about four inches long, splits into two inch-broad valves. Each valve usually bears two dark brown seeds, about the size and shape of common beans, one attached to each edge on opposite sides of the valve's center. The drying valve bends slightly back, becoming somewhat concave on the outer surface. It is thereby converted into a little twirler, with wings symmetrically weighted, that gyrates as it falls. When a gust of wind strikes the tree at midday, the air is full of them, each whirling rapidly around as it descends slowly, while the breeze carries it away from the parent tree.

What a contrast with the Red-flowered Poró, whose thick-shelled, scarlet seeds, conspicuously exposed by the splitting of pods still attached to the tree, hang there for months, vainly trying to entice birds, who cannot digest them, to swallow them and carry them afar! I wonder what circumstances caused the development of this method of seed dispersal, so ineffectual when the tree grows in dooryards, fence-rows, and plantations, where it is usually propagated by setting out living branches rather than by seeds, and whether the Red-flowered Poró's pods evolved from those of the Orange-flowered Poró or some other of the hundred species of *Erythrina* widespread in the tropics of both hemispheres.[1]

Among our native trees, the jacaranda, *Goethalsia*, mayos, and Campana, all of which readily invade clearings, have winged, wind-borne seeds; but most other forest trees are disseminated by frugivorous animals, chiefly birds, rodents, monkeys, and bats. As far as I know, no tree at Los Cusingos has wind-pollinated flowers, but some hold their inflorescences so high that I have been unable to study them. Pollination by wind, frequent in northern coniferous or deciduous forests with one or a few kinds of trees, would be inefficient in tropical forests, where trees of one species may be widely scattered among many other species, whose leafy crowns would impede the transfer of pollen by breezes. Without animal carriers of pollen, the great diversity of tropical forest trees could probably never have arisen. For trees dependent upon winged creatures for pollination, this diversity is advantageous. If such trees grew in almost pure stands over large areas, and all bloomed at once, they might lack enough pollinators to fertilize more than a small fraction of their flowers, leaving the remainder sterile, unless self-pollinated. The many different arboreal species in a tropical woodland diminish competition for pollinators by flowering at different times.

At the edge of the forest that greets my vision whenever I lift my eyes from my paper stands an arborescent *Piper* with large, obliquely cordate leaves. It is a member of a huge genus, widespread in moister forests and thickets throughout the tropics of both hemispheres. Among its multitudinous species in the Americas are a few herbs, many shrubs, slender trees up to thirty feet high, and a few vines that attach themselves to trees by adventitious roots. All are easily recognized by their stems, which are

---

1 An account of the Red-flowered Poró and its visitors is included in the present author's *A Naturalist in Costa Rica* (1971).

swollen at the nodes; simple, alternate leaves; and spikes of minute, green flowers, which are usually compactly massed. On different species, the spikes are from an inch to two feet long, finger-thick or thinner, stiffly erect, arching or pendulous. Beyond the tropics, pipers are scarcely known; but their much smaller, herbaceous relations, the peperomias, are grown in northern greenhouses and homes for their handsome foliage. Many species of *Piper* have a pleasant, spicy aroma, and one, *Piper nigrum*, furnishes the familiar pepper of dining tables. Black pepper is prepared from the unripe fruits of this shrub of the Oriental tropics, white pepper from its ripe seeds. Other Old World species are sources of less widely known condiments, but the American members of the family are rarely used by man.

Known in Costa Rica as *cordoncillos* (little cords) from the shape of their inflorescences, these plants flourish in tropical American rain forests and clearings among them in such a great and bewildering variety of forms that nearly everyone who has made extensive botanical collections has found species new to science. From my own collections in Costa Rica, William Trelease, an authority on the Piperaceae, named many new species, most of which are now included in long lists of synonyms of previously described species in the *Flora Costaricensis* by William Burger (1971), who wrote that "the taxonomy of the neotropical species of *Piper* is in a state of chaos."

The biology of these abundant members of tropical American floras is likewise very inadequately known. The tiny flowers, consisting of a single pistil and usually four stamens, devoid of sepals, petals, nectar, and fragrance, are in most species so closely packed along the spike that it is difficult to distinguish them without dissection. Accordingly, it is not easy to learn how they are pollinated. Minute insects that crawl over the spikes and small, pollen-gathering bees appear to be their chief pollinators. It is equally difficult to learn how the fruits, best described as diminutive, one-seeded berries, are disseminated. One may

*Piper obliquum*: Twig with Fruiting Spikes and Cross Section of Petiole,
Showing Corpuscles Eaten by Ants (inset) ▶

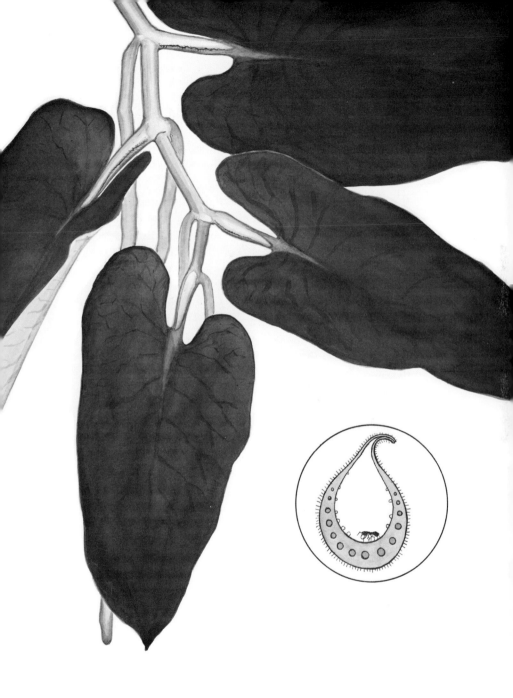

watch long without seeing any animal take the slightest interest in them. Over the years, I have seen only two species of birds, the Scarlet-rumped Tanager and the Tawny-bellied, or Spot-crowned, Euphonia, eat parts of spikes, which to me are most unpalatable. In Trinidad, the Snows (1971) likewise saw two members of the tanager family, the Blue Tanager and the Violaceous Euphonia, consume fruits of *Piper*. They describe how the Blue Tanager breaks off a length of spike and lays it across a branch while it plucks pieces from it. These fruiting spikes are certainly not a favorite food of tanagers, and it is difficult to believe that they alone are responsible for the wide dissemination and abundance of *cordoncillos* in tropical America. Could nocturnal bats help to disperse them?

In some species of *Piper*, the petioles are margined by thin wings that enclose and protect developing leaves and floral spikes. In some of these *cordoncillos*, the wings wither and fall as the leaf matures, but in others they are retained, with interesting consequences. Among these is the tall *Piper* (a member of the *P. obliquum* complex) that I view at the forest's edge as I write. The petioles of the large leaves are so strongly incurved that their thin edges meet and press together, enclosing a canal that extends most of the petiole's length of one and a half to nearly four inches. Ants of the innumerable species that inhabit the tropics seldom neglect to establish their colonies in such sheltering nooks in plants. Those almost invariably present in the petioles of these *cordoncillos* are pale brown, sluggish, and innocuous. The tiny workers are only about an eighth of an inch (three millimeters) long. Other members of the colony, who have enlarged heads and might be regarded as soldiers, are bigger, up to three sixteenths of an inch (five millimeters) in length.

At the sheathing base of each petiole, just beneath the axillary bud, the ants gnaw away soft tissue to make a narrow hole and gain access to the solid, succulent pith. Then, working from both ends of an internode, they extend their excavations upward and downward until they meet, forming a hollow that finally stretches the length of trunk or branch. The medullary cells surrounding the cavity divide to form a phelloderm, or wound tissue.

Not only does the tall *cordoncillo* at the forest's edge provide lodging for the ants, it also nourishes them. The smooth, glossy wall of the canal along the upper side of the petiole is thickly covered with tiny, pearly white corpuscles, the smallest of which are hardly visible to the naked eye, the largest about one hundredth of an inch (a quarter of a millimeter) in diameter. Each corpuscle is the outgrowth of a single epidermal cell, from which it is cut off by a wall. Each is a single large cell, enclosed by a thin membrane and packed with granules that resemble those in the multicellular protein corpuscles of Cecropia trees. It contains little, if any, starch. The larger of these corpuscles are about the size of the ants' eggs, from which they can be distinguished by their spherical rather than elongate shape. Apparently, the petiole yields a constant succession of these pearly bodies.

To observe the behavior of the ants, I cut away one side of a petiole attached to a segment of stem and placed it in a box with a transparent lid. Ants busily carried the pearly bodies back into the stem through the perforation at the base of the petiole. A worker might approach, feel, and leave several corpuscles before it found one that was satisfactory. To detach the corpuscle from the epidermis often required strenuous effort by the tiny ant, who sometimes abandoned a refractory one to try another. The nutritious qualities of these corpuscles are recognized by ants of other kinds, including the little black ones that live in crannies in the wooden walls of my study, who picked up and carried away some that I offered to them.

With enclosed spaces where the ants can dwell in safety, and a special food for them, these *cordoncillos* appear to be as well adapted to entertain their hexapod guests as Cecropia trees and bull's-horn acacias, both of which are much better known as antplants. No one who has come into close contact with the fiercely stinging *Pseudomyrmex* ants that inhabit the hollow, paired thorns of the acacia shrubs and eat the protein bodies at the tips of their tiny leaflets can doubt that they are an effective garrison; they protect the host plant from encroaching vegetation as well as from other insects and browsing animals. Whether, as has been alleged, the stingless *Azteca* ants of Cecropia trees protect them in any way is a debatable question that I have discussed in another book (1977).

It is still more questionable whether the *cordoncillo's* tiny ants benefit the hospitable plant, which is less in need of defenders, because its foliage is less attractive to insects and browsing mammals than the Cecropia leaves are. Unlike the Cecropia's *Azteca* ants, the *cordoncillo's* ants do not swarm out and over a person who touches the tree, biting weakly where they can reach tender skin; the *cordoncillo's* sluggish little ants have neither bitten nor stung me. On the other hand, they do not, indirectly, bring disaster to the tree, as the *Azteca* ants do when big Lineated Woodpeckers peck open the Cecropia's trunk and branches to feast upon the ants and their pupae. The perforations that the ants make beneath the *cordoncillo's* axillary buds do not prevent them from growing into vigorous branches or, apparently, harm the tree in any way. If species of *Piper* can give such generous hospitality to ants without evident recompense, why not Cecropia and other ant-plants?

## 11. *White-crested Coquettes*

 EARLY on the sunny morning of November 1,
1936, I entered a small coffee plantation near
my cabin in the valley of the Río Buena Vista,
hoping for a better view of a plumed hummingbird, new to me,
that I had glimpsed too briefly a few days earlier. The *Inga* trees
that shaded the coffee shrubs were flowering profusely, and hummingbirds of several kinds were probing the fluffy clusters of long,
white stamens. Among them was the hummingbird that I sought,
and several more who seemed to be females and young of the
same kind. Every time the plumed male whom I most wanted to
see came into view, a larger hummingbird drove him away. Once,
while he rested, a Snowy-breasted Hummingbird struck him with
its breast, but this time the plumed one did not change his
perch.

The perch to which the plumed hummingbird returned to
rest after each visit to the *Inga* flowers was an exposed twig of a
coffee shrub, only five feet high. Here I could examine at my leisure the splendors of this three-inch gem, who was not at all shy.
His upper plumage was largely metallic green, with a narrow
white band across his rump, a feature unusual in hummingbirds.
His tail was chestnut-rufous, with a narrow dusky band near the
ends of the central feathers. When he spread it fanwise, I could
see that it was double-rounded. Whenever he looked straight toward me, his cheeks, chin, and throat appeared dull black, but
they flashed brilliant green when he turned so that I viewed

them obliquely. Contrasting with this was a pure white chest, bordered by the deep cinnamon that covered his remaining underparts, except the white beneath his tail. His bill, straight, rather short, and narrowing from a broad base to a sharp point, was coral red with a black tip. As though this attire were not sufficiently elegant, his head was adorned more elaborately than that of any other hummingbird that I had seen. On his forehead was a low shield of feathers, black when viewed from directly in front but bronze when seen from the side. Behind this rose a white tiara that narrowed from a broad base to a slender tip that stood well above his crown. From each side of his head sprang a tuft of plumes, brilliant green to dark according to how I viewed them, which tapered to a long filament that projected far behind his neck. He was my first White-crested Coquette.

The females who hovered around resembled him closely in body plumage, but lacked all his head adornments. Their white throats had only scattered spots of green, and their bills were black instead of red.

During the minutes that I needed to write a detailed description of the ornate male, he obligingly remained perching close in front of me. When I had finished, I approached slowly to within arm's length before he flew. Later, he returned to rest less than a yard above my head, so great was his attachment to that particular coffee shrub. A young male, still without head plumes, his white throat only tinged with green, permitted me to come almost as close. When I met these extraordinarily confiding hummingbirds, I had already passed nearly a year in my cabin beside the Río Buena Vista. I surmised that they had come from the vast forests that still surrounded the narrow cultivated valley, and had little experience of man. None of the hummingbirds that I frequently saw in the valley was half so tame.

The White-crested Coquette lives chiefly on the Pacific slope of southern Costa Rica, from about 1,000 to 4,000 feet above sea level. From this center of abundance, it crosses to the Caribbean slope in central Costa Rica, where the continental divide is rela-

◄ White-crested Coquette (male)

tively low, and it extends sparingly into Chiriquí Province in western Panama. It is rarely seen in the forest, perhaps because it remains high, visiting the flowering crowns of tall trees. I have met it most often in plantations, gardens, and other clearings with abundant blooms. The *Inga* trees planted to shade coffee plantations, formerly more widely than now, are especially attractive to it. Near the plantation where I first met the White-crested Coquette was another small grove of shaded coffee, where, in early November, I found a number of others, some of whom were scarcely less confiding. In the years when long hedges of *Stachytarpheta* bordered my dooryard, many coquettes came to share the nectar of the small purple flowers of this straggling shrub of the verbena family with a variety of other hummingbirds. Flowering trees that attract them include the Mayo, the Copalchí, and the Cerillo. They appear to wander widely in search of nectar; their presence at Los Cusingos is sporadic and unpredictable.

I have seen coquettes in female plumage so much more frequently than males in full regalia that I have wondered whether the latter wear their adornments throughout the year, or go into "eclipse" after the breeding season. I have recorded males in full nuptial attire chiefly from August to March, an interval that includes the breeding season; and males acquiring green throats, crests, and ear tufts from late May to early October.

I have watched only a few courtship displays. In late October, a female coquette rested on a low, slender twig beside the flowering *Stachytarpheta* hedge, while a male hovered in front of her, oscillating rapidly from side to side in a most peculiar lateral flight, such as only hummingbirds, of all feathered creatures, appear capable of performing. Always keeping his breast toward the quiescent female, he swung now toward his left wing, now toward his right, alternating his direction with surprising suddenness. The length of his sideward swing between the opposite turning points seemed not to exceed one foot. The female always turned her head so that her bill pointed directly toward the dis-

White-crested Coquette (female); *Stachytarpheta* ▶

playing male. Soon she rose slowly above her perch, hovering on the wing as only a hummingbird can, while he continued to float in front of her, now oscillating more slowly than before. After a few seconds, they separated.

At the end of April, when the only coquettes at the hedge were in female attire without head plumes, one of these unornamented individuals perched on a *Stachytarpheta* bush, while another, equally plain, hovered in the air, facing it, a few inches away. After this had continued for less than a minute, the first hummingbird slowly rose into the air; and the one who had been hovering ascended with it, still facing it, and now began to swing rapidly from side to side, only a few inches in each direction. After a few seconds, they flew away. This performance resembled that of the adult male that I had watched earlier, but the lateral oscillation was shorter and less regular. I wondered whether the performer was an adult male in eclipse plumage or an immature individual.

I have never found a singing assembly of White-crested Coquettes, nor read of their occurrence in any related species. But for nearly a month from the end of December into January, when bright sunny days returned to the valley, at least four males in their most resplendent attire—the largest number I have ever seen together—behaved in a manner that might have been the coquettes' equivalent of a typical singing assembly. One of these males perched alternately on several thin, exposed, dead twigs of the orange trees and a big *Inga* tree in the pasture behind the house. On one or the other of these twigs, from twenty to forty feet up, he rested for long intervals, turning his head from side to side, stretching or scratching. He was always silent; I detected no movements of bill or throat that might reveal utterances too weak to reach my ears or above my range of hearing, such as I have often discerned in other species of hummingbirds. While he rested well above my head, I could find no angle from which his throat appeared other than black.

At times this male was visited by one, two, or even three oth ers as elegant as himself. Pursuing one another, they traced erratic courses high in the air, after which two might alight close together, face to face, with coral red bills wide open, and almost touching each other, in what looked like a threatening attitude. Sometimes one supplanted the other on his perch. One morning, while one of these males rested quite relaxed, stretching and preening at his leisure, another alighted nearby and extended his head toward him, with bill closed or slightly open, as though trying to gain the preener's attention, or to induce him to join in a chase. They reminded me of two male manakins resting close together between their display stations during intervals of inactivity at their courtship assembly. After a while, the two coquettes flew together over the hilltop and were lost to view, as such pursuits usually ended.

Although I could not learn where the visiting coquettes were stationed, each appeared to know where to find his rivals. During the many hours that I watched, I failed to see a female coquette. In the five Januarys that have passed since I found these males together, I have seen no more among the orange trees, and few elsewhere. In this, too, the coquettes' courtship gathering, if such it was, differs from a typical hummingbirds' singing assembly, which is in the same place year after year.

White-crested Coquettes begin to nest in December, when rains become lighter and flowers more abundant, and continue until the drought becomes severe in February. I have not watched the construction of the tiny open chalice of downy materials, well covered on the outside with gray or greenish gray foliaceous lichens, but doubtless it is done by the female alone. Although usually placed in rather exposed sites, these nests are so small and inconspicuous that I would not have noticed any of them if the coquettes had not revealed their situations by their activities. The first that I found was about sixty feet above the ground, fastened to the upper side of a slender stem of a dying orchid plant that hung below the mossy branch of a dead tree at the forest's edge. The next four nests were sixteen to twenty-one feet up on slender twigs in the open crowns of Guava trees in the garden or surrounding pastures. Situated well out from the trunk and only slightly shaded and screened by foliage, they were easily seen after one's attention had been drawn to them. The sixth nest was on the exposed end of a tall, slender bamboo shoot, about sixty feet above a stream. It, too, was only sparsely shaded by foliage.

Each of the four nests whose contents I could ascertain held the hummingbird's usual two eggs or young. In the first nest, eggs had been laid in December, as I could tell by the date when the parent began to feed nestlings so far above my head. In three other nests, eggs were laid either in late December or early January. In one nest, they were laid in January, and in another in February. By early March, this latest set of eggs was abandoned, probably because food had become scarce in the dry weather.

While I sat at early breakfast on January 28, 1947, I noticed a coquette attending her nest in a Guava tree in front of the window, where it had apparently been built while I was absent from the farm. Well covered with gray lichens, the tiny cup was saddled over a slender branch where a lateral twig gave some support at the base, but most of the structure rose free into the air. Through the window I watched the female incubate all of a sunny morning and all of the following afternoon, when the sun shone intermittently through a light overcast. In nearly twelve hours, she incubated for thirty-eight intervals, ranging from about 1 to 34 minutes and averaging 10.4 minutes. Her thirty-nine absences lasted from less than 1 to 23 minutes and averaged 7.1 minutes. She spent 59.4 percent of the day on her eggs. In the morning, when she was more active than in the afternoon, both her sessions and recesses averaged shorter. Although she came and went more often before than after midday, the range of her sessions and absences was nearly the same in both halves of the day.

As she approached or left her nest, the coquette flew haltingly, with short advances separated by momentary pauses, when she hovered on wings vibrating too rapidly to be seen, and jerked up and down by raising and lowering her tail. Like other incubating hummingbirds, she often brought contributions to her nest. Between 6:30 and 7:45 A.M., she added nine small pieces of lichens or similar materials, which she stuck to the outside of a cup already so well covered that there seemed no space for more. After 7:45, I could detect nothing in her bill when she returned; but the way she wiped her bill over the outside of the nest after settling in it suggested that she was spreading cobweb over it. She continued wiping her bill over the nest until early afternoon.

A Snowy-breasted Hummingbird often came to rest in the nest tree, which appeared to be his preferred station. Whenever he approached the nest, the much smaller coquette quickly drove him away. Maternal solicitude gave her the force to chase away this larger and rather aggressive hummingbird.

Eight years later, my wife and I watched another coquette incubate in a Guava tree throughout a day when brilliant morning sunshine was followed by an afternoon of increasing cloudiness, although no rain fell. This female filled the day with thirty-seven sessions that ranged from less than 1 to 78 minutes and averaged 13.4 minutes. Her thirty-eight recesses varied from less than 1 to 22 minutes and averaged 5.7 minutes. She incubated with the high constancy of 70.2 percent. Her attentiveness, however, fluctuated greatly with the time of day and was especially low between 8:00 and 10:00 A.M., when she devoted much time to the nest itself, sometimes sitting for a minute or less, flying off to search for material, then returning in a minute or two to add it to her structure. Her thirty sessions before noon averaged only 8 minutes in length and her thirty-one absences averaged 4.7 minutes. In striking contrast to this, her seven sessions after noon averaged 36.1 minutes and her seven recesses averaged 10 minutes.

In the hour and a half between 8:30 and 10:00 A.M., this hummingbird appeared to bring something to her nest at least eleven times. Although once she came with a tuft of seed down almost as big as herself, most of the material was small; often it was invisible. Frequently when we could detect nothing, she settled in the nest, then bent over and rubbed her bill carefully over the outer surface, apparently applying cobweb. As she did this, she spread her wings over the nest's rim. At other times, she seemed to knead the material in the bottom of the cup with her feet. She was last seen to add cobweb at 12:50 P.M., after which she gave no more attention to the nest itself and attended her eggs far more steadily.

At the latest nest, Darwin and Barbara Norby, who were studying with me, made a day-long record of incubation. In twelve hours, they timed forty-nine sessions on the eggs that ranged from 15 seconds to 18 minutes and averaged 6 minutes. Fifty-one absences varied from less than 1 minute to 22 minutes and averaged 8 minutes. The eggs were covered only 42.9 percent of the day. This abnormally low attentiveness suggested that the coquette was now, at the end of a dry February, having difficulty finding enough to eat. A few days later she abandoned her eggs, as already told.

In the Guava tree in front of the window, the eggs hatched on February 5 or in the following night. During the first five hours of February 8, I watched the female coquette attend her two nestlings. Twelve times she brought them food and spent from 22 to 54 seconds delivering it. Since I could see nothing of the babies except rarely the tip of a bill, I could learn no more details. The mother brooded them eighteen times, in sessions that ranged from 2 to 19 minutes and averaged 7.1 minutes. Her seventeen absences lasted from 3 to 18 minutes and averaged 9.4 minutes. She was at the nest for 43.2 percent of the five hours, including the time devoted to both feeding and brooding.

On February 15, when the two nestlings were about ten days old, I again watched for the first five hours of the day. Although the morning was cloudy and cool, the coquette did not brood after her first departure at 5:42 A.M. On each of her nine visits with food, she appeared to regurgitate several times to both nestlings alternately. However, from the window I could see little of them until late in the morning, when they raised their heads well above the nest's rim at mealtime.

By February 25 I could see much of the twenty-day-old nestlings' well-feathered bodies protruding above their nest's rim, while I again watched from the window through the first five hours of the day. On this bright, cool morning, they were not brooded. On each of their mother's twelve visits to the nest, she regurgitated to both nestlings. On some visits both were fed twice, alternately; on others one was fed twice and the other nestling once; and sometimes each received only a single portion. When the parent regurgitated to a nestling only once, it appeared not to desire more. The young hummingbirds were active, preening a good deal, and at intervals rising in the nest to flap their wings vigorously, exercise they often took just after receiving nourishment, first one and then the other.

One of these young White-crested Coquettes left the nest before 7:45 A.M. on February 27, and the other flew from it in my presence forty minutes later. It appeared to sever contact with its nest quite spontaneously, and soon after leaving it was fed by its mother on a neighboring bough of the Guava tree. These young hummingbirds were in the nest twenty-one or twenty-two days.

At no time was a male coquette seen to take an interest in any of these four nests. On the morning when I found the fourth nest, a male flew past it without stopping; aside from this, none was noticed near any of them. Although the most magnificent of the trogons, the Resplendent Quetzal, is a faithful attendant of his eggs and young, the most ornate hummingbird in Central America remains strictly aloof. Each follows the pattern of behavior widespread in his family.

# 12. Oil Palms
## and Their Guests

IN front of my window an African Oil Palm, one of two that sprang from seeds given by a friend years ago, lifts the tip of its topmost frond seventy-five feet into the air. The other, slightly lower, stands on the opposite side of the house, farther from the forest. Both have massive trunks ragged with persisting bases of dead fronds, which do not fall away cleanly, as they do from the more slender trunks of our tall native palms in the forest, but break off above the attachment of the leaf-stalk. Each palm bears a wide-spreading crown of huge, feathery fronds, of which the youngest, still folded, rises like a tall green rod at the center of the rosette. In great plantations in the lowlands of Costa Rica and other humid tropical countries, these palms are grown for the commercially valuable oil in their fruits. A few find their way to higher elevations as ornamentals. Careful gardeners trim the decaying bases of the fronds and even whitewash the trunks, making the palms neater but less interesting to a naturalist.

In the humus that collects among the persisting bases of the fronds, a variety of plants take root and flourish, covering the trunk with verdure that hides its unsightly raggedness. The fern *Nephrolepis pendula* drapes the trunk with slender, pendent fronds up to five yards long. The narrow ribbons of *Vittaria* hang less conspicuously in compact, verdant clusters. Stems of the curious fern *Oleandra costaricensis* stand out like slender rods bearing long, narrow leaves. Aroids of several kinds grow on the trunks,

but orchids are absent. An epiphytic shrub of the potato family, *Lycianthes synanthera*, of which I wrote in *A Naturalist on a Tropical Farm* (1980), flourishes on the palm trunks, as do strangling figs, which we try to remove before they become menacingly big and heavy. Even plants that nearly always grow in the ground, such as the pokeweed *Phytolacca rivinoides*, a species of *Costus*, and *Pothomorphe umbellata* of the Piper family, have sprung up among the old leaf-bases, from seeds carried by birds.

The oil palms attract as great a variety of animals as of plants. The brown fruits, about an inch and a half long, are borne in massive clusters amid the bases of living fronds where they are difficult to see. Each contains one extremely hard seed surrounded by oily, fibrous, yellow or orange pulp that is eaten by Golden-naped and Red-crowned woodpeckers, Garden Thrushes, Scarlet-rumped and other tanagers, Buff-throated Saltators, and Cinnamon-bellied Squirrels, as well as by domestic chickens who come across fallen fruits.

When Black Vultures began to come in numbers to share the feast, we feared that they might bring diseases or foul the surroundings, so we tried unsuccessfully to discourage them. However, our fears were unfounded. Although as many as two dozen have been present at one time, either in the crowns of the palm trees eating the oily pulp or waiting for their turns in neighboring trees, they have not been troublesome. The most objectionable feature of these omnivorous scavengers is the uncouth sounds they make when two disagree. One morning toward the end of March, two vultures stood in contact on a high, thick, exposed branch of a neighboring Orange-flowered Poró tree. For many minutes they continued to preen, mostly each its own plumage, but at intervals one nibbled the feathers of its companion's lower neck or shoulder, just as many smaller, more attractive birds do with their mates. Perhaps to vultures, vultures are beautiful!

Vocally, White-faced Monkeys are hardly more endearing than Black Vultures. Occasionally an outburst of the most blood-

◄ Black Vulture on Oil Palm Frond

curdling cries, suggesting nothing less than mayhem, apprises us
that a troop of monkeys, not in perfect harmony, is approaching
the oil palm nearer the forest. Their less objectionable utterances
include high-pitched, birdlike notes, barks, and mild coughs.
The monkeys advance through the clump of timber bamboos,
taller even than the palm, that stands between it and the forest's
edge. Nimbly they run across an arching spray of bamboo that
touches an arching frond of the palm, neither of which sinks
much beneath their light weight. Mothers come with babies
draped across their shoulders. Of all the palm tree's visitors, they
are most interested in their human watchers, not only when we
stand on the ground but even when we look through a window.
They owe to their wariness their survival in an isolated tract of
forest not immune to poachers and they do not quite trust us. As
they peer intently down from a high palm frond, their brown
eyes in little wizened faces appear perplexed and troubled, as
though they were already oppressed by the unanswerable questions that worry their relatives who stand erect and wear clothes.

The two biggest visitors to the oil palm, the monkeys and the
vultures, compete for their fruits. Sometimes, when a vulture
finds monkeys in the palm near the forest, without alighting
there it flies to the palm on the other side of the house, which
the monkeys cannot reach without running over the ground, as
they are reluctant to do. Or the monkeys, passing through the
bamboo, may drive the vultures from the palm. But the black
birds are not always intimidated. I watched one continue to eat
while the monkeys stood aside, threatening it with horrid shrill
screams. Or else, while a vulture finishes its meal at leisure, the
monkeys go to the opposite side of the palm's thick crown to eat
fruits that are apparently less ripe and desirable. One afternoon a
vulture continued to eat, unperturbed, while three or four monkeys jumped around it as though they were dancing. When two
more of the big birds alighted near the ends of fronds, a monkey
advanced toward them, grimacing, showing its teeth, and wav-
ing its lifted arms, as a person might do to shoo away a domestic

animal. These vultures flew off without trying to reach the fruits. Evidently, some are bolder than others.

All these visitors to the palm's crown eat only the pulp, or pericarp, of the fruit and drop the seeds, each enclosed in a shell so hard that it turns the edge of a machete's blade. Fallen seeds are picked up by the wholly terrestrial Agoutis, who share the chickens' corn and compete with them for scraps of food from the kitchen. Sitting with arching back on its fat hindquarters in the shade of a palm tree, the Agouti holds the dark seed in its little forepaws while, with sharp, grating sounds, it gnaws a small round hole in the thick shell—a lengthy process. When the opening is wide enough to admit its lower incisors—as I judge from its movements, although I cannot see the teeth—it re-volves the seed in its forepaws until it has scraped out all the nu-tritious white meat. The ground is littered with perforated shells that the Agoutis have dropped.

When the Agoutis are satisfied, they may bury excess palm seeds, sometimes covering the little holes with fallen leaves or other ground litter. Some of these cached seeds are retrieved, but many are not, with the result that palm seedlings spring up all over the garden and in the surrounding pastures, often at a good distance from the parent trees. If we did not continually remove these unwanted seedlings, we would before long be surrounded by a forest of oil palms. My only complaint about these amusing and innocuous rodents is that they make us pull up so many palm seedlings. As I bend over to uproot them, I speculate upon the role of Agoutis in the ecosystems of tropical American forests. I have never seen an Agouti bury a seed in the forest, where they are shy and bound away, with startled notes and conspicuously raised pelage on their rumps, the moment they spy a man. At the forest's edge, I have watched them perforate the thinner shells of, and remove the meat from, the seeds of *Protium* trees after they or the birds above them have eaten the mealy, strongly scented, white arils that surround them. I have little doubt that the Agoutis' habit of burying food makes them the chief disseminators of fairly large tree seeds that are rarely swallowed by birds. Hence they are important agents in the perpetuation of these forests.

Recently we noticed an aspect of the Agoutis' lives that I omitted from the account of these mammals in *A Naturalist on a Tropical Farm*. Through much of October, a female with two half-grown young came morning and afternoon when we fed the chickens with maize, which the juveniles held in their forepaws and ate, just as their mother did. They also buried food in adult fashion. About the first of November, the dam began to wean her offspring, whom we called "the Twins." This was a gradual process; after rebuffing the Twins on one day, she would permit them to follow and suck her on the following day.

About this time, the Twins formed the habit of resting under the big Rose-Apple tree on the lawn after their morning meal. They sat with foreparts elevated or lay prone, close together or in contact with each other. At intervals one caressed or groomed its companion, who held its head turned upward, with eyes almost closed, while the other ran over it with its pink nose and appeared to lick it with its tongue. Then the recipient of this attention did the same for its partner. More rarely they groomed their bodies. When one walked away, the other stood upright, its forelegs hanging limply by its sides, until the first returned. For over half an hour, with brief intermissions, they remained resting quietly together.

Through November, the Twins continued occasionally to groom each other. I was absent for most of December; but after my return they came to eat corn as in the past, then rested beneath the Rose-Apple tree. The last time I saw them together was on December 27, when for about half an hour they lay flat on the grass, their rumps only a few inches apart, their bodies diverging at an angle of about sixty degrees. I did not see them groom. During much of the two months when the Twins remained intimate, a third young Agouti of about the same age ate near them while we fed the chickens, but never rested with them. Adult Agoutis

are such solitary animals, each remaining alone except during the short intervals of sexual attraction or when followed by dependent young, that the continued intimacy of the Twins after weaning surprised us. These defenseless animals might be more social if their solitary habit did not increase their chances of survival in forests where larger animals prey upon them.

African Oil Palms attract hungry creatures not only with their own fruits, but also with those of plants that grow on their shaggy trunks. Tanagers, saltators, honeycreepers, and other birds eat the pea-sized, yellow fruits of *Lycianthes synanthera*, which ripen from August to October. They are a favorite food of lovely, blue-and-green Bay-headed Tanagers, who seem to prefer these hard berries, more bitter than sweet, to the bananas that we offer them on the feeder.

The *Costus* that roots high on the palm nearer the forest has slender, branchless, green stems about six feet high, with large, glossy, obovate leaves arranged in an ascending spiral. Each stem is terminated by an inflorescence with closely overlapping bracts that resembles a smooth, dull red pine cone about eight inches long. One by one, the bracts loosen to permit the emergence of large, red-and-yellow flowers with the peculiar structure typical of the ginger family. Later, the bracts bend outward to expose their bright red inner surfaces and a contrasting white pod, surmounted by three red sepals. This pod is so thin and transparent that through it one can distinguish the white arils that embrace the tiny, angular, black seeds. Each aril consists of many slender, crooked filaments that become entangled with those of neighboring arils, so that, after the pod splits irregularly, they hang together in a cottony mass. The filaments contain many small oil droplets, but no evident starch.

A bird that relished these arils was a Streaked Saltator, who ate freely until chased away by a Garden Thrush (who did not take any), then returned and devoured many more. Orange-collared Manakins and Ochre-bellied Flycatchers also gathered them, while clinging to the cone or flying past. Scarlet-rumped

*Costus:* Opening Cone with Exposed Pods at Base; Two Arillate Seeds ▶

Tanagers sampled the arils, but swallowed them sparingly. A female was troubled by the filaments, one of which fell on her crown and stuck there until she shook it off. Other Scarlet-rumped Tanagers of both sexes repeatedly visited the *Costus*, but seemed to drop more of the arils than they ate. These arils of a monocotyledonous plant did not attract the birds so strongly as those of the dicotyledons described in chapter 6.

The oil palms continue to grow higher and higher, spreading huge fronds above huge fronds. They are closer to our windows than they should be, and some day they must come down— which will be a problem.

# 13. *Boat-billed Flycatchers*

EARLY in March, a Boat-billed Flycatcher started her nest in the top of a guava tree outside the dining-room window, where in a later year a White-crested Coquette Hummingbird raised her young. Except by behavior, I could not distinguish the female of this biggest of the flycatchers at Los Cusingos from her mate. Stout birds about nine inches long, they were olive on back and rump, browner on wings and tail. Each had a black crown, separated from the black cheeks by broad white superciliary stripes that nearly met on the back of the head. Their throats were white, the rest of their underplumage bright yellow. Their strong, notably broad, black bills were responsible for their name. Their eyes were brown, their legs and feet black.

The more familiar Great Kiskadee is confusingly similar to the Boat-bill in size and coloration, but very different in habits and voice. It may be distinguished by its narrower bill and rufous coloring on the wings, which the Boat-bill lacks. When I taught ornithology at the University of Costa Rica, I made the ability to distinguish between these two species, both of which occurred on the campus, a test of the students' competence in identifying birds. Five smaller species of flycatchers have color patterns almost identical with that of the Boat-bill and Great Kiskadee. One wonders why this pattern has been acquired by no less than seven species of flycatchers in four genera. What advantage does it confer on its wearers?

Boat-bills are treetop birds who frequent the highest boughs of the crowded giants of the forest and wander over all sorts of open country where trees are not too stunted or widely spaced. Across the whole length and breadth of the tropical American mainland, from Mexico to northern Argentina and from the Atlantic to the Pacific, these tolerant birds inhabit arid as well as extremely rainy regions. They may be found in coffee plantations with light shade, pastures with scattered trees, and riverside fringes of trees in open country. Over much of their wide range, they extend from sea level up to about 6,000 feet, and once in Costa Rica I saw a single individual nearly 1,000 feet higher. They appear to migrate altitudinally. During my year at Montaña Azul, they were not rare around 5,500 feet in July and August, after which they vanished and were not seen again until the following April. Like many other birds of the treetops, they rarely delay long in one place, except at their nests, but each day roam widely, in pairs or families of from three to five.

Boat-bills include both insects and fruits in their diet. Unlike kingbirds and some of the other larger flycatchers, they rarely catch insects on long, spectacular aerial sallies, but prefer to pluck them from leaf or limb by means of a quick dart from a perch, usually without alighting beside them. Many of their victims are of substantial size, and often they are green. In the drier months early in the year, when big cicadas chirr and buzz loudly among the trees, they are often captured by Boat-bills. Snatching one of these noisy insects from twig or trunk, the flycatcher carries it to a convenient perch, against which it beats its prey resoundingly. After knocking the cicada several times against the branch, the bird turns it with a slight toss of the bill, then beats it until it has been thoroughly pounded on all sides. Then the bird gulps down the tough, dry morsel. It would be interesting to know whether the Boat-bills distinguish the male cicadas, which are little more than hollow sound chambers, from the females,

Boat-billed Flycatcher, Usually Concealed Orange-Yellow Crown Patch
Exposed, with Cicada ▶

which contain more nourishment, and whether they eat only the latter.

Among the fruits that Boat-bills eat are small wild figs, berries of *Miconia*, *Cissus*, and *Palicourea guianensis*, and arillate seeds of *Protium*, *Alchornea*, and *Dipterodendron*. The birds often pluck berries much as they catch insects, by flying up and pulling one from its stem without alighting. However, if they find a satisfactory perch within easy reach of a cluster of berries, they may rest there while they gather them. Soft berries, such as those of melastomes, are swallowed directly; but I have watched a Boat-bill fly up to a long, dangling fruiting spike of a Cecropia tree, tear away a short length, with its tiny, crowded green fruits, and beat it vigorously against a perch before swallowing it with an upward toss of its head, exactly as though it had captured and swallowed a cicada.

One morning in August, a Boat-bill flew into a tree in front of the house with a big brown feather in its bill. After beating it against its perch, it dropped the plume. As it floated slowly downward, the mate of the first bird darted out and caught it. Then the second Boat-bill perched in the tree and knocked the feather against a branch. Soon it dropped the feather, only to shoot out and catch it as it wafted downward and then strike it against the branch once more. Next, the bird carried the plume to a neighboring tree and continued to beat it. None of this knocking was hard; it seemed not to be done in earnest. Finally, the bird with the feather released it, and the pair flew away together. They appeared to have been playing.

Perching or flying, a Boat-bill often repeats a loud, rather high-pitched *choip choip choip choip*, its usual call note. When the bird is near, this note sounds slightly raucous; but two or three Boat-bills answering one another from distant treetops are pleasant to hear; they sound like soft chimes. Another of the Boat-bill's notes is a prolonged, whining *churr*, usually delivered while the bird perches. Boat-bills who nested around the house that we occupied in Venezuela often called *yoi yoi yoi* in a most peculiar nasal tone, such as I have not heard in Central America.

Like a number of other flycatchers, the male Boat-bill has a special song that he sings in the morning twilight, and later in the day only when he is greatly excited, as by a clash with a neighbor. This most melodious of the Boat-bill's utterances consists of a clear, ringing *cheer*, repeated over and over, and punctuated at irregular intervals by a slurred note of quite different character that sounds like *bo-oy*. Rarely, a Boat-bill introduces his whining *churr* into his dawn song, but the far-carrying clear notes always predominate. On cool mornings in early January, I have heard a Boat-bill practice his dawn song tentatively; but usually it is late February or even March before he sings persistently. Thereafter, I have heard his song at daybreak well into June, and sometimes in July. A Boat-bill who sang in late September and early October was probably without a mate. This spirited, stirring performance begins in the earliest gray dawn and continues for many minutes, usually while the yellow-breasted bird perches in a high treetop. One Boat-bill I watched in early April sang without intermission for twenty-five minutes, and continued haltingly for ten minutes more. Usually the song ends before sunrise.

In March, when the female Boat-bill built in the guava tree in front of the dining-room window, her mate sometimes sang at dawn in a tree twenty or thirty yards away, rarely in the nest tree. On some mornings, I heard a dawn song, probably his, coming from a greater distance, and on other mornings I failed to hear it. Possibly he then performed too far away to be audible; one morning, when I heard him in the distance, he came to finish his monologue near the nest tree.

Other male Boat-bills sing more consistently, over a longer interval. Sometimes one performs in the tree where later his mate, perhaps attracted to it by his singing, will build her nest. In a tall wild fig tree beside a rivulet flowing between pastures, a male sang sporadically in January, more consistently and at greater length from late February onward. Toward the end of March, his mate started her nest in this fig tree. After this nest fell, she built another in a much lower tree at least a hundred yards away. The male continued to sing in the top of his tall fig tree, but later in the day he went to guard the new nest. This second nest was also prematurely lost. If the female built another, it was so far away that I failed to find it. Nevertheless, the male continued to sing at daybreak in his fig tree, where I last heard him in June.

Another female built in the top of a lofty ojoche tree where her mate sometimes sang, but after her nest was finished he performed in another tree about two hundred feet distant. When, after the loss of nestlings, the female built again about five hundred yards away, her mate sang at daybreak in a tree about midway between the sites of the first and second nests. Probably, when the nest is placed in the tree where a male has been singing his twilight song, he moves to a more distant tree to avoid attracting attention to eggs and young.

*Nesting*

Here in the valley of El General, Boat-bills sometimes begin their nests in late February, but few start before March, when the bird in the guava tree began. Only about twenty-five feet above the ground, her site was among the lower of the thirty nests whose heights I have estimated, all in Costa Rica except for one in Guatemala and three in Venezuela. These nests ranged in height from twenty to about a hundred feet from the ground, with eight of them above fifty feet. The lowest were among foliage at the tops of small trees, on branches too long and slender to be climbed, although I could view the contents of a few in a mirror attached to a long pole. Some of the higher nests were in crotches of stout branches, occasionally against the main trunk, and often quite exposed. Although nearly all the nests were in living trees, three, apparently all the work of the same female, were in crotches of charred, nearly branchless dead trees standing in a recent clearing, gaunt and visible from afar. One nest was well hidden in the midst of a densely leafy mistletoe high on a leafless tree. All the nests that I have seen were in isolated trees in dooryards, pastures, and plantations, or at roadsides. If Boat-bills ever breed in the forests over which they wander, their nests have eluded me.

Like the dozen others that I have watched, the Boat-bill who built in the guava tree beside the house gathered all her materials from trees, never from the ground. Usually she found them at a good distance from her nest, often at points beyond view. She struggled hard to break the dead twigs that formed her nest's foundation from treetops, and gathered lengths of dead vines in the same strenuous fashion. More hard work was needed to pass long, stiff, often branching pieces through the boughs around her nest. When a toilsomely acquired piece was knocked from her bill while she struggled with it and fell to the ground, she never descended to retrieve it, but preferred to fly afar for another piece. After she finished the coarse foundation of her open cup and started to line it, she laboriously tore long, fibrous roots from orchids, ferns, and other plants that grow high on mossy trunks in tropical forests. Then she flew to her nest with the longer pieces trailing far behind her and carefully coiled them into the bottom of the cup.

The Boat-bill in the guava tree chiefly worked late in the day. I seldom saw her visit her nest while I ate breakfast. She came more often at lunchtime, and sometimes continued to build until mid-afternoon. Whenever I watched, her visits were so widely spaced that I tired of waiting for her to reappear. So leisurely was her pace that she needed about two weeks to finish her nest. Other Boat-bills have come more often, earlier in the day; but at best they bring contributions to their nests rather infrequently, perhaps because they work so hard to gather them. A female building high in a fig tree brought pieces forty-one times in four hours of the early morning, or at the rate of about ten times per hour. She worked at her nest for at least ten days. Another, whose site was high in a dead tree beside a river, brought material nineteen times from 7:00 to 8:00 in the morning and fourteen times in the next hour. This was late in the season, in April instead of in March, when probably the nest was more urgently needed for eggs.

While a female Boat-bill builds, her mate perches close by the nest, indolently, or languidly preening his feathers. At intervals he bestirs himself to follow her on trips to gather materials. Returning, he may bear a twig or a rootlet, sometimes a very long one, which he may either promptly drop or continue to hold while he rests near the nest, until he accompanies her on another excursion. When she returns with a contribution to her nest, he may follow her with the same piece that he carried off. One male brought the same root three times to the fig tree where his mate was building, and thrice carried it away. At other times, the male Boat-bill continues to hold his piece until he drops it to seize a passing insect; once he held it for eleven minutes by my watch. It never seems to occur to him that he might deposit the material on the nest or pass it to his partner, thereby saving her much hard work; and she does not try to take it from him. I have watched a number of nests without ever seeing a male contribute any material to it; his role is to watch and to guard. In all this, he resembles male tityras, both the Masked and the Black-crowned, who rarely drop into the nest cavity the pieces that they frequently carry back and forth while their mates build.

Early one afternoon, soon after the nest beside the house was started, the male Boat-bill sat in it and rapidly repeated low, intimate notes suggestive of contentment. I knew he was the male because, while he delivered this "nest song," his mate perched close beside him, holding a stick that she later added to the nest. At the same time, Vermilion-crowned and Gray-capped flycatchers were singing rather similar nest songs while they examined possible nest sites in neighboring orange trees with their mates. Probably this stimulated the Boat-bill to sing, too; I have repeatedly noticed that the nest song of one pair of flycatchers evokes similar utterances from neighboring pairs of the same or different species. Through the remainder of the period of nest building, I heard this low, "confidential" song, so different from Boat-bills' usual loud notes, a few times more from both the male and the female. After the female started to incubate, I did not hear it again until the day the eggs hatched. At other Boat-bills' nests, I failed to hear the nest song, probably because these higher nests were farther away and I passed less time near them.

When finished, the Boat-bill's nest was a broad, shallow cup, with an internal diameter of about four inches and a depth of one and three quarters inches. The loose, bulky foundation was made of coarse, stiff materials. In one nest this consisted of about equal numbers of crooked, dry twiglets and slender, leafless stems of epiphytic orchids, including one fourteen inches long. In the foundation of another nest were many dry vines. In yet another, the foundation and outer layers were composed almost wholly of small, epiphytic orchid plants with green, leafy shoots, chiefly of a species of *Dichaea*. In the linings of various nests I have found slender, flexible rhizomes of creeping epiphytic ferns, orchids, and other epiphytes, some very long, many partly decayed, but a few still green; dry tendrils; and a few short twiglets. Nothing in these nests appeared to have been gathered from the ground. Looking up through the bottoms of some nests, I have seen flecks of sky through the open fabric. Only a fairly large bird with a strong bill could build a nest of materials that are usually difficult to detach from the trees where they grow.

Although the Boat-bill's nest was long ago correctly described by Euler (1867) as a slight, frail, open structure, certain later writers have confused it with the bulky roofed nest of the Great Kiskadee. Once, in Guatemala, I found both of these birds, so similar in appearance, but so different in voice, habits, and temperament, nesting in the same tree in apparent amity. The kiskadee's domed nest with a side entrance was in the main fork, the Boat-bill's much slighter structure on a slender branch, far above.

Empty Boat-bills' nests are sometimes occupied by other birds. When eggs were lost at the same time from the neighboring nests

of Boat-bills and Blue Tanagers, the latter promptly took possession of the flycatchers' nest, lined it more softly, and laid eggs in
it. On another Boat-bill's nest, a Gray-capped Flycatcher built a
roof and a side entrance, converting it to her own use.

The Boat-bill in the guava tree beside the house appeared to
have finished her nest by March 20, but she did not lay her first
egg until March 31. Her second egg, which was also her last, was
laid three days later. Including this, six of the nests that I could
examine had two eggs or nestlings, and six contained three eggs
or nestlings. The eggs are usually laid at intervals of two days. I
timed the laying of two eggs, each the second in its set. One appeared between 10:00 A.M. and 12:05 P.M.; the other between
11:30 A.M. and 1:08 P.M. The dull white eggs, measuring about
29.7 by 21.5 millimeters, are thickly speckled and blotched with
dull brown and pale lilac over the entire surface, most densely on
the thicker end. Even if I could not look into a high nest, by
watching its attendants I could usually learn the month when
eggs were laid in it, which in twenty-two nests in the valley of El
General was as follows: February, one; March, five; April, seven;
May, seven; June, two.

As the female Boat-bill builds without help, so she incubates
without help. The bird in the guava tree started to incubate on
the day before she laid her second and last egg, but another female was not seen incubating until the day on which she completed her set by laying the third egg. In the interval between the
laying of the first and the last egg, one member of the pair was
almost always to be found guarding the nest from a nearby perch.

In April 1949, Darwin and Barbara Norby helped me to keep
what we hoped would be an all-day watch on a nest situated in-
accessibly on an exposed limb of a Cecropia tree in the pasture
behind the house. After our vigil had continued more than ten
hours, it was abruptly terminated, at 4:15 in the afternoon, by a
drenching thunderstorm. We had timed sixteen of the female's
sessions on her eggs, which ranged from 15 to 77 minutes and
averaged 30.2 minutes. An equal number of absences varied

from 2 to 19 minutes and averaged 8.3 minutes. The female
Boat-bill covered her eggs for 78.4 percent of the ten and a quarter hours that we watched. During shorter watches at two other
nests, the females incubated with similarly high constancy: 77
percent of six hours at one of the nests, 87.6 percent of four and
a half hours at the other, where one of the female's sessions continued for an hour and a half. No other flycatcher that I have
watched has covered her eggs so constantly, and few birds of
other families have done so unless they were liberally fed by their
mates, as in the case of jays and goldfinches. I have never seen a
male Boat-billed Flycatcher feed his mate, but at every nest that
I have studied, he has guarded the eggs during her absences.

The first nest that I watched while the female incubated was
most attractively situated in the top of a small Ceiba tree, which
at the end of April was renewing its foliage with bright red young
leaflets. The big, heavy bill, boldly marked black-and-white
head, and part of the yellow breast of the flycatcher were visible
above the nest's rim. Amid the brilliant new foliage, with the
blue sky showing through its gaps, she made so lovely a picture
that I longed for the skill to paint her with a few dazzling white
clouds drowsing overhead.

At this nest, the movements of the two partners were admirably coordinated. With two exceptions in the course of the morning, the female remained patiently warming her eggs until her
partner arrived to guard them. He always flew silently into the
Ceiba tree, and the moment he arrived, the female as silently departed. Until she returned, he continued to watch over the nest,
sometimes while perching close beside it, sometimes resting at
the ends of branches several yards from it, more rarely standing
on the nest's rim. While on sentry duty, he frequently preened
his feathers. His exercise of guardianship was limited to driving
such innocent and unwitting intruders as a Vermilion-crowned
Flycatcher and a wintering Yellow Warbler from near the nest,
with aggressive forward darts and loud, warning clacks of his
heavy bill. Without harming them, he served notice that they

were trespassing. When his mate returned from her usually brief recess, he greeted her with ringing cries that sounded like *choip choip* or *choee choee*, then promptly flew away, while she at once settled on the eggs, often uttering low, soft notes of contentment. The male Boat-bill's noisy departure contrasted sharply with his silent arrival.

Only twice during the morning did the female Boat-bill leave her eggs before her mate arrived. The first of these departures occurred when she heard or saw him rush to attack a party of Chestnut-mandibled Toucans who had appeared on a hilltop about five hundred feet away. As soon as the toucans came within view, she dashed off to help her mate harry these nest-robbers. After the great-bills had vanished into the neighboring forest, the male Boat-bill came promptly to guard the vacant nest until his mate, who doubtless had taken advantage of her excursion to snatch a little food, returned two minutes later. The whole episode demonstrated the closest cooperation between the partners in guarding and defending the nest.

Toward the end of the morning, after she had been sitting for an hour without relief, the female grew restless and hopped from the nest to perch close beside it, facing it, while she preened. After eight minutes of this, her mate still delaying his arrival, she returned to her eggs. But after sitting only two minutes more, hunger overcame her attachment to her nest, and she flew away leaving it unguarded. Five minutes after her departure, the male came to the unattended nest and stood guard over it until, after only two minutes more, the female returned to resume incubation. At this nest, the male was in view only while the female was absent.

During four of the female's five absences from a nest in a riverside *Inga* tree, the male stood sentinel in the treetop. When she began her recess at half-past ten, he had already been resting there for half an hour, preening much of the time. Now, when she flew off to forage, he followed. A flurry of excitement among the trees by the river, beyond view, suggested that the male Boat-bill had left the nest tree to drive away an enemy. As soon as the excitement died away, he returned to a perch in the riverside tree overlooking the nest; he stood guard during each of his mate's absences. Among intruders driven from near the nest that morning were a female Black-crowned Tityra, a Vermilion-crowned Flycatcher, and a Garden Thrush. When pursued by the male Boat-bill, the thrush dodged through the boughs of the nest tree, refusing to leave, until the female jumped from her eggs to help her mate chase the brown trespasser, who then retreated to a neighboring tree.

At the nest in the guava tree beside the house, the male guarded from a neighboring treetop rather than in the nest tree. Since I knew exactly when the eggs had been laid in this conveniently situated nest, I hoped to learn the length of the Boat-billed Flycatcher's incubation period, which was not known. By the afternoon of April 20, seventeen days after the last egg had been laid, neither had hatched. At noon on the following day, the pair were attending their nest. Shortly afterward, a violent rainstorm blew up and continued for about an hour, forcing me to delay my inspection of the nest with a ladder and a mirror attached to a long pole. When at last I could raise the mirror above the nest and see its contents, it was empty! A Chestnut-mandibled Toucan had passed by the house as the storm was ending, and this for me was sufficient explanation of what had happened. On the ground beneath the nest I found the cap of one of the shells, neatly severed from the body of the shell by the bill of the chick within, not roughly broken off by a predator. Hence I had no doubt that at least one egg had hatched, after about eighteen days of incubation. Eight years later, I studied a nest in which all three eggs hatched seventeen days after the last was laid.

I have seen newly hatched Boat-billed Flycatchers only as images reflected from a mirror. They are typical passerine nestlings, with the bright yellow interior of the mouth characteristic of the flycatcher family. They are fed largely, if not wholly, with insects by both parents, and kept almost constantly guarded, as I saw long ago in Guatemala, and have since verified at a number of nests in Costa Rica and Venezuela. After feeding, the female broods, remaining until her partner arrives with food, when she flies off. After he has delivered what he brought, the male lingers upon the rim of the nest or close beside it, standing guard, until she returns to feed and brood once more. During his periods of sentinel duty, the male never, as far as I have seen, covers the nestlings; he only watches over them. While the nestlings are only a few days old, the female may vary this routine by moving to a point close beside the nest when her mate arrives with food, to resume brooding as soon as he has fed the nestlings, leaving him free to fly away and hunt for more.

At a nest far beyond reach in a mistletoe bush high in a *Zanthoxylum* tree, the nestlings, estimated to be five days old, but whose number I could not learn, were fed only seven times in three hours, four times by their father and three by their mother. She brooded for four periods ranging from thirty-four to forty-five minutes and totaling a hundred and fifty-four minutes. She also stood guard on the nest's rim for five minutes, after interrupting her brooding to drive away an intruding Yellow-bellied Elaenia. The male stood guard for three intervals of nine, three, and eight minutes, which corresponded with his partner's brief absences for food—all that she took during the three hours. Except for one interval of two minutes, the nest was constantly attended.

Eight days later, this nest in the mistletoe held a single nestling, easily visible from the ground as it rose to take food or stood to preen. In three hours and twenty minutes, the young Boat-bill was fed sixteen times, or at the rate of 4.8 times per hour. Since its mother did not now brood after each feeding, I could not always distinguish the parents; but the male fed the nestling at least six times, the female at least five. The latter brooded for a total of seventy-five minutes. Sometimes the well-feathered young flycatcher stuck its head out from beneath its mother's breast. During seventy-five additional minutes, one or the other of the parents, chiefly the father, rested in the nest tree or close beside it, guarding the nestling. In all, the young bird was attended, one way or the other, for a total of one hundred and fifty minutes during the two hundred minutes that I watched, or three quarters of the time. That the male rested in the nest tree expressly to guard the nestling, and not merely because this was a place as good as another for loafing, was amply demonstrated by his prompt departure each time his mate arrived to take charge.

After six more days, I was surprised to find this young Boat-bill, who had long been completely feathered, still in its nest in the mistletoe. In two hours and twenty minutes, it was fed only nine times, or at the rate of 3.9 times per hour, by both parents. As far as I could see, it was given only insects, some of which were very large, including a cicada that it swallowed with difficulty. The young bird was guarded, from points near the nest, for a total of seventy-one minutes, by both parents, and brooded a total of forty-five minutes, presumably by its mother only. Thus it was under parental vigilance for one hundred and sixteen out of one hundred and forty minutes, or six-sevenths of the time. Almost ready to fly, it seemed not to enjoy being sat upon on a bright, warm morning, and persisted in sticking head and shoulders out in front of its mother's bright yellow breast, sometimes preening parts of its plumage that she did not cover. At times the young bird's restlessness caused its mother to leave the nest and watch close beside it. Thus, on the same visit to the nest tree, she alternately brooded and guarded the nestling. It seemed that habit made her brood long after this was necessary; if she had not remained to guard, she probably would not have covered the nestling.

This young Boat-billed Flycatcher left its inaccessible nest twenty-three days after I first saw the parents take food to it. The following year, three nestlings, reared in a nest into which I could look with a mirror, departed spontaneously when twenty-four days old. At this age, they could fly so well that one covered over a hundred feet on a rising course. Because young Boat-bills often grow up in nests situated at great heights, they need to fly competently as soon as they leave. On the morning when the three fledglings left home, their parents were watchful and anxious, loudly protesting my approach to their offspring, who closely resembled them.

After three fledglings departed the nest in the Cecropia tree in the pasture behind the house, the parents were so vigilant and excitable that I could not approach within a hundred yards without stirring up a storm of protests. When I suddenly emerged from the forest adjoining the pasture, an anxious Boat-bill would notice me almost immediately and fly up to scold. Then one or both of the parents would follow me over the pasture, often darting angrily above my head, and alighting upon low boughs of the guava trees to complain, while their young remained hidden.

After they fly, young Boat-billed Flycatchers stay with their parents for months, continuing in their company long after they cease to be dependent upon them for food. Three young Boat-bills who left their nest in an Algarrobo tree in Venezuela on May 1 continued to roost with their parents in a neighboring Rose-Apple tree at least into the third week of July. The flocks of three, four, or five individuals that wander through the treetops through most of the nonbreeding season appear to consist of parents with full-grown young. In 1942, three young were fledged in a tree behind the house. During the latter half of that year, and through January and February of the following year, five Boat-billed Flycatchers used to pass through the garden morning and evening, flying down to the river in front of the house before sunrise, and returning to the coffee grove behind it late in the afternoon. They straggled one behind another instead of flying in a compact flock, and while resting in the shade trees around the house repeated their long, drawled *churr*. These were doubtless the pair who had successfully nested nearby, with their three offspring. Toward the end of January, I noticed slight signs of discord in this family, but it held together more than a month longer. After the male started to sing his dawn song at the beginning of March, the family was reduced to the mated pair.

As already told, on March 10, 1943, the female of this pair began to build in the guava tree in front of the dining-room window. She did not succeed in rearing a brood here, and apparently was equally unsuccessful at a distance. Through the second half of the year, I now saw only two Boat-bills in the garden instead of the five who had frequented it in 1942. If a pair fails to produce offspring, it seems to remain alone into the following year.

In October and November of a later year, a pair of Boat-billed Flycatchers, who apparently had reared no progeny in the preceding nesting season, roosted nightly in a small tree of *Inga spectabilis* in the pasture. Here they slept about twenty feet above the ground, always separated from one another by a yard or two—never in close contact, as mated Black-fronted Tody-Flycatchers roost. Although they could have concealed themselves well amid the coarse compound leaves of the tree, they perched on the leafless bases of stout twigs, where with a flashlight I could readily see them from below. However, the foliage formed a thick canopy above them on those rainy nights. When I directed the beam of light upon them, their heads were always exposed instead of turned back among their feathers. They sat motionless while I peered up at them. In Venezuela, a male Boat-bill had the habit of resting in the late afternoon within a yard of his incubating mate. Sometimes he delayed there for about half an hour, while daylight faded. I looked for him to roost so close to the nest, but in the twilight he silently flew away.

Despite the watchful care of parent Boat-bills, they lose most of their nests. Because of repeated failures, a pair that started to build in late February did not have fledglings until early June; even this brood might have been lost if I had not rescued the nestlings when the branch that supported their nest crashed down in a windy rainstorm. Most late nests appear to belong to pairs who have not yet produced flying young. I know of only one

occasion when a successful nesting was followed by an attempt to rear a second brood. This female continued to incubate in the mornings, but was often absent in the rainy afternoons, into the third week of July, after which she abandoned her nest.

It is difficult to obtain an accurate measure of the success of nests usually so high and inaccessible. Of nineteen in which incubation appeared to have begun, and of which I learned the outcome, eleven failed and eight, or 42 percent, yielded at least one fledgling. Here in El General, the chief despoilers of Boat-bills' nests appear to have been Chestnut-mandibled Toucans, until they vanished from the valley. Fiery-billed Araçaris, which remain in reduced numbers, doubtless also took eggs and young. Although I have seen both of these great-billed birds pillage nests of a variety of smaller birds, I have never caught one in the act of plundering a Boat-bill's nest. However, on a number of occasions, nests were empty just after we saw a party of toucans pass by. Once I watched a Chestnut-mandibled Toucan peer into an unfinished Boat-bill's nest, while both the male and female darted angrily at the intruder.

In the feathered world, I have seen few antipathies so strong as that of Boat-billed Flycatchers to Chestnut-mandibled Toucans, and to a lesser degree to the smaller Fiery-billed Araçaris. In other parts of the flycatchers' vast range, they doubtless have to contend with other species of these great-billed nest-robbers. Toucans, more than any other predators, seem to be responsible for the almost constant guard that Boat-billed Flycatchers keep over their eggs and nestlings. Instead of waiting for the toucans to approach their nests, they often advance to meet them while still far away, then continue to harry them until they return to the forest. As long as the toucans perch, the flycatchers dare not approach within reach of the long, mobile bills, but on the wing, the toucans cannot defend their backs. This is the flycatchers' opportunity, and sometimes they pounce boldly upon the back of a flying toucan. However, they are careful to separate from

◀ Boat-billed Flycatcher Pursuing Chestnut-mandibled Toucan

him before he alights and can turn his beak backward, with possibly disastrous consequences to the much smaller flycatcher. Exceptionally, the sight of a distant party of toucans sends a Boat-bill hurriedly to its nest from the elevated perch where it has been watching.

One rainy afternoon in November, while I watched through a window as three Boat-billed Flycatchers, with a few Vermilion-crowned Flycatchers and other birds, caught insects among the surrounding trees, a hawk swooped down without warning and seized a flycatcher, whose cries were piteous to hear. The raptor, which I had not seen well enough to identify, dropped with its victim to the ground on the far side of the hedge, where the Boat-bills, instead of fleeing like the smaller birds, darted down upon it, snapping their bills. I rushed out for a closer view, but before I could reach the gate in the hedge, the hawk had vanished with its victim. Apparently this was a Vermilion-crowned Flycatcher and not a Boat-bill, as I had at first supposed; for three of the latter were still in the garden. The energy of the Boat-bills' attack upon the hawk was the more remarkable if the victim was of another species.

Boat-billed Flycatchers have been accused of being quarrelsome, but this has not been my experience with them. Courageous in the defense of their nests against toucans and other predators much larger than themselves, they are good neighbors to smaller birds. I have never seen a Boat-bill persecute them or take their eggs or nestlings, as Great Kiskadees sometimes do. Possibly Boat-bills too fussily chase small, inoffensive birds from near the Boat-bills' nests; but many other parent birds are equally anxious when they have eggs or nestlings to defend. Because some of the Boat-bills' notes sound petulant or disagreeable to us, we should not hastily conclude that these utterances reveal a bad temper. Perhaps to the Boat-bills themselves that long, whining *churr* is the sweetest and most endearing of sounds.

# 14. Fascinating Weeds

TWO or three times each year, the local representative of the Guardia de Asistencia Rural, familiarly known as "the policeman," brings me a printed sheet to be signed in duplicate, one copy for him and one for me. I am directed to chop down the vegetation along the edge of the public road adjoining my property. If this is not accomplished within fifteen days, so the order reads, public employees will be sent to do the work, and I shall be charged, as a fine, twice what they are paid. Since public employees are not notable for exerting themselves, their work would probably cost me, not twice, but three or four times as much as if I have it done promptly. Accordingly, I look for a young neighbor who swings his machete mightily, and, after agreeing on a price, set him to attacking the weeds along the roadside.

If the verge were not occasionally cleaned, in this rainy climate, it would before long grow up into a dense roadside thicket. Nevertheless, I am reluctant to obey the order, especially when it comes toward the year's end; for in December and January, as the wet season passes into the dry and sunshine increases, a great variety of flowering herbs would brighten the roadside if they were not mercilessly slashed down. Most of the white, yellow, pink, blue, and purple flowers belong to widespread, common weedy plants, but here and there among them a native displays more impressive blooms. Riding along the Inter-American Highway in southern El Salvador in November, years ago, I was delighted by the profusion of large morning glories of many shades of blue, lavender, purple, and white. On earlier horseback journeys through the highlands of Guatemala at the same season, masses of red, blue, and purple salvias, interspersed with yellow and white composites, cheered my way. Here the verges had not recently been chopped.

Every man's hand seems to be set against weeds, those unwanted, usually herbaceous plants of many families that spring up profusely, especially where man has destroyed the native vegetation. Formerly, in the tropics, the long machete was the weapon generally turned against them. Now chemical herbicides are displacing this agricultural tool. Some of the neighbors spray these weed-killers along their roadsides, making them look more barren and desolate than when the vegetation is mowed down. In the coffee plantations, herbicides are widely used. I have never spread them at Los Cusingos, either on the verge or inside the farm, for I do not know their long-term effects upon soil, vegetation, or fauna. Nevertheless, after I have enjoyed studying the uninvited growths, I must treacherously (as I sometimes feel) attack them in the pastures, before they shade out the grass, and in the *milpa*, lest they compete too severely with the maize.

The plants that we designate by the pejorative "weeds" are mostly hardy, adaptable species of wide distribution that play a role in nature's economy that becomes increasingly important as man destroys the natural vegetation over ever vaster areas. They cover with verdure places that people have left bare and unsightly—roadsides, embankments, abandoned fields, vacant lots, even trash heaps. They reduce erosion, bring new life to exhausted soil, and with their flowers often brighten spots that we have made ugly. More annoyingly, in fields and flower beds, they spring up vigorously on the bare soil between our cultivated plants, as though to vindicate the old adage that nature abhors a vacuum. Although the agriculturist and gardener may curse

*Sida acuta* ▶

weeds for the labor and expense they cause, they are by no means an unmitigated evil. To the botanist, they are highly instructive.

Fascinated by weeds, I devote to them attention that some of my acquaintances lavish upon orchids. As a hobby, plebeian weeds have many advantages over aristocratic orchids. Well able to shift for themselves, they require no laborious cultivation. Never imported at great expense, they spread over the Earth without deliberate human aid. I need not go in search of them; they come and settle around me. I never fear that they will be stolen, as orchids often are, especially here in the tropics, where they are mostly kept outdoors. They do nothing to foment the competitive spirit; nobody covets my weeds or vies with me to have the rarest or most costly specimens or the largest collection, as frequently happens among orchid fanciers.

Weeds may not have such large, spectacular flowers as many orchids display, but, if one looks closely, their modest florets are often charming. Of simple construction, they are readily polli-nated by a variety of agents, and most of them set seeds—often, as in composites and mints, only one or a few to each flower. In strong contrast to this fecund simplicity, the elaborate flowers of orchids require such special conditions for pollination that, even in species growing in their natural habitat, only a small minority may be fertilized. To compensate for the many orchid flowers that remain barren, the few that are pollinated develop pods with enormous numbers of minute, wind-blown seeds. So diverse in their floral structures, the thousands of species of orchids are monotonous in their method of dispersal, displaying few of the curious devices that have spread common weeds over the Earth.

Among the most abundant of tropical weeds are the broom-weeds, which thrive in pastures, neglected dooryards, along roadsides, and in similar open situations. Rural housewives, who call them *escobillas*, gather the tough, wiry stems, tie a bundle of them to the end of a stick, and make an effective besom. They belong to the large genus *Sida*, of the mallow family, and, like many other members of the family, open their flowers only briefly.

*Chaptalia nutans*; Plumose Achene (inset) ▶

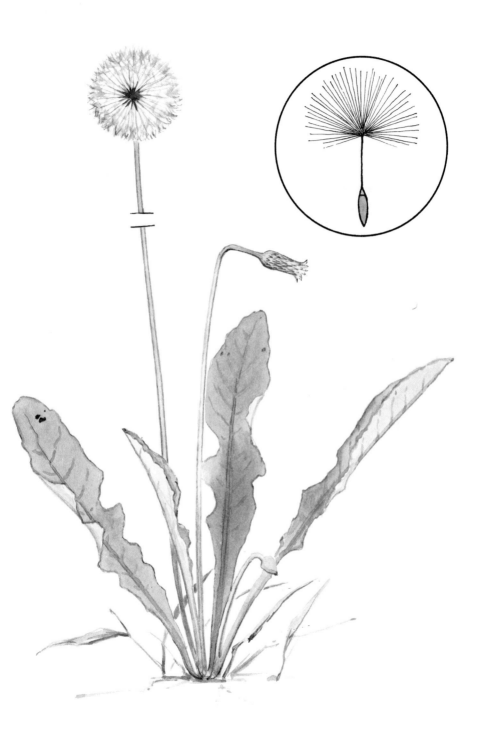

In November, before the end-of-the-year cleaning of pastures, I gave much attention to three kinds of broomweeds that flourished in the riverside pasture. The most abundant was *Sida acuta*, sometimes known as *escobilla negra*, which from stumps left by previous pasture cleanings produced ascending branches, about two feet high, with small, serrate leaves in two ranks. Its pale yellow, five-petalled flowers are slightly over half an inch broad. On bright mornings, the flowers that first received the sun's rays were open by about 7:40, while those most shaded were not fully expanded until an hour later. On cloudy or rainy mornings, few flowers opened before 8:00, but half an hour later many had expanded.

Even before the petals were fully spread, the many stamens clustered at the center of the flower had released their large, yellow pollen grains, covered with the minute spikes typical of the mallow family, and the stigmas appeared to be receptive. I could detect no fragrance or nectar; but the White Peacock Butterflies, who frequently visited the flowers, might have found a little sweetness in them—or perhaps they ate the pollen, as some butterflies are known to do. Small, stingless *Trigona* bees, some with black and some with yellow abdomens, busily filling the pollen baskets on their hindlegs, were evidently the chief pollinators. Other visitors were small, plain white butterflies and very tiny bees. Between 10:30 and 11:15 A.M., after about three hours of anthesis, the flowers closed, those in sunshine first, never to open again. In the Almirante Bay region of western Panama, where I observed it half a century earlier, *Sida acuta* opened its flowers much later, from 11:00 A.M. to between 1:30 and 3:00 P.M. These two populations of broomweeds, separated by the high Cordillera de Talamanca, are evidently genetically different.

Scattered among *Sida acuta* in the riverside pasture were many plants of *S. rhombifolia*, whose more erect stems, up to four feet high, were preferred by a neighbor for her brooms. Their

*Synedrella nodiflora*: Marginal Achene (left) and Two Central Achenes ▶

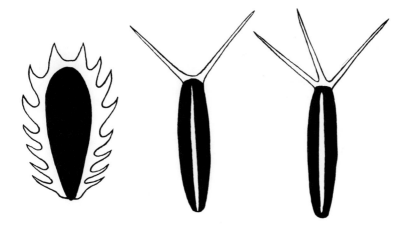

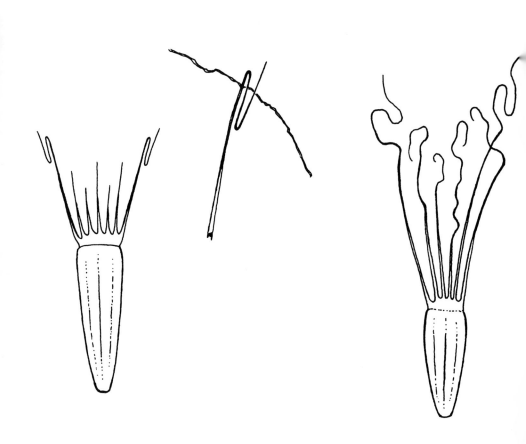

flowers, also pale yellow, were about the same size as those of the related species, but they did not open until around noon, after those of *S. acuta* had closed. At this season, afternoons were usually cloudy, and rain often fell during much or all of the three hours, or a little more, when the flowers of this tall broomweed were open. Likewise scentless, with little or no nectar, they attracted the White Peacocks less often than did the flowers that opened on sunny mornings. During a lull in the rains, stingless bees visiting the tiny white florets of nearby Button Mints neglected the broomweed. It was interesting to observe how these two closely related broomweeds prevented, or minimized, hybridization by opening their very similar flowers at different hours of the day.

Growing less abundantly among these two species of broomweeds was a third that did not quite correspond to any description available to me. The stellate hairs on its stem, the undersides of its leaves, and its calyces allied it to *S. rhombifolia*, and the slender pedicels that bore the flowers were intermediate in length between those of the two neighboring species. It almost looked as though, despite their different times of anthesis, the two other species had hybridized; but this would not account for the red "eye" at the center of each pale yellowish or buffy flower, which bloomed in the forenoon at the same time as those of *Sida acuta*.

When mature, the dry fruits of these broomweeds split into from seven to twelve divisions called carpels. Each is a tiny brown nutlet with two short beaks, or none at all, enclosing a single triangular seed. Although these seeds lack evident devices for dispersal, the plants that bear them have somehow managed to spread through the tropics around the globe, probably largely with cultivated plants.

Of all the plants at Los Cusingos, none so resembles the Dandelion of temperate regions and tropical highlands in its manner of growth as *Chaptalia nutans*, another member of the composite

◀ *Pseudelephantopus spicatus*: Achenes from El General (left) and Northeastern Costa Rica

family. Less aggressive than the Dandelion, it grows scattered about our lawn, chiefly where shrubs give it a little protection. The lyrate leaves, smoothly green above, but densely covered with woolly white hairs below, hug the ground in a rosette. From its center one or two thin, leafless stems, woolly like the undersides of the leaves, grow straight up, exceptionally as much as two feet, and each bears a cylindrical flower head that nods obliquely downward, as the plant's specific name suggests. The inconspicuous pink rays of this compact head surround a much greater number of white disk flowers. When the seeds mature, the head stands erect, and the involucral bracts bend out and down, exposing a cluster of one-seeded fruits, called achenes, each with a long, slender beak tipped with a halo of fine whitish filaments, the pappus. The soft, feathery mass of plumed achenes closely resembles that of a Dandelion, which children used to blow upon to tell the hour by counting the few fruits that remain clinging to the receptacle after the majority have floated, parachutelike, away.

The methods the 20,000 or more species of the composite family have evolved to disperse their one-seeded fruits are of fascinating diversity. Very many, like the Dandelion and *Chaptalia*, use the breezes. A few, like the shrubs and small trees of the tropical genus *Clibadium*, some of which grow in tall thickets at Los Cusingos, produce berrylike fruits that are eaten by birds. Many others attach their fruits to fur or clothes by various means. Of these, a few surround the whole flower head with hooked spines, so that the achenes are transported in a packet, in the manner of Burdocks and Cockleburs. As a child, I stuck burlike heads of Burdock together to make little, prickly green baskets. More often, each achene has its own device for attaching itself to some unwary animal, so that the seeds are dispersed singly. This is the method of the highly successful bur-marigolds of the genus *Bidens*, widespread in the Western Hemisphere. The achenes, which may be flat or long and slender, are crowned with two or more stiff little spikes covered with tiny, backwardly directed prickles,

*Pavonia rosea*: Flower and Seed Pods ▶

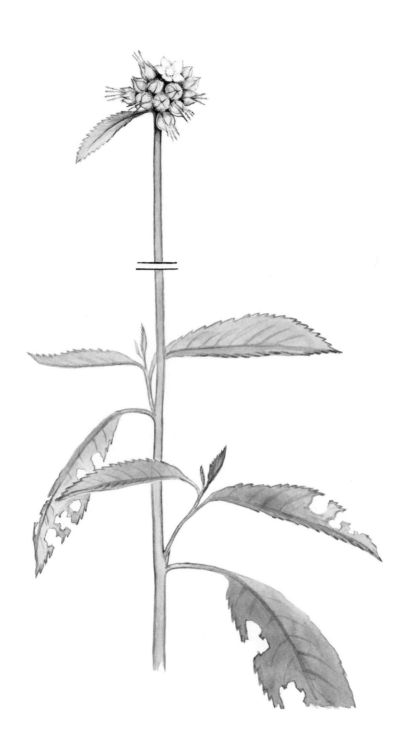

which make them stick tightly, and often annoyingly, to garments. One of these bur-marigolds (similar to *Bidens riparia* if not
the same) springs up sparingly in our garden and too abundantly
in the coffee and banana plantations, where it grows six feet
high. It bears large, finely divided leaves and small yellow flower
heads, with one to three short rays, or often none. Like many
other composites, it blooms as the rainy season nears its end, in
November and December. As soon as the weather turns dry, its
slender achenes, tipped with four barbed spikes, are ready to
cover our clothes as we walk through the plantation.

Another composite, *Synedrella nodiflora*, has two curiously
different achenes. The small heads of yellow florets nestle inconspicuously in the axils of this low herb that grows sparingly in
shady spots in the pasture. The four or five ray-florets produce flat
achenes margined by broad, hooklike projections. From the five
minute, yellow disk-florets arise much narrower achenes, crowned
by two or three straight spikes, which lack barbs and do not appear to be very effective in attaching the seeds to disseminators.
Although I could make them stick to the rough fabric of my trouser legs, they soon fell off as I walked—in strong contrast to the
tenaciously sticking barbed achenes of bur-marigolds. The hooklike projections that surround the flat achenes of the ray-florets of
*Synedrella* seem even less effective in attaching them to anything;
I could not learn their function.

Very different is the mode of attachment of the achenes of
*Pseudelephantopus spicatus*, a low, tough herb whose flower heads
are arranged on long, slender spikes. Each narrow head contains
four tightly clustered florets, whose lobes radiate outward from
the center of the tetrad, so that the whole head resembles a single flower with about twenty narrow, white petals. The flowers
open around nine o'clock on sunny mornings, and many are
closed again by two in the afternoon. The achenes that follow
them are tipped with bristles of two kinds. Those in the center
are straight, smooth, and of different lengths. At the sides are

Carpel of *Pavonia rosea* (left); Achene of *Bidens* ▶

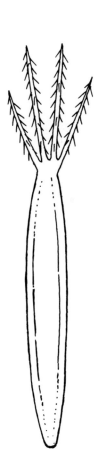

two longer, stouter bristles, which at the top bend sharply downward, then upward again, forming a double hook that directs the
hairs of animals, or the fibers of clothes, into the tight first bend,
where they are held so tenaciously that they carry the achene
until it is scraped or pulled away, often at a distance from the
parent plant. Beside the Río Tortuguero, on the opposite side
of Costa Rica from Los Cusingos, I found a dense stand of this
same species that had purple instead of white florets. The bristles
on the achenes were longer than those at Los Cusingos, with curious curls that seemed less effective in catching hold of hairs or
threads.

Another weed widespread in tropical America is *Pavonia
rosea*, of the mallow family, which sometimes becomes a shrub
four or five feet high and bears pretty pink flowers, clustered at
the ends of long peduncules. The mature fruit splits into five sections, or carpels, each containing a single seed. Crowning each
carpel are three long, stiff, strongly barbed spikes, which take
firm hold of fur or garments. It is instructive to compare this one-
seeded division of a fruit with the bur-marigold's one-seeded
achene, which botanically is a whole fruit.

Very abundant in shady places in our garden is a herb of the
Amaranth family called *Cyathula prostrata*. I considered it only a
pest, with nothing to compensate for its annoying habit of covering my trouser legs with tenaciously sticking little burs, until
careful study revealed it to be one of the most interesting of all
our weeds. It has thin green stems that sink down and root at the
nodes, and on their ascending ends, which become about two
feet high, bear pairs of thin, smooth, oval leaves, and floral
spikes up to ten inches long. Along the upper part of the slender
axis, the flowers are arranged in crowded clusters or glomerules.
Lower, these glomerules are more scattered, and below the lowest is a long, naked stalk. The minute green flowers, with no dis-
cernible odor or nectar, have five sepals, five stamens, and a
pistil that produces a single seed. When they open between 8:30

*Cyathula prostrata*: Inflorescences, Fertile Flower (right inset); Flower Trans-
formed into Bur. Both Greatly Enlarged ▶

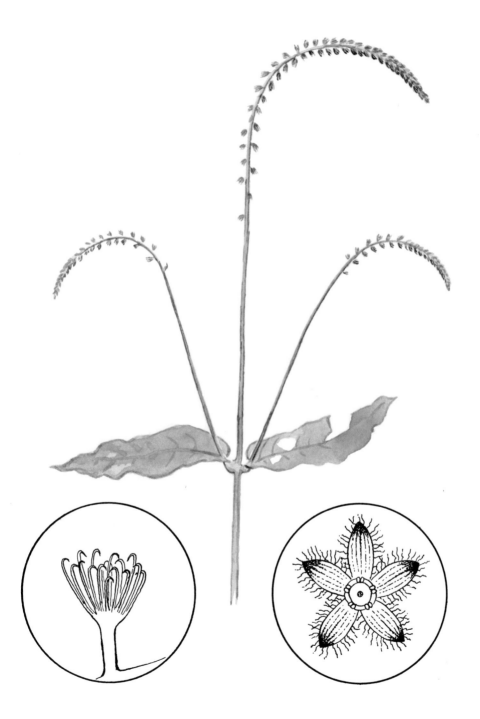

and 9:00 in the morning, they are visited by pollen-gathering *Trigona* bees, tiny beetles, and other small insects. Between 4:00 and 4:30 on clear afternoons, they close, never to open again.

Close scrutiny reveals that each flowering spike has two zones of open florets. The first, near the apex, is separated from the second by a band about half an inch wide where the flowers remain closed. The glomerules are arranged along the spike in irregular spirals, which may ascend either from left to right or from right to left. In the younger part of the inflorescence, each glomerule consists of only two florets. In each doublet, the first to open is on the side the ascending spiral first reaches; then, after an interval of several days, the other member of the pair opens in the second, more basal, zone of anthesis. If the spiral is dextrorse, ascending from left to right, each open flower in the first, or apical, zone is on the left side of its glomerule. In the second, basal, zone, each open flower is on the right side of its glomerule. If the spiral is sinistrorse, ascending from right to left, the first flower to open in the apical zone is on the right side of its pair, and the second, in the basal zone, is on the left.

When three flowers occur in a glomerule, the third usually develops and opens well after the other two, nearer the base of the spike, and at the side of the triad rather than in the center. Rarely, nearer the apex of the spike, a third flower arises between the first two.

In addition to two or three fertile florets, each glomerule finally contains two, or more often three or four, sterile flowers, each of which consists of a dozen or more little hooked bristles, with none of the usual floral parts. Since the hooks might impale pollinating insects, the sterile flowers develop later than the fertile ones, on the lower part of the spike, where no more fertile flowers open. One or two of these hooked structures stand beside each of the lateral florets of a triad. The fertile flowers set the seeds; the sterile flowers aid their dispersal by attaching the glomerules to the fur of quadrupeds or the clothing of humans. Among

*Salvia occidentalis*: Flowering Plant; Enlarged Single Flower with Glandular
Calyx (inset) ▶

the many plants that bear flowers of two or more kinds, the most usual differentiation is into male and female, or perfect and unisexual flowers. In certain other plants, including many compositions, some hydrangeas, and a number of species in the madder, or coffee, family, the flowers at the edge of an inflorescence are much more colorful than those in the center. Flowers so highly modified that their sole function is to disperse the seeds of closely associated flowers are far more rare, and make *Cyathula* unique among plants that I know.

In addition to plants that attach their fruits to animals by means of hooks, there are others that employ sticky glands for this purpose. One of these is *Salvia occidentalis*, a straggling herb whose slender stems, rooting where they lie along the ground, ascend at their ends to bear small, serrate, ovate leaves and flowers in clustered verticels on a long, leafless axis. The two-lipped blue flowers, with white streaks on the lower lip, are barely a quarter of an inch long. It is difficult to believe that this widespread tropical weed is closely related to the splendid Scarlet Sage of flower gardens. In sunshine the flowers open around eight o'clock in the morning, those in shade perhaps half an hour later. Among the insects that visit them, the largest I have seen, and apparently the most effective pollinators, are small *Trigona* bees, bigger than the flowers, from which they appear to take nectar instead of the pollen they busily collect at many other kinds of flowers. Early in the afternoon, corollas begin to drop from their calyces; by 4:30 P.M. most have fallen; but a few, which have probably not been fertilized, remain attached and open until evening. The little calyces are thickly covered with stalked glands, which stick them to clothing and doubtless also to the fur of animals. Each encloses one or, rarely, two seeds, the other members of the tetrad usual in the mint family having aborted.

Another plant that disperses its seeds by means of sticky glands is *Drymaria cordata*, a delicate, slender-stemmed starwort

*Drymaria cordata*: Flowering Shoot; Part of Glandular Pedicel Much Enlarged
(inset) ▶

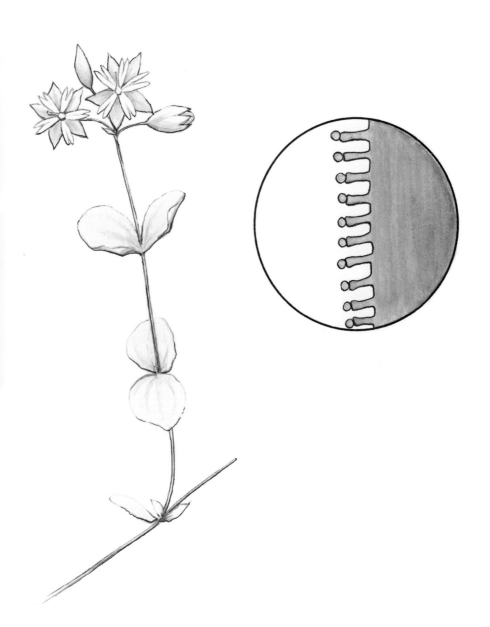

or chickweed with small round leaves and tiny flowers with five white petals, each so deeply cleft that there appear to be ten. They open around the middle of the morning and close at noon, or a little later, after about three hours of full anthesis. Instead of being on the calyx, as in *Salvia occidentalis*, the stalked glands densely cover the pedicel below it. When this sticks to a passing animal, it readily breaks away from the plant along with the seed pod, enclosed in green sepals. This starwort thrives in moist, shady spots, often close to houses. When Garden Thrushes gather mud for their nests in such spots, they sometimes include pieces of it, which, in rainy weather, root in the layer of mud in the nest's thick wall and send up leafy sprouts all around the sitting bird and her mottled blue eggs, forming an attractive aerial garden.

Different again in its method of dispersal is the *china*, *Impatiens sultani*, an ornamental introduced from the Old World that has become naturalized in tropical America, and flourishes beautifully on moist roadsides as well as around dwellings. Regarding it as a weed, fastidious gardeners expel it from their gardens; but its thick, fleshy stems often take root and thrive where they are cast away. Less difficult to please, we permit the exuberant *china* to brighten the shady sides of our house throughout the year with large flowers of varying shades of red, pink, and orange. At a touch, its turgid green pods explode like those of the touch-me-nots or jewelweeds of northern lands, shooting the seeds to a distance.

In pastures and along roadsides flourishes one of the most curious of all the weeds, *Cuphea carthagenensis*, a slender herb of the loosestrife family, rarely two feet high, with small elliptic leaves and six tiny purple or lavender petals attached around the edge of the green calyx. This calyx and the seed pod that it encloses split along the upper side to release five or six minute seeds. Each epidermal cell of the seed coat is almost filled with a coiled, hairlike ingrowth of its outer wall—a most unusual structure. These hairs appear to be strengthened by spiral thickenings

◀ *Cuphea carthagenensis*: Shoot with Flower and, at Bottom, an Open Pod

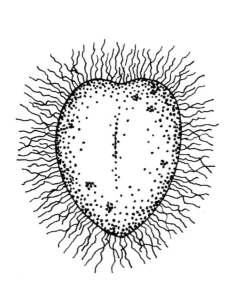

that are in fact corrugations of their thin walls. Placing a seed in water, through the microscope I watched the hairs emerge through the epidermis, turning, sleevelike, inside out as they elongated. After a night in water, the seed was so thickly surrounded by fine filaments, up to one millimeter (⅟₂₅ inch) long, that it appeared to be covered with mold.

Using high magnification, I watched the filaments continue to lengthen. The part of the hair that was already everted resembled a colorless fungal hypha without transverse walls, and the still infolded end of the hair was contained in this tube. The folds of this uneverted part were now much closer together and no longer appeared to be spiral; they resembled the folds of an accordion or camera bellows almost completely closed. As this infolded end of the hair slid forward in its transparent sheath, at the advancing edge I could see the folds straighten out as they passed from the included to the external part of the hair. I seemed to be watching a many-segmented annelid worm sliding out of a transparent tube. When I concentrated attention on the apex, I was reminded of the advancing pseudopod of an amoeba. After a filament reached its final length by turning completely inside out, its walls might be almost smooth or more or less strongly folded. Some filaments resembled long, spirally coiled springs— differences that I could not explain. The emergence of the hair from its cell, and its continued elongation, appears to be caused by the swelling of mucilage in the epidermal cell.

These amazing structures are, as far as I know, found only in the seed coats of certain species of *Cuphea*. In the way they emerge by turning inside out, they remind one of the nematocysts, or stinging hairs, of *Hydra* and sea anemones. Their function is obscure. Possibly they make the seed more readily transportable by water flowing over the ground in a heavy rainstorm. Or they may help the seed to germinate by absorbing water, like roothairs, which they resemble, although they develop in a very different way. I suspect that such filaments would be more useful

◄ *Cuphea carthagenensis:* Seed Surrounded by Everted Filaments; Part of Filament Greatly Enlarged

to species of *Cuphea*, like *utriculosa*, that flourish on rocks beside, or emergent from, swiftly flowing streams. They might an-
chor seeds that are borne downstream by the current. I have
been trying to find seeds of this streamside *Cuphea* to learn
whether they have similar structures.

The reader will have noticed that the flowers of nearly all the
weeds mentioned in this chapter have short lives, rarely as much
as a full day, sometimes of only a few hours. In *A Naturalist in
Costa Rica*, I gave examples of a number of other plants, some of
which spring up unbidden in our lawn and pastures, whose flowers are equally ephemeral. These simply constructed flowers,
which depend upon no specialized pollinators, stake their lives
on being promptly fertilized. In this they differ strikingly from
many orchids, which may remain open for weeks or months,
waiting for the proper pollinator to arrive, but wither promptly
after they have been fertilized.

The refined mind delights in contemplating the forms or con-
figurations of things, which are most diverse and loveliest in the
living world. The scientific mind is not satisfied until it can relate the forms of organic structures to their vital functions. Common weeds, no less than rare orchids, can yield the high satisfaction that we feel when we can explain symmetrical or curious
forms in terms of useful functions. I recall the exclamation of
pleasant surprise when I showed the two types of achenes of *Synedrella nodiflora* to my friend Rafael Lucas Rodríguez, professor of
botany at the University of Costa Rica, who painted most of
Costa Rica's thousand species of orchids before his untimely
death while I worked on this chapter. A most versatile man, he
delighted in forms and patterns so various as those of orchids,
weeds, and Scottish plaids.

# 15. Black-striped Sparrows

THE first bird that I heard this morning in early May, as on many another morning through long years, was the Black-striped Sparrow who roosts amid dense shrubbery in front of the house. In the dim light of early dawn, he began drowsily with subdued notes, alternately high and low. After several repetitions of this leisurely performance, he was sufficiently awake to greet the new day with his full song. Beginning slowly with notes of varying tone, he gradually increased his tempo until, with rising pitch, it became almost a trill. Its rhythm has been well compared to that of a ball bouncing to a halt, or that of steam escaping from the cylinders of an old-fashioned locomotive gaining speed. This charming performance, unique among bird songs that I have heard, was repeated with many variations as daylight waxed. Sometimes the sparrow continued much longer to repeat the distinctly spaced notes, omitting the final acceleration. Sometimes a brief prelude introduced a cascade of clear notes rising high. A delightful call to arise and be active!

Soon, when I threw out maize, the songster and his mate came hopping over the lawn to share the grains with chickens, White-fronted Doves, Rufous-naped Gray-chested Doves, and Agoutis. Beautiful in their clear shades of olive-green and gray, the two sparrows were so similar that I could not distinguish between them. About six and a half inches long, they had gray heads boldly marked with four black stripes, one along either

side of the crown and a narrower streak on either cheek, passing around the eye. The rest of their upper plumage was bright olive-green, and the bend of each wing was canary yellow, conspicuous when they flew. Their throats were dull white, their chests and sides light gray, and their abdomens white. Their thick bills were black, their eyes brown, and their legs and feet grayish flesh-color.

The sparrows picked up the larger grains of maize, too big and hard to be manageable, only to drop them promptly. They chose the smaller grains and spoiled ones disdained by the well-fed hens, which were more easily broken in their bills. Later, they flew up for the bananas or halved oranges that I daily place on the feeder. Or the pair would appear beneath the kitchen window, seeking grains of cooked rice or scraps of tortillas. Farther afield, they would eat the berries of melastomes and other shrubs, and the white arillate seeds of small *Lacistema* trees, escaping from red pods at no great height, but they would never ascend to lofty treetops to share the arils eagerly sought by a great variety of other birds. Much of their foraging would be done on the lawn, or beneath neighboring thickets, where amid fallen leaves they would find insects, spiders, and an occasional small lizard or tiny frog, all without scratching in the manner of Large-footed Finches and towhees.

Although these sparrows now hop over our open lawn with feet together, never walking with alternate steps, they were not always so confiding. Over a range extending from Honduras to Venezuela, Colombia, and the Pacific slope of Ecuador, Black-striped Sparrows are mostly shy inhabitants of low thickets that afford concealment and sites for their nests, but are not so dense that they lack open spots, grassy or bare, where the birds can forage on the ground. A neglected pasture, with a maze of cowpaths through lush vegetation not much more than head-high, is a favored habitat. They live also in weedy fields, plantations of coffee, sugarcane, pineapples, or bananas, and fields of maize, especially if these plantings are not too free of weeds. A few may lurk in the overgrown margins of rural roads, venturing forth into the roadway when traffic is absent. Although Black-striped Sparrows prefer humid regions where rain forest is the natural vegetation, I have not met them inside old forest or even heavier second growth. In Costa Rica I have occasionally found them as high as 5,600 feet above sea level, but at this altitude they were seen only in the milder weather from March to early August, when they evidently came up the mountainside from lower levels.

Never flocking, Black-striped Sparrows live throughout the year in pairs, which for months after a successful nesting are accompanied by their full-grown young. When a mated bird alights beside its partner after a brief separation, they greet each other with a rapid flow of queer, whining notes, delivered simultaneously with falling inflection. The greeting ceremony of birds that I heard in Ecuador sounded much the same as that of the sparrows around our house. This greeting song, if song it may be called, is given throughout the year, and, simple though it be, is the most elaborate utterance that I have heard from an undoubted female. To maintain contact when separated, members of a pair call back and forth with dull, nasal notes, deliberately repeated. A high, sharp whistle or squeal, usually given just once as a sparrow takes wing, may apprise the mate of its movements. The sparrows express alarm or apprehension by rapidly repeating their dull notes, which change to a rapid flow of hard, sharp notes as a potential enemy approaches their nest.

Although at dawn they may rise to the lower bough of a tree, Black-striped Sparrows usually sing inconspicuously amid low vegetation. At Los Cusingos they sing in every month, but most freely during their long nesting season from February to July or August. A hot, dry March, or continued gloomy weather in June, may decrease their singing without wholly silencing them. As I write this on a rainy afternoon, a sparrow among the wet shrubbery outside has continued to sing, mostly with slower tempo, rarely with the accelerated finale. Birds of many kinds sing most freely when they are separated from their mates or mateless; a Black-striped Sparrow in the garden, who long remained solitary after his partner was killed while incubating in May, was exceptionally songful throughout the remainder of the year.

More than any other bird in our garden, the sparrow sings at night. Often a single clear song rings out in the stillness preceding dawn, whether the night be dark or moonlit. After an interval, it may be followed by another solitary song; or many minutes may pass silently before the sparrow begins sustained singing at break of day. Sometimes, when I arise early to reach a distant nest before the birds become active at dawn, the alarm clock is answered by the song of the sparrow outside, also aroused by its bell. More rarely, he sings just once early in the night. These sparrows appear to sleep lightly. The only bird who has come to a light at Los Cusingos was a Black-striped Sparrow who, one dark night in June, flew through the open bedroom door and singed his feathers by flying over the kerosene lamp. Placed on a curtained shelf for safety, he passed a quiet night, and at dawn flew out through the doorway.

Although Black-striped Sparrows were not uncommon in the hills south of Lake Valencia in north-central Venezuela, they remained so well hidden amid dense thickets that nearly a month passed before I saw one. After the long drought was broken by showers toward the end of April, they exposed themselves more often and began to sing. They had such a varied repertoire of clear, cheerful verses, delivered in a rich, full voice, that I regarded them as the best songsters in the region. But I never heard from them anything that remotely resembled the accelerated song typical of Black-striped Sparrows a thousand miles away in Central America, which belong to a different race.

I have only once seen a Black-striped Sparrow engage in that puzzling activity, widespread among birds, called "anting." Although at higher latitudes this is usually performed on the ground, here in the tropics I have invariably seen it done in a tree or shrub; even a bird so terrestrial as the Black-striped Sparrow rose well above the ground to ant. Resting close beside a silken nest of Spinning Ants in the Rose-Apple tree beside the house, he repeatedly rubbed something along the inner sides of his slightly raised wings—the movement typical of anting. Since at that moment my binocular was not at hand, I could not detect in his bill the ants that I was sure he held.

Although Black-striped Sparrows are generally pacific birds, one was responsible for the most violent assault that I have witnessed at our usually peaceful feeder. While a sparrow stood there eating banana, a female Scarlet-rumped Tanager alighted on the board to take her share. Rushing at the tanager, the sparrow made her fly upward; then, continuing the attack, it darted up beneath her and struck her breast hard with its feet. Promptly separating, the two birds went different ways. In a moment, the tanager returned to the table, while the sparrow flew away. Possibly the attack was motivated by territorial exclusiveness, as soon afterward the sparrrow's nest was built almost beneath the feeder, which no bird tries to monopolize.

*Nesting*

Although once, near my cabin by the Río Buena Vista, I found a single nest with eggs in it at the end of January, Black-striped Sparrows in the valley of El General rarely start to build their bulky roofed nest until February or March. Seldom on the ground, most nests are placed low, in clumps of grass or weeds, bushes, and tangles of vines, more rarely in a pineapple plant or among the bases of bananas, sugarcanes, and other cultivated plants. In our garden, where the short grass offers few very low sites, nests have tended to be higher than amid thickets and weedy fields. Wherever it is placed, the bulky structure needs ample support. Ninety nests ranged in height from ground level to nine feet, but only sixteen were below six inches, and only fourteen above four feet. Eighteen were between six and twelve inches; the remaining forty-two nests were rather evenly distributed between one and four feet. The highest nest was nine feet up, in a dense tangle of the tall, canelike stems of the terrestrial orchid *Arundina graminifolia* beside my study. Another high nest was eight feet up, in a great clump of the golden-spray orchid *Oncidium* growing between the sprouts of a pollarded tree. The doorway faced up a steep slope, which diminished the distance that the sparrow had to rise to it. An equally high nest was also on a steep slope, in a wide, dense bush of *Thunbergia erecta*. A nest at six feet was in the crown of a tree fern standing in a pasture. Somewhat lower nests were on stiff fronds of the cycad beside my study door. A broad base sometimes tempts the sparrows to nest at exceptional heights.

I was familiar with the secretive Black-striped Sparrow for years before I succeeded in learning details of its behavior at the nest. Nests amid tangled growth sometimes faced a small open space, where my blind would be closer in front of the shy bird's doorway than she would tolerate; yet I could not move it farther back without so much clearing of vegetation that she would probably have deserted her eggs. Even when the site permitted me to set up the blind at a good distance and gradually advance it to within satisfactory range of the nest, the sparrow would persistently remain away. Only after they began to frequent our dooryard and share the feeder's bounty did some of them become confident enough to be watched at the nest. Before long they would build or attend their eggs close in front of the blind, which they might watch me erect while they sat in the nest. Sometimes I could watch them from a window or across the lawn without concealing myself. Other birds, too, became easier to study at their nests after they had for years enjoyed the food and protection that we give them.

After watching the construction of eight nests for a total of twenty-three and a third hours, during which four hundred and thirty billfuls of materials were brought to these nests, I concluded that all the effective building is done by the female sparrow. While she works, her mate loiters nearby, very rarely picking up a bit of material, which he may drop on the way to the nest, and almost as rarely taking food, which he eats if his toiling partner is not at the nest to receive it. She gathers her materials on or near the ground, and approaches the nest by hopping over it or flying low over obstructing vegetation. The pieces for the base are often so large and coarse that she cannot carry two of them in her bill; some are so heavy that they bear her to the ground when she tries to fly. Noticing her predilection for strips of monocotyledonous leaves, I tore large, dry leaves of the Caña de India into strips and placed them on the lawn, where a building female promptly found them and took them to her nest. At a later stage of construction, when the sparrow needs finer pieces for her nest's lining, she gathers a whole sheaf of them in her bill.

The sparrows build chiefly in the early morning, while dead leaves, moist from dew or the previous afternoon's rain, are still pliable. After eight or nine o'clock on a clear morning, when dead vegetation becomes dry and intractable, little work is done. However, I have thrice known nests to be started after the middle of the afternoon. On one of these occasions, only a few pieces were laid in place; but on another, the sparrow surprised me by her concentrated activity at this late hour. As sunshine broke through clouds after a mid-afternoon shower, I noticed her starting a nest in a thunbergia shrub at a corner of the house. After bringing fifty-five billfuls in one hour, she had a bulky foundation well concealed amid the bush's crowded stems. While she toiled, her mate hopped over the lawn, picking up grains of maize that the chickens had left. He sang far less than a migrating Swainson's Thrush in the surrounding trees.

Early next morning, in bright sunshine, the female resumed building with great energy, carrying sixty-seven billfuls to the nest in fifty-eight minutes. This intense activity seemed to tire her, for in the following hour she brought only twenty-two billfuls, building up the nest's rear wall to its full height and starting to extend the roof forward from it. After half-past eight, she did little until three o'clock in the afternoon, when, following a

brief shower, she resumed active building. On the second morning, when she was bringing finer materials for the lining, she came
to the nest much less often than on the first, but she worked hard
pulling fine rootlets from the ground. Before midday, the nest appeared to be finished, although a little more fine lining was added
that afternoon and on the third morning. This sparrow built during parts of four days, but by far the greater part of the work was
done in one late afternoon and two early mornings.

   This nest was built in mid-April. In May a nest was completed in two and a half days. More often, Black-striped Sparrows have spread building over five or six days; and early in the
season, in March, one worked at her nest for six or seven days.
One female spent two days on the foundation, walls, and roof of
her nest; on the third day, she mixed fine with coarse materials;
and on the fourth and fifth days she gathered fine pieces for the
lining. No other female has worked as rapidly as the one who
brought sixty-seven billfuls in fifty-eight minutes. The next most
active building that I have recorded was thirty-three trips with
material in an hour, and, for a shorter interval, twenty-three in
twenty-five minutes.

   The finished nest is a large, oven-shaped structure with a
wide, round doorway in the side. The thickness and complete-
ness of the roof varies greatly; in many nests it covers the whole
chamber and is compact enough to shed heavy rain; in others,
especially those built late in the season, a slight, loose roof may
extend over only the back of the nest, so that the opening faces
obliquely upward. However, some late nests are as well built as
early ones. At times the top of the nest is peaked rather than
domed; the high roof gives the doorway an oval shape, much
higher than wide. Occasionally a nest tilts over backward, until
the doorway faces the sky, and appears to have been built without a roof.

   The materials of the nest are usually coarse and include dead
leaves, grass blades, lengths of dry vines, tendrils, weed stems,
pieces of bracken fern, and roots—according to what the locality

affords. One nest was built on the ground in a banana plantation, amid grass and beside a large, dry banana leaf, several strips of which, still attached to the massive, prostrate midrib, had been pulled over the top, giving excellent concealment and protection from rain. The lining is of fine grass stems or fibers. The bulky, rather untidy nests often measure six or seven inches in diameter, with a chamber slightly over four inches high and three inches wide. The doorway, much larger than the sparrow needs to pass easily in and out, is about three inches in diameter.

One female laid her first egg on the morning following the completion of her nest. Others have rested for one to three and, rarely, four days before they laid. Black-striped Sparrows regularly deposit the first egg of a set before sunrise or soon afterward, usually between 5:30 and 7:00 A.M. Most females sleep over the single egg—I have known seven who did and only two who did not—and lay their second egg after an absence the following morning, usually between 7:00 and 8:30, rarely after 9:00. Thus, the interval between the laying of the first and second eggs is definitely more than twenty-four hours and sometimes as long as twenty-five or twenty-six. This schedule contrasts with that of the tanagers who nest in our garden and lay both of their eggs at nearly the same early hour.

In Costa Rica, and apparently also in Panama, Black-striped Sparrows nearly always lay two eggs. I have found eighty-three nests with this number of eggs or nestlings, and only one with three eggs. This nest, the first that I found in Costa Rica, evidently belonged to an exceptionally vigorous female, who was incubating this unusually large set at the extremely early date of February 14, 1936. When a bird nearly always lays two eggs, nests with a single egg or nestling must be regarded with caution, for one could have been lost. However, in three nests that I followed carefully during the interval of laying, I am confident that only one egg was deposited. Two of these nests replaced earlier nests from which eggs or nestlings had been lost. The other single egg was laid late in the breeding season, in July. The immaculate white eggs average 25.2 by 18.4 millimeters. Ninety-three sets of eggs in the valley of El General were laid as follows: January, one; February, five; March, seventeen; April, twenty-three; May, nineteen; June, fifteen; July, ten; August, two; October, one.

Only after Black-striped Sparrows began to live in the garden and eat at the feeder did they permit me to watch them incubate from the blind. As she built unaided, so the female warms her eggs with no help from her mate. For eleven hours I watched one who nested in a privet hedge, timing seven sessions on the eggs that ranged from 33 to 99 minutes and averaged 59.4 minutes. Her nine absences lasted from 12 to 25 minutes and averaged 19.4 minutes. She sat for 75 percent of the eleven hours. In the following year, I watched a nest that a female, probably the same individual, had built among the flowers of a Golden-trumpet bush on the front lawn. In twelve hours I timed seven completed sessions of 47 to 94 minutes, with an average of 70.3 minutes. Eight recesses ranged from 13 to 35 minutes and averaged 21.9 minutes. The sparrow incubated with a constancy of 76 percent. As described in *A Bird Watcher's Adventures in Tropical America* (1977), I studied this nest during the bloody revolution of 1948, when I was often interrupted by rumors that the mercenaries who roamed over the valley, plundering, burning, and killing, were approaching our neighborhood. Once I had watched this second female incubate continuously for two hours and five minutes when I was called away by one of these false alarms.

These sparrows sat in their nests facing outward. Each was fed on the nest by her mate once during my watches. When the first egg among the Golden-trumpet flowers was on the point of hatching, the male came with a small lizard and, finding his mate absent, swallowed his offering. When this female left her eggs during the first days of incubation, she usually turned sharply, to hop slowly and laboriously through the densely branched bush and emerge a minute later on the side behind the nest. Before her eggs hatched, she often neglected this precaution and went directly from her doorway, which faced the open lawn. Once clear of the bush, her first act was often to stretch her wings after her long confinement. After she had hopped or flown a short distance, she would give the sharp signal call for her mate. As soon as they met, often on the feeder, they joined their voices in greeting. After an excursion with her partner, and sometimes another visit to the banana on the nearby board, she returned to her nest inconspicuously by working her way through the dense bush that supported it. In the preceding year, too, the female often began and ended her recess by eating banana. Although in the mornings each male often escorted his mate when she returned to her nest, in the afternoons, like many other male birds, he was neglectful. Infrequently he chased a trespasser, such as a Buff-throated Saltator, from near the nest.

The shortest of seventeen incubation periods that I have determined could have been no more than thirteen days plus two hours, and no less than twelve days plus twenty hours. Usually the period is between thirteen and fourteen days; often it is a few hours more than fourteen days; and occasionally it is as long as fifteen days, in each case counting from the laying of the second egg to the hatching of the second nestling. This nestling often hatches six or more hours after the first, as a result of the female's sleeping on the first egg before she lays the second. She promptly eats the empty shells.

Newly hatched Black-striped Sparrows have pink skins, thinly shaded by tufts of gray down. Their eyes are tightly closed, and their mouths are red inside, with conspicuous yellow flanges at the corners. They develop rapidly, and their feathers begin to expand when they are six or seven days old. Three days later they are well covered, at least on the parts exposed while they lie in the nest, with olive-green plumage. At first their mother broods them about as constantly as she incubated the eggs, but each day she spends less time covering them until, after their feathers expand, she no longer warms them in the daytime. She sleeps with them until their last or next-to-last night in the nest. Their father never broods them, but, soon after they hatch, he brings food. If he finds his partner brooding, he passes it to her, and she may spend several minutes patiently coaxing a tiny nestling to take a large item difficult to swallow. As days pass and the mother broods less and feeds more often, the two parents frequently arrive together and stand side by side in the wide doorway delivering food, which they bring in their bills rather than in the throat or deeper regions, as many birds do. This consists chiefly of larval and winged insects, including grasshoppers. Tiny frogs vary the nestlings' diet, and a pink, caudate object that one gulped down with difficulty seemed to be a new-born mouse. Although the parents continue to eat banana at the feeder, they only rarely bring this or other fruit to nestlings.

Because while feeding nestlings their father rarely sang, it was difficult to learn how many times each parent brought food. Two nestlings a day or less old were fed eighteen times in five hours, at least nine times by their father, seven by their mother, and twice when I could not identify the feeder. Two nine-day-old nestlings were fed twenty-seven times in three hours. When ten to twelve days old, two nestlings received ninety-nine meals in eleven hours, which was at the same rate of 4.5 times per hour for each of them. Coming with food, the cautious parents hopped over the smooth lawn for a few or many yards to enter the Golden-trumpet bush behind the nest and pass inconspicuously through its crowded stems to the doorway. Leaving, they were less consistent, sometimes retracing their course through the midst of the bush and sometimes flying straight out from the front. When they carried away a white dropping, they usually chose the easier, more conspicuous route.

On the morning preceding the nestlings' departure from the Golden-trumpet bush, they were active and restless, preening a great deal. As they took their meals, they buzzed harshly, then often rose in the nest and stretched forward, revealing their streaked breasts while they looked in the direction taken by the departing parent. Three times, after being fed, a nestling jumped up on the doorsill only to promptly return inside. It appeared that they were about to leave; but after mid-morning they rested quietly in the nest, where I found them the following dawn. When a parent arrived with the day's first meal, a nestling hopped out in front of the nest, but returned promptly. One preened vigorously. A few minutes before sunrise, first one, then the other severed contact with the nest, while the parents were approaching with food but still distant. The adults did not try to induce the young birds to leave; their emergence appeared to be quite spontaneous, as is usually true of undisturbed nestlings.

When the parents arrived and found a fledgling at the edge of the bush, they promptly led it away by running over the lawn in front of it with short, rapid steps, wings and tail dragging, in a display similar to the "rodent run," of which I shall presently have more to say. The young sparrow followed hopping after them. When several well-grown pullets approached, their curiosity aroused by the excitement among the sparrows, the adults fluttered in the faces of the much bigger domestic fowls, first bewildering them, then making them turn and run away. Soon the fledgling gained the shelter of a neighboring bush, whereupon its parents flew up into a higher shrub and greeted each other with their queer notes.

The second fledgling lingered in the Golden-trumpet bush, calling at intervals with a sharp *tup*, until, accompanied by its parents, it hopped rapidly over the grass to a larger bush of the same kind, twenty-five feet away. When I left my blind and approached this bush, the parents protested with sharp, metallic notes that I had not previously noticed, and also with deeper calls. The older of these nestlings was then a few hours less than thirteen days of age; the younger, between twelve and twelve and a half days. In all, I have known ten nestlings to leave five nests when approximately eleven days old. Eleven left seven nests when twelve days old, and four left two nests when about fourteen days old. Usually they leave the nest in the morning, but one departed on a rainy afternoon.

Soon after leaving the nest in the Golden-trumpet bush on April 28, the two fledglings vanished, and for the next fortnight they remained so well hidden amid dense vegetation that I could not find them, although I knew they were alive because the parents continued to carry billfuls of banana to them. Not until May 13 did one of them expose itself where I could see it. Ten days later, their mother started another nest in a neighboring Golden-trumpet bush. While she built, a juvenile with a streaked breast twice came near the nest without being repelled by her, although its father chased it mildly. On this day, it ate the little black berries of a nearby tree of the melastome family, but was also fed by a parent. On May 30 their mother completed her new set of eggs, and on the following day, when it was forty-five or forty-six days old, I last saw a juvenile receive food from a parent.

By June 12, at the age of fifty-seven days, these young sparrows were visiting the feeder and helping themselves to banana. They appeared still to be exploring the edibility of the objects around them, for I saw them pick up fragments of wood, bark, and leaves, mandibulate them a little, then drop them. Two weeks later, I twice saw the two juveniles on the board together; each time, one drove away the other, who waited nearby until the first had finished his meal. The young sparrows also tried to chase birds of other kinds from the table, manifesting a degree of pugnacity unusual among the guests who eat there. Such churlish behavior often appears to result from feelings of insecurity on the exposed board.

By the end of June, these juveniles no longer accompanied their parents, who had lost their eggs from the second Golden-trumpet bush and, unknown to me, had built yet another nest in a more secluded situation. When I watched the parents attend this latest brood on July 6, the young hatched in April did not appear, but they continued to meet their parents on the feeder. A few days later, a parent chased one of them in front of the house. Although the juveniles continued to come to the board for banana for the next month, their visits became furtive as a result of much opposition from the parents, who were now carrying food to their latest offspring. I last saw the parents pursue the juveniles on August 8, when they were nearly four months old and had become difficult to distinguish from adults.

Like many other birds who leave low nests before they can fly well, Black-striped Sparrows appear always to stay well hidden amid low, dense vegetation for about two weeks after their departure, first becoming more active and visible when four weeks old. They begin to find some food for themselves when about six weeks old, but are dependent upon their parents for a while longer. Although I did not see the juveniles from the Golden-trumpet bush being fed after their forty-sixth day, other parents, more indulgent or less occupied with later broods, have continued to give at least an occasional meal to young two months old. Some parents become antagonistic to offspring little over two months old, but in other families adults and young remain amicably together for over half a year. A pair who raised only one fledgling permitted it to accompany them through much of December. Although it is unusual to see more than two Black-striped Sparrows together after the winter solstice, in the following February four, indistinguishable in their adult plumage, foraged together in the garden with no sign of antagonism. I wondered whether the parents were tolerating their previous year's offspring after it had found a mate.

When they appear after their fortnight of hiding, the month-old sparrows have fully expanded plumage conspicuously different from that of adults. Their upper parts are less greenish, more olive, and their head stripes are less prominent because they contrast less with the ground color. Instead of being clear light gray, their underparts are strongly tinged with pale olive, and on the breast are dark streaks that older individuals lack. At two months of age, the juveniles have noticeably begun to acquire adult plumage. The stripes begin to disappear from the breast, which loses its greenish cast as it becomes clear light gray. The molt of the dorsal plumage proceeds more slowly, so that three-month-old sparrows, with only a few lingering streaks below, are still dingy above, with head stripes less sharp and clear than they will become. When nearly four months old, juveniles have become difficult to distinguish from their parents. Those hatched late in the nesting season acquire full adult dress when about two weeks younger.

Like most other birds, especially those that nest on or near the ground, Black-striped Sparrows suffer heavy losses of eggs and nestlings. Of fifty-six nests that I found at all stages, only twenty-two, or 39.3 percent, yielded at least one fledgling. Since nests found with incubation well advanced, or with nestlings, are already a selected set, having escaped perils to which other nests have succumbed, one expects a rate of success higher than with nests kept under observation from the beginning. Nevertheless, of twenty-six of the above nests found no later than the laying of the second egg, eleven, or 42.3 percent, were successful. Probably the slightly more favorable outcome of these nests that were exposed to predation and other losses during a longer period of observation can be attributed to the fact that many were in the garden, which we try, not with brilliant success, to keep free of predators. In this smaller sample of nests, forty-seven eggs were laid, thirty-three hatched, and nineteen young fledged—70 percent of the eggs hatched, 40.4 percent of the eggs yielded fledged young.

Probably most nest failures are caused by snakes, which invade our garden, most frequently while birds are nesting, and have often been caught in the act of raiding the nests of other birds. The only predators that we have witnessed in flagrante delicto at the sparrows' nests are Cinnamon-bellied Squirrels and a Double-toothed Kite that snatched nestlings from the cycad beside my study. This surprised me, as I had watched a nest of this kite for many hours without seeing it bring anything but insects and an occasional lizard to its young. No matter what their principal diet, hawks, kites, and falcons appear capable of devouring nestlings that are readily available.

To compensate for their frequent failures to rear young, Black-striped Sparrows try repeatedly. One pair, whose nest among the Golden-trumpet flowers has received so much of our attention, built four nests in a season and raised young in the second and fourth. As far as I have seen, the sparrows always build a new nest for each brood, more or less distant from the preceding nest, whether this was successful or not. One female started to build a new nest only three days after she lost her eggs. In two cases, the interval between the loss of eggs and the start of laying in the new nest was nine and ten days. Three females resumed laying only eight days after they lost nestlings. On two occasions, twelve days intervened between the departure of nestlings at the usual age and the start of laying for another brood. Other intervals between a successful nesting and the resumption of laying have been much longer, up to sixty-four days; but I cannot exclude the possibility that in this long period the female built other nests that I failed to find.

Less concerned or less bold than many small birds, Black-striped Sparrows have nearly always prudently retired when I visited their nests, at most complaining with staccato notes from a safe distance. Perhaps, unlike many birds whose nests are low, they do not often try to lure me off with a distraction display because such displays are rarely given unless the bird has a suitable stage for them; and the nests of these sparrows are often situated amid dense vegetation, where the birds might become entangled, an easy prey for predators, if they acted as though disabled. However, when I approached a nest whose exceptionally high doorway faced the open lawn, the sparrow dropped to it and hopped slowly away in a hunched attitude, in a rudimentary distraction display. When I followed, she continued to lead me on.

Although a few cases of birds giving distraction displays in front of snakes have been recorded in print, in my experience small parent birds attack snakes much more often than they try to toll them away. On the only occasion when I saw a bird luring a snake, a Black-striped Sparrow, whose fledglings were evidently hiding nearby, was the chief actor. The sparrow ran or hopped over the ground with rapid, short movements, while a slender, brown ground snake, three or four feet long, followed it closely. After they had gone a few yards, the bird flew up to a perch and the serpent remained lying in the grass. I have never seen this kind of snake pillage a bird's nest, but I suspect that it does so at night.

While I sat at breakfast one morning in May, I looked through the window and saw a rat or large mouse emerge from a patch of high grass and chase a sparrow, who hopped rapidly away with the rodent galloping in pursuit. Only after the bird had led the rodent a good distance, keeping just beyond its reach, did the former take wing. Why the nocturnal animal pursued the sparrow in full daylight was an enigma to which I had no clue until some years later, when I watched a parent sparrow bring to its nestlings an object that appeared to be a baby mouse. Did the sparrow arouse the rodent's ire by trying to steal her young?

My best opportunity to observe the Black-striped Sparrow's lure display came when, from a blind, I watched a parent lead away a fledgling who was in an exposed situation just after leaving the nest. As already described, the parent ran over the lawn with short, rapid steps, wings and tail dragging, in what appeared to be a rudimentary example of the "rodent run" display that is best developed in shore birds who nest on the tundra, where Arctic Foxes prey heavily on their eggs and chicks, but is also employed by Australian wren-warblers and by Green-tailed Towhees in the western United States. One may wonder why a bird gives the same, or very similar, displays in front of potential enemies, such as a snake or a man, and its own fledglings. The element common to both situations appears to be "progeny in peril." In one case, the parent tries to lure the intruder from its eggs or young; in the other, it leads its fledglings from a dangerously exposed situation to the safety of cover. I have seen a Gray-striped Brush-Finch, which also forages on the ground, guide exposed fledglings to cover by a similar display.

For swifter predators, Black-striped Sparrows have a more adequate distraction display. In Puerto Limón's shady seaside park, I watched a pair of these sparrows with two full-grown juveniles with streaked breasts and a fledgling that had left its nest so recently that it could barely fly. Apparently, the absence of dense, tangled vegetation in this carefully groomed park was responsible for the fledgling's presence in the open at an age when it should have been in hiding. I wished to see whether the juveniles would feed the fledgling, who appeared to be their younger brother or sister; but, although all five kept close together, they gave it nothing. Presently a nursegirl and child came by, accompanied by a dog who, seeing the birds on the bare ground, rushed toward them. The fledgling was so far from cover that I was certain it would be in the dog's jaws before I could intervene, but a vigilant parent saved it. Instantly placing itself in front of the animal, it fluttered over the ground just ahead, luring it swiftly away from the helpless young bird. The dog was still vainly pursuing the parent when the young passed out of sight amid the shrubbery. Distraction displays, like nest building and many of birds' other activities, follow innate patterns; but to adapt these patterns successfully to all the varying circumstances of birds' lives requires something difficult to distinguish from judgment or intelligence.

As I finish this chapter on a rainy afternoon, the Black-striped Sparrow sings calmly in the garden. May he continue to do so through long years!

# 16. *Selfishness, Altruism, and Cooperation*

 DURING the last half-century, the study of evolution has become increasingly gene-oriented and mathematical. Evolutionists have considered in great detail the distribution of these bearers of heredity among organisms and their flow through populations. This concentration of attention upon genes rather than the creatures that bear them has led to exaggerated views of their importance, not in forming and regulating living bodies, which is undeniable, but in a wider philosophical sense. In the words of Richard Dawkins (1976), "they swarm in huge colonies, safe inside gigantic lumbering robots. . . . They are in you and me; they created us, body and mind; and their preservation is the ultimate rationale for our existence . . . we are their survival machines."

One can hardly read this for the first time without feeling shock, as though one had been struck or rudely insulted. One asks, Can it be true that I, with all my experiences and accomplishments, all my hopes and aspirations, exist only as a "throwaway" machine for the preservation and multiplication of these unseen bodies distributed throughout my tissues, of which I was wholly ignorant until I learned about them in biology class? Where does the value of existence lie, in the living, feeling animal or in its ultramicroscopic genes? Which came first, the genes or the bodies that bear them?

Dawkins's book seems to imply that genes preceded bodies in

the evolution of life, which is doubtful. The earliest living things, the eobionts, lacked nuclei and probably multiplied by simple fission, each blob of primitive protoplasm pinching itself in two and dividing its substance, including whatever organelles it may have had, equally between its daughter blobs. As organisms became larger, more complex, and more solid, multiplication by fission was no longer practicable; half of a man or any other vertebrate, or half of an insect, could hardly produce a whole man or insect. The alternative was to produce gametes or propagules, each of which contained, in extremely compact form, "directions" for the development of similar organisms. This was the indispensable condition for the evolution of all the more advanced plants and animals. Such directions are carried in the coils of DNA by the genes. The stages of this development, which occurred in the far distant past, can no longer be reconstructed; but it makes as much sense to say that bodies acquired genes as the prerequisite for reproducing as they became larger and more complex as to say that genes developed bodies for their own multiplication. Insofar as life has meaning and value, it certainly resides in the whole organism, not in its invisible genes.

These genes are declared to be "selfish," incapable of supporting any behavior that does not redound to their own multiplication. The uncritical perusal of the writings of sociobiologists such as Dawkins might leave the impression that genes are calculating little demons, scheming to multiply themselves, at whatever cost to other beings or even to the organism that bears them. Actually, they can be called selfish only metaphorically. As far as we can tell, they act blindly or mechanically, like other molecules; but, if they cause their bearers to survive and reproduce more than the bearers of other, more "altruistic," genes in the same population, they will eventually supplant the latter, all as automatically as, according to Gresham's Law, base coinage will drive from circulation intrinsically more valuable coinage of the same legal value. Therefore, the argument goes, all living

Arctic Loon with Spectacled Eider Ducklings ▶

things must be insuperably selfish; altruism, if it somehow arose, as by a mutation, could hardly persist.

This confronts advocates of the selfish gene with the problem of showing how acts that appear altruistic are not what they seem to be, while those who believe that altruism is not always an illusion need to explain how it could arise in the face of the obvious tendency of animals that devote all their resources to their own survival and reproduction to prevail in the population. An apparently altruistic form of behavior widespread in the animal kingdom is that of warning companions, who may include different species, of the approach of danger. Would not the bird who sounds the alarm when it spies a hawk have a better chance of escaping if it silently took cover, leaving unsuspecting companions to fall into the raptor's talons? It might thereby reduce the number of competitors for food, a mate, or nesting space. How can it fail to act in a way most likely to maximize the number of its own genes that are perpetuated? The supporters of the selfish-gene doctrine have devoted much ingenuity to suggesting ways by which, against all appearances, the seeming altruist in fact improves its own chances to survive and reproduce.

Selfishness, like altruism, is a psychic or moral quality that cannot be imputed to genes without attributing to them minds of their own. An animal may not know that its genes are impelling it to behave in a manner that will promote their own multiplication. It may even be moved by helpful or generous impulses. As mentioned in chapter 8, many young birds help their parents, or even less closely related adults, to feed and protect the nestlings and fledglings of the mated pair. We can point out certain advantages of this behavior: the young helper remains in relative safety on the parental domain instead of hazardously seeking one of its own; it gains experience that will make it a more competent parent in later years; in a stable population that rather fully occupies available habitat, its best chance of breeding may be to stay with its parents, whose territory it may eventually inherit. It thus works to the advantage of the young bird's genes. But the helpful bird need not be aware of this. He is probably as innocent of scheming calculation as the human child who helps his parents without thinking that he may some day inherit from them.

Or take the curious case of the cichlid fishes in Nicaragua's Lake Jilóa. Unlike the many fishes that lay their eggs and abandon them, cichlid parents guard their eggs and fry, sometimes nourishing them with secretions from their own skins. In this freshwater lake, each of a number of broods of the large, predatory *Cichlasoma dovii* was guarded by one or, rarely, two males of the smaller, herbivorous *Cichlasoma nicaraguense*, who drove away other fishes that would have swallowed the young *dovii*. Because they were helped by these unrelated adults, the parent *dovii* exerted themselves less strenuously to protect their progeny. The helpers were apparently individuals who could not obtain holes for breeding in the lake's rocky wall, or who had lost their own young.

Naturally, the diving biologist who discovered this extraordinary situation looked for some advantage that the voluntary helpers might derive from it, as evolutionary theory demands. The only possible advantage that occurred to him was most indirect. The recipients of this aid prey upon fishes who compete for breeding sites with *C. nicaraguense*. By helping to rear predators who would reduce the number of their competitors, the assistants and their kin might have more breeding sites and increase the number of their progeny (McKaye 1977). But are we to suppose that the helpful fishes had thought this out? They were satisfying thwarted parental impulses, and, if they acted consciously, may well have been motivated by altruistic feeling. Our genes do for or to us many things of which we are unaware. They may exploit an animal for their own multiplication without revealing this to it.

One of the corollaries of the selfish-gene doctrine is that organisms cannot act for the good of their species. At most, they can act to increase the fitness, or reproductive potential, of close relations who share many of their genes, as contemplated by the concept of kin selection. The index of relatedness employed by expositors of kin selection, based upon the probable distribution of rare genes rather than of whole genetic complements, may mislead the unwary who do not keep this limitation constantly in mind. Thus, it is asserted that full brothers and sisters will, on average, have half of their genes identical. It is true that the probability that a particular rare gene will be found in two siblings is one in two. Moreover, it is true that if male and female parents are completely heterozygous, without a single pair of shared identical genes, siblings that are not identical twins are not likely to have more than half of all their genes in common. However, it is probable that parents will be more or less homozygous, with pairs of identical genes, and that exact copies of many genes will occur in both of them, in which case the offspring are likely to share much more than half of their genes.

The method of calculating used by advocates of the selfish gene leads to more surprising results the farther they carry it from siblings. Thus they say, often without warning us that they refer only to rare genes, that the probability that a particular gene will be shared by third cousins is 1 in 128. Although this may be true of a rare gene, it can hardly be true of all the genes, rare and common, taken together, for identical copies of many genes must be widely diffused through an interbreeding population. An animal with whom I shared no more than 1 in 128 of my genes would probably not be human at all, possibly not even a primate. I surmise that I share more than 1 in 128 of my genes with my horse. Since each gene is held to govern the manufacture of a different protein, if we knew all the kinds of proteins present in two animals, we would have an accurate measure of their relatedness. Recent studies of blood proteins indicate that nearly 99 percent of human genes are identical with those of chimpanzees and gorillas (Pfeiffer 1980).

By focusing attention upon the differences, rather than the similarities, of the genetic complements of members of a species, certain evolutionists support their dogma that organisms cannot act for the good of the species. Perhaps the common genes, which must be in the majority, outweigh the "selfishness" of the rare ones and support behavior that helps those like themselves to multiply. Although rare genes may be the precursors of evolutionary change, the common, widely diffused genes of tested value perpetuate a species. The gene, or the animal that it controls, that does nothing for the benefit of its species is certainly behaving stupidly, for a gene can survive only in a species, never for long in an individual destined to die. Moreover, in organisms that reproduce sexually, the genes of any particular individual can be transmitted to posterity only in closest association with those of some other member of the species. What is reproduction if not for the good of the species, the indispensable means of its survival? While perpetuating its own genes in its progeny, the individual also helps to perpetuate its species.

Finally, the individual dies for its species. That an organism with the great capacity for self-renewal that many animals have should become senile and die is an enigma not easily solved. Of the many explanations of senescence that have been advanced, the most convincing is that it is genetically determined—programmed by the genes, as the final stage of a process that begins with the first cleavages of a fertilized ovum and continues through growth and maturity. Death from senility appears to have evolved by mutation and selection, like other characteristics of organisms, because without it evolution would be greatly impeded. Individuals have limited adaptability; only by means of a succession of slightly differing individuals can a lineage change enough to meet all the stresses of changing environments or to take advantage of new opportunities for expansion and perhaps progressive development.

The old make way for the new, until species are altered beyond recognition. However much its fossils may differ from any creature now alive, a species that has left living descendants is not really extinct, but simply altered. (In most cases, we do not know enough to distinguish between extinct species and altered species; but for the philosophical understanding of evolution, recognition of the difference is important.) *Tyrannosaurus rex*, the great carnivorous dinosaur, has evidently left no descendants and must be classed as extinct; but if *Homo erectus* is, in fact, ancestral to *Homo sapiens*, it is not an extinct but an altered species, which survives in us. The organism makes the supreme sacrifice for the benefit of its species; however much it may resist, it is compelled to do so by its genes.

Those who deny that the individual can act for the good of the species overlook the subtle interactions between competition and cooperation, one of the most pervasive aspects of the living world, to which we shall presently return. It is undeniable that individual organisms, with different genetic complements, compete with others of their kind for food, living space, and mates, and each may be regarded as trying to multiply its own genes at the expense of those of its neighbors. Such competition between genotypes may lead to evolutionary change. But evolution can occur only in populations, never in individuals; and unless the competing individuals also cooperate to perpetuate the species, it will vanish from the Earth.

Contributing to the survival of the species while multiplying one's own genes can hardly qualify as altruism, unless the care of dependent young, as in many of the more advanced animals, is regarded as an expression of altruism—it is undoubtedly the origin of much altruistic behavior. Accordingly, we still must ask how altruism can arise when, as is obvious, the genes most successful in multiplying themselves, by whatever means, will automatically prevail in a population. How can evolution avoid making all organisms consistently selfish?

In the first place, we should notice that the kinds of altruism contemplated by sociobiologists are often extreme. They consider in what circumstances the risk or sacrifice of an individual's life to save other individuals of the same species would be the kind of behavior that evolution might support. In what circumstances could a person imperil his own life to save another from drowning without jeopardizing the very gene(s) responsible for his altruism? This is presumably a rare gene, so that the probability that the drowning person bears it can be determined by the index of relatedness. For one's child, or a full brother or sister, the relatedness is one half. Accordingly, if one lost one's life while saving two of one's children, or two brothers, the frequency of the altruistic gene would probably not be reduced. If one perished while saving three such closely related individuals, the altruistic gene would probably be more abundant than if they had been left to drown. The risk involved in life-saving should not be omitted from the calculus. When the risk is slight, one might rescue a distantly related person, or even a stranger; when the risk is great, or death certain, an individual mindful of his genes would incur it only to save his children or his brothers— not even his wife, who, if not otherwise related to him, is unlikely to bear the same rare gene. Needless to say, in an emergency no one sits down to make such a calculation before he acts.

Natural selection sets limits to self-sacrifice, even by parents for their offspring. If, without continued care by their parents, the offspring would perish, natural selection will tend to eliminate such extreme parental devotion, and the parents will be innately inhibited from taking great risks. Thus, among birds, whose nestlings will die without parental care, the adults, however agitated they may become when their nests are, or appear to be, endangered, seldom jeopardize their lives by boldly confronting an animal able to destroy them. Occasionally, however, parental zeal overcomes prudence; birds hardly larger than a sparrow have pecked the hand that I placed upon their nests; and I have watched them attack snakes that could swallow them whole. Such imprudent behavior is understandably rare among all animals whose young are dependent upon a single parent, or at most a pair. Among more social animals, whose progeny have many potential attendants, the situation is different. When honeybees and certain large wasps attack, their barbed stings remain so firmly embedded in the victim's flesh that they pull out the departing insect's viscera. Nevertheless, the loss of a few such self-sacrificing defenders need not jeopardize a populous hive or vespiary. Males in troops of baboons and herds of horned grazers often defend their young by confronting a powerful enemy.

The altruism chiefly considered by sociobiologists entails the reduction of an individual's ability to leave progeny—technically, its fitness—in order to increase the fitness of another individual. Loss of life, as by sacrificing it to save another, is obviously total loss of fitness. Fitness might be reduced by sharing scarce food, by relinquishing an opportunity to mate, or by helping to rear offspring not one's own. According to the principle of kin selection, such sacrifice of fitness is likely to persist in a natural population only when the beneficiaries are so closely related to the self-sacrificing one that the genes responsible for such abnegation are thereby increased, or at least not diminished. Birds who postpone breeding for a year or more while they help a nesting pair usually, but by no means always, attend their younger siblings, so that cooperative breeding is compatible with the principle of kin selection. Hardly reconcilable with this principle is the deliberate sacrifice of fitness by human couples who refrain from begetting all the children that they would like, in order to preserve a world in which future parents could have two or three children, instead of the single one that is now approved by the government of overcrowded China. To suppose that all people who remain childless are influenced by such generous motives would, of course, be to overestimate human altruism. Many may remain childless simply because they are too selfish or lazy to undertake the burdens and reap the rewards of raising children.

When we survey all the evidence, it appears that genes for altruism that reaches beyond close kin exist only precariously in natural populations. How, then, can we account for the helpfulness to unrelated members of the same species, and even to animals of different species, that we frequently witness not only among humans but among nonhuman animals? We must, I believe, attribute such altruism to minds not minutely controlled by the genes—to free mental activity, which permits animals to extend cherishing behavior beyond their own dependent young, for which it originally evolved, and which, at the higher levels, generates sympathy, compassion, and similar sentiments. Although genes govern the development and functioning of brains, they must in many cases, for their own survival, allow some freedom of choice to the minds these brains support. For example, the kind of site in which a bird builds its nest is, in a general way, determined by its heredity. But if the site were too minutely prescribed by the genes, the bird might squander precious time seeking what it cannot find. For efficiency, the bird should be able to choose, among the great variety of sites most localities afford, that which most closely approximates the hereditary type; and we do indeed find, in the same species in the same locality, a considerable variety of nest sites. The more mind develops and intelligence increases, the greater its liberation from strict genetic control—liberation that reaches its maximum in man. Such freedom might be regarded as a concession to their subjects by those invisible despots, the genes that, without consulting our wishes, shape our bodies and determine the quality of our minds.

An example of altruistic behavior that is obviously not programmed by the genes is the care of unrelated young by adult birds and mammals. I refer not to the cooperative breeding widespread among permanently resident birds of warm lands, but to the occasional feeding or guiding by breeding adults of young not their own. Sometimes a bird attends nestlings in a neighboring nest of its own species, perhaps against the actual parents' opposition. More frequently reported, probably because more obvious to casual observation, are instances of a bird of one species assiduously attending young of a different species. Among the many recorded instances are those of a House Sparrow feeding fledgling Eastern Kingbirds, a male Cardinal nourishing fledgling American Robins, a pair of Mountain Chickadees attending nestling Williamson's Sapsuckers, and a female Eastern Phoebe bringing food to nestling Tree Swallows. A pair of Arctic Loons adopted five Spectacled Eider ducklings, guiding them, carrying them on their backs, and feeding them from their bills, as loons feed their own young but ducks do not (Abraham 1978). Ducks, grouse, and shorebirds admit strayed or orphaned young into the broods they guide and protect, where the downy ducklings or chicks can safely search for their own food. These are only a few examples of the many avian helpers and foster parents that have been reported (Skutch 1976).

One does not often find interspecific helpers; in many years of bird watching, I have noticed only three, a female Tropical Gnatcatcher who for two weeks fed and brooded two nestling Golden-masked Tanagers, a male Blue Honeycreeper who repeatedly gave food to a much larger young Scarlet-rumped Tanager, and a female Blue Honeycreeper who fed a fledgling Yellow-green Vireo. Nevertheless, in view of the number of cases that are continually reported in the ornithological literature, and the extremely small proportion of the activities of all the birds that are witnessed by people who record them, I surmise that every species of small altricial birds has from time to time fed young of every other species of rather similar habits with which it associates over a wide range. From fishes to man, individuals without dependent offspring satisfy their parental impulses by feeding and protecting young creatures not their own.

Often the avian helper is a parent who has lost its own brood, or who has reared its young to independence without exhausting its parental impulse. Sometimes it appears simply unable to resist the appeal of the nestlings' gaping mouths or their pleading cries. The propinquity of two nests of different species may lead parents to feed their neighbor's brood. A bird that builds an open nest may attend alien nestlings in a hole or box; or one may place food into gaping mouths that display a bright color different from that of its own nestlings. That the mouth which receives the food need not closely resemble that of the feeder's young is at-

Male Blue Honeycreeper (left) and Young Scarlet-rumped Tanager ▶

tested by the strange, well-authenticated case of a Cardinal who repeatedly fed seven goldfishes in a pond (Lemmons 1956). These cases of interspecific helpers reveal the ability to recognize similarities despite striking differences, and to engage in helpful activities that are certainly not narrowly dictated by selfish genes. Whatever the motivation of these feathered helpers, their behavior is altruistic objectively—which is the only criterion we can apply to the conduct of nonhuman animals whose minds are closed to us.

A shocking example of the horrors that selfish genes can instigate is provided by the male Langur Monkey who murders all the infants in a harem he wrests from another male, so that the females will sooner become pregnant with his own progeny. Similar infanticide has been reported of lions (Wilson 1975). The lawgiver Moses, as recorded in Numbers 31, also demonstrated how selfish genes operate when, after proclaiming "Thou shalt not kill," he commanded his Israelites to slay all male children and all pregnant females of the defeated Midianites, preserving only the virgins for breeding. From these revolting examples of selfishness, it is pleasant to turn to the birds who, when they replace a lost parent, help the surviving parent to raise a brood of their stepchildren. The replacement of one parent by another of the same species and sex is likely to be overlooked without close watching of marked birds. Nevertheless, fostering of nestlings, and sometimes also of fledglings, by stepfathers has been reported of the Yellow-bellied Sapsucker, Williamson's Sapsucker, Eastern Bluebird, Prairie Warbler, and Dark-eyed Junco. This is not unexpected when one recalls that birds frequently help mated pairs to feed young of the same or different species (Kilham 1977, Crockett and Hansley 1977, Pinkowsky 1978, Nolan 1978, Allan 1979).

When we remember the altruistic behavior of helpers and foster parents, which often entails strenuous exertion and may involve considerable risk (a male Yellow-bellied Sapsucker who replaced a father killed by a raccoon promptly met the same fate), the prevalence of the alarm signals to which we earlier referred will hardly surprise us. With a negligible expenditure of energy, and probably no added risk to itself, the alarm-giver may save companions who include close relatives, as well as birds or quadrupeds of other species that may be within hearing or sight. On another occasion, it may benefit from the warning cry of a companion. Selfishness carried to the extreme of withholding a substantial service so cheaply given would probably be self-defeating. The strained attempt to show how the alarm-giver might directly increase its chances of escaping predation seems wasted ingenuity, when it is so obvious how it benefits indirectly by moving amid associates who are also vigilant and quick to warn of danger. A principal advantage of joining the flocks of mixed species of small birds that wander through the woods of all lands is that the many watchful eyes and voices ready to sound the alarm when a predator approaches more than compensate for the conspicuousness of these loquacious companies.

Altruism need not be self-sacrificing, and some of its most precious manifestations, in man and other animals, result in gain rather than loss to the altruist. Altruism has much in common with the more spontaneous forms of artistic creation and with play, especially the latter. All are outlets for energy or other resources that an animal may have in excess of its needs for survival and reproduction. These activities yield satisfaction or enjoyment to the individual who engages in them, and may benefit it in ways that are neither foreseen nor calculated. Play develops muscles and coordination and may improve social relations. Drawing, painting, singing, decorating one's possessions are wholesome outlets for energy that might otherwise find mischievous expression. Similarly with altruism, which among humans is often the dedication of spare time or energy to activities that not only help others but bring the altruist satisfying social contacts, enlightening experiences, and a gratifying feeling of being benevolent and useful. Often, too, the large-scale altruism called philanthropy is a means of unloading excess wealth, which selfish people too often use to their own detriment. However, altruism need be neither exacting nor conspicuous. A few words of encouragement, comfort, or sympathy may be as altruistic as material aid, and in certain situations more helpful. Beauty, which uplifts the beholder's spirit with no cost to the beautiful creature, might be regarded as unconscious altruism.

Correspondingly, the bird or other animal who helps to rear another's offspring appears to apply its excess energy to a satisfying activity. A bird that is sexually immature or without a breeding territory, but well able to find more food than it needs, gives the excess to its younger siblings, or sometimes to unrelated nestlings or fledglings. In so doing, it gains experience that will later enable it to breed more successfully, lives in greater safety among vigilant companions, and probably finds its activites pleasant. A parent who has lost its brood, or has raised its young to independence without exhausting its parental impulses, satisfies them by attending a neighbor's young. The urge to feed others, upon which the survival of most avian species depends, has become so strong that it often impels birds to offer food persistently where it is neither needed nor wanted. Juvenile apes and monkeys fondle infants not their own, as little girls play with dolls, and thereby become more closely associated with the infants' mothers. Heifers lick and groom calves that they could not bear, and such "aunting" appears to be widespread among the more social mammals. Helpfulness, or altruism, should offer no more difficulty to evolutionary theory than play or artistic creation. It is probably no coincidence that dolphins, who are among the most playful of mammals, are among the more altruistic, supporting newborn young and injured companions so that they may breathe air, and even coming to the aid of human swimmers in distress. Possibly they take a quasi-parental interest in swimming bipeds, so much less secure in the water than they are.

Most admired, because most spectacular or "heroic," and because approved by religions, are the manifestations of altruism that involve grave personal risk, or the sacrifice of life, limb, wealth, comfort, or biological fitness. As I earlier pointed out, natural selection sets limits to sacrifice in all except the most highly social animals, such as bees, wasps, ants, and termites; nothing could be more futile than for a parent to lose its life, or to be severely maimed, defending young who without its constant ministrations would surely die. Even among men, extreme self-sacrifice is often ethically indefensible, and a sacrificial morality leads to paradoxical situations.

If, in circumstances where food is critically short, as in a lifeboat on the high seas, one person starves himself so that another may live, the altruist is probably of greater moral stature than the beneficiary, so that, unless he is much older, his death would be a greater loss to society. The poor swimmer who jumps into deep water to save a drowning person takes a foolish risk; his loss may bring sorrow and hardship to those who love or depend upon him. To deny oneself desired children because the Earth is becoming perilously overcrowded—a sacrifice of biological fitness—is, in present circumstances, misspent altruism, because others less worthy to become parents practice no such restraint. Voluntary limitation of parenthood may lead to racial deterioration, in consequence of the greater fecundity of the least intelligent and responsible; the population problem can be solved only by legal control. If to give is more blessed than to receive, the truly altruistic person should be the recipient rather than the giver, for thereby he enables the latter to achieve blessedness. If almsgiving confers sanctity, the best society might be one with great economic inequalities, so that many might win the merit of beneficence, perhaps credited to them in heaven. The proper beneficiaries of altruism, if parental care can rightly be so called, are dependent young of all kinds. It is more enlightening to view the devoted parent as passing on to his offspring a debt that he incurred to those who gave him life and that he cannot directly repay.

In an ideal society, universal friendly cooperation would prevail, but material charity would be rare. Cooperation and reci-

procity promote self-respect, good will, and equality; almsgiving
fosters feelings of inadequacy and dependence, and is as likely to
generate envy as gratitude. Nature provides many examples of
cooperation among organisms of the same or different species,
but few that resemble almsgiving. Among simple organisms, including corals, sponges, bryozoa, and myxomycetes, or slime
molds, many individuals unite to form a colony that often ex-
hibits considerable complexity of structure and specialization of
functions. Among more advanced animals, the most widespread
and closely coordinated cooperation is that between a male and
female parent in the rearing of young, which is the prevailing
system among birds, less common among mammals, cold-blooded
vertebrates, and invertebrate animals. In cooperative breeding,
of which fresh examples are yearly discovered among tropical and
subtropical birds, cooperation becomes more inclusive. Such cooperation, by complete individuals, each of whom could live and
rear young with only a single partner of the opposite sex, differs
profoundly from the more complex cooperation widespread in
insect societies composed of different castes, each composed of
individuals so incomplete that they could neither live nor reproduce alone. Fully to explore cooperation among animals and
plants would require volumes.

Cooperation and competition frequently coexist and interact
in subtle ways, as is nowhere more evident than in human society. People who cooperate to establish and preserve a society
compete incessantly for status and wealth, which apart from the
society would mean little. Similarly, mammals and birds who
find certain advantages in living in herds or flocks compete for
high rank in a hierarchy, or "peck order," and the benefits this
brings. In a flourishing tropical forest, trees of many kinds cooperate to maintain a habitat in which they thrive, while with silent persistence they compete for space in the sunlit canopy.
Male birds that gather in courtship assemblies, or leks, including
manakins, hummingbirds, grouse, and Ruffs, cooperate in attracting females to a traditional locality, while they vie for the

privilege of mating with these females, whose choice is uncompelled. Throughout the living world, individuals cooperate to perpetuate their species while they compete to multiply in the species any special genes that they may have.

Failure to appreciate the intimate relations between cooperation and competition is responsible for the one-sided theories, the narrow views, the hard alternatives that biologists too frequently propose to us. In its infinite diversity and complication, nature blends opposites in ways that confuse us. While evolutionists argue vehemently whether natural selection operates upon individuals or upon groups, it does both simultaneously, as is clear from the differential survival of individuals and the extinction of populations or whole species no longer well adapted to changing environments. While they deny that individuals can act for the good of the species, individuals continue to perpetuate their species while multiplying their own genes. While they proclaim that genes are inevitably selfish, the bearers of these genes perform acts of altruism. While they dogmatically assert that, simply by the logic of numbers, all species must reproduce as rapidly as they can, there are many instances of restrained reproduction. From lichens, in which fungi and algae unite in a symbiotic association that can flourish where neither alga nor fungus could thrive alone, to birds that build nests with many chambers for many pairs, and men who cooperate in the most diverse ways, fertile cooperation pervades the living world. As life ascends to higher levels and minds escape strict control by genes, the capacity for cooperation and altruism increases, but unhappily not without a concomitant capacity for hatred and destruction. To make the whole Earth a single harmoniously cooperating community of the most diverse creatures, devoid of enmity and violence, would be evolution's finest achievement.

# 17. *The Naturalist's Progress*

PROBABLY most people who take more than a casual interest in nature began their careers as collectors. Delighted by the beautiful or strange objects on which their eyes fell as they wandered through woodland and meadow, they wished to clutch and retain them. A glittering pebble, a colorful molted feather, a brilliant flower, or a curious shell has started many a boy and girl along the naturalist's long road. Desire to possess shining objects is not peculiar to mankind; a number of birds, especially bowerbirds and members of the crow family, display it in high degree.

At this earliest stage of collecting, as among crows, jays, children, and even certain adults, little attention is paid to the wholeness of a specimen. It is not as an example of a certain class of natural productions but as a brilliant or unusual trinket that the attractive object is acquired. In the forested parts of tropical America, one often sees the bright yellow breast of a toucan, or its huge and colorful bill, cut from the bird and stuck up as an ornament on the wall of a rustic cabin. The first skins of birds of paradise to reach Europe were prepared without legs by the natives of New Guinea, who evidently thought that the whole value of the specimen lay in the gorgeous plumage, from whose beauty the quite commonplace avian legs and feet only detracted. This naïve attitude was responsible for the name Linnaeus gave to one of these mutilated specimens of a brilliant bird, which, by the rules of zoological nomenclature, it still bears, *Paradisea apoda*, "the footless bird of paradise." Similarly, when children and amateurs collect flowering herbs, they preserve only the blossoms, with perhaps a bit of stem and a few leaves, neglecting the roots, which add nothing to the beauty of their specimens, although they tell the botanist much about the plant's mode of growth.

With those who become earnest naturalists, this kind of collecting is a transient phase, leading to a more mature interest in natural objects as wholes, all of whose parts are significant. If collecting is long and strenuously pursued, so many specimens accumulate that some system for arranging them becomes imperative. This brings us to the second stage in the naturalist's progress, the effort to classify the productions of nature. To do this intelligently, one must pay attention to the structure of the objects to be classified; the more detailed and intimate our knowledge of their structure, the sounder our system of classification will become. It is also helpful to trace the development of the animals or plants in question, for often a study of their earlier stages reveals relationships that are masked when they mature. Investigation of the functioning of the organism, its chemical constitution, and its behavior also contributes greatly to understanding its relationship. Thus anatomy, histology, embryology, physiology, biochemistry, and ethology are pressed into the service of taxonomy, or the science of classification. Many researches in these fields have been instigated by the desire to improve or substantiate a scheme of classification.

As the naturalist continues his long journey through the vast and infinitely varied realm of nature, he becomes increasingly curious about the reasons for the endless array of forms, colors, and habits that it presents to him. No longer content with admiring, possessing, or even classifying the productions of nature, he wishes to account for them; and this brings him to the third stage in his progress, the search for explanations in terms of causal factors or of utility. Every child and savage can see that the toucan's bill is extraordinarily large and brilliantly colored, but what is its

significance? How does this bird of the tropical forests happen to have a beak so much bigger and more conspicuous than those of its neighbors of whatever size? How does it help him to fill his vital needs? Or is it actually a hindrance to the bird, an evolutionary freak that natural selection somehow failed to eliminate?

By what course, in response to what needs, and by the action of what agents of selection did the birds of paradise acquire their gorgeous plumage? And from asking these questions in respect of some of the more striking of the colors and structures of organisms, we proceed to ask them about those that are less obtrusive. We may wish to know the function of a little hook on the tip of a small bird's bill, or of certain curious outgrowths on the legs of a bee, or why a certain moth's wings are mottled with shades of gray rather than being as brilliant as the wings of some other moths. The attempt to answer a few of these multitudinous questions may occupy us agreeably for years and exercise our intelligence to its limits.

In making his collection, or trying to answer some of the questions that occur to him, the naturalist commonly treats living things as though they had no will or purpose of their own; and often he deals with them as though they were wholly devoid of feeling. But occasionally a more sensitive and thoughtful naturalist stops to wonder about the inner life of the creatures he studies. How do *they* look upon the world? What feelings or thoughts might they have? Do they observe us while we watch them? He may be led to such questionings at an early age by a sort of natural sympathy, or he may be more tardily brought to them by some of the investigations he has been pursuing.

Thus, the most probable explanation of the origin of the bright colors and ornamental plumes of birds of paradise and many other beautiful animals of diverse orders is that they were acquired by the process known as sexual selection. If the females of any species mated with slightly more brilliant males in preference to duller ones, this should lead, in the course of genera

◄ Naturalist and Scarlet Macaws

tions, to their ever greater beauty and grace. But this explanation makes certain assumptions about the psychic life of the animals in question, for it attributes to them aesthetic responses or something quite similar, and it thereby introduces us to that vast, unexplored realm, the inner life of nonhuman creatures. The effort to enter this realm, whether by the bold exercise of imaginative sympathy or by groping analysis, constitutes the fourth stage in the naturalist's progress.

When the naturalist who began his career by regarding nonhuman creatures as hardly more than potential specimens begins to suspect that they may have feelings and thoughts, volitions and purposes of their own, he has reached, by a long, circuitous path, the attitude of every untutored child and primitive man, who never doubts that animals of all kinds, and perhaps even trees and other plants, enjoy an inner life not greatly different from his own. And when he reflects that his acts may affect their happiness, bringing them pleasure or pain, joy or sorrow, the morally mature man, be he a naturalist or otherwise, begins to ask how he should govern his dealings with them. How should he conduct his life in order to bring the minimum of pain, or the maximum of contentment, to these other sentient lives that encompass him? He desires ethical guidance, a code of morals that will regulate his relations, not merely with other members of his own society or of his own species, but with all beings that may somehow be benefited or harmed by his acts.

Obviously, moral problems, often perplexing enough even within the narrow context of human society, become vastly more complicated when extended to cover the whole living community. Nevertheless, no thoughtful and compassionate person can contemplate man's relations with the rest of the living world without ardently desiring their improvement, and perhaps detecting a number of ways in which this might be done. This desire to be moral in our dealings with all living things, this searching for ethical principles to regulate our treatment of them, marks the fifth stage in the naturalist's progress; it follows di-

rectly, almost inevitably, from the fourth stage, in which the naturalist begins to wonder about the quality of consciousness in the
animals he observes. Certain other cultures reached this point
millennia ago, by a route very different from that we have traced;
but Western civilization, with its own peculiar background, seems
most likely to attain it by the roundabout path of the naturalist.

Of the many who take the first steps along the naturalist's
long road, only a few persevere until they arrive at the fifth stage.
Even fewer reach the sixth, which we enter when we ask: "What
is the significance to me of this so varied world in which I find
myself?" This, of course, is the supreme question that religion
and philosophy have long tried to answer, each in its own manner; hence it cannot be regarded as one peculiar to the naturalist. But it seems to acquire greater breadth and depth when one
reaches it along the route of the naturalist, who was first attracted
by the beauty and strangeness of nature's productions; who laboriously collected and tried to classify them; who endeavored to
explain the function and mode of origin of some of them; who
speculated about the inner life of the creatures that display such
a vast variety of forms and colors; who thence became concerned
about his treatment of them as affecting their own welfare.

Far more than the philosopher whose days have been passed
in academic cloisters, far more than the mystic who has striven
to reach the Godhead by averting his gaze from the world around
him and sinking into the inmost depths of his own being, the
student of nature is aware of the endless diversity of creation, of
the intricate interactions among its myriad forms, of the startling
contrasts between supreme beauty and appalling ugliness, between tender love and violent rage, between beneficent growth
and destructive fury, that this baffling world presents. He wishes
to know for what purpose, if any, he has been thrust into its
midst, what ultimate significance is to be found in his presence
here, to what end the whole vast, confusing pageant is moving.
This last question seems to include in its wide scope the answers
to some of the earlier questions, so that if we could answer it con-

vincingly, we might also know the answers to them. If, for example, one were sure of the significance of one's own life, one could better understand life's meaning for other creatures.

These final questions evidently carry us far beyond the "scientific" study of nature. We often forget that science is the deliberate effort to solve certain limited problems by limited means. The scientist investigates the phenomena manifest to his five external senses, with or without the aid of instruments that report to them; he has decided to employ in his researches only the data these senses yield to him. In the attempt to understand the relations between these phenomena, this has proved to be an efficient method; the scientist's success in his self-appointed task proves the wisdom of the limitations he has imposed upon himself. Nevertheless, these same limitations have placed vast segments of reality beyond reach of the scientific method. No one is more poignantly aware of this than the naturalist who follows his chosen path as far as it can take him.

# 18.  *Windows of the Mind*

I count myself fortunate to have lived most of my life where balmy air and paucity of pestilent insects have made window glass and metallic screens superfluous. When we throw open our wooden shutters before sunrise, nothing separates us from the outer air. Gentle breezes, the fragrance of flowers in the garden or the neighboring forest, butterflies and airborne seeds drift in through the windows unimpeded. Through them the loveliness of plants and the grandeur of distant mountains greet our eyes, unmarred by anything ugly or sordid.

Unless the windows of our minds are also open, the windows of our houses may admit air and daylight but little to nourish the spirit. I often wish that the windows of my mind were as transparent as the glassless window through which I look. Much that enters through the window fails to enter my mind, because my senses, on which I am wholly dependent for verifiable knowledge of the surrounding world, do not report it. In the cases of a wide range of electromagnetic waves and of magnetic fields, I can prove this by turning on a radio or looking at a compass—indeed, even when I close all windows and doors with solid wood, I cannot exclude them. I have little doubt that I am surrounded by other radiations, emanations, or influences whose presence I cannot demonstrate. Our increasingly subtle technology has not yet provided instruments that translate them into signals to which my senses respond, and they do not directly affect my mind in a wholly convincing manner. Moreover, far from being attentive to all the signals that my senses report to me, I am blind and deaf to many of them, as everyone must be to avoid distraction. I do my best to heed those that seem most significant, and regret that they fail to reveal much that I ardently wish to know.

When I watch the creatures of which I have told in the foregoing chapters, I witness fascinating sequences of activities, integrated patterns of behavior admirably adapted to preserving their lives and perpetuating their species. If these creatures experience no satisfaction or enjoyment in living and acting, all their strenuous activity is as a moving picture on a screen, which may be of absorbing interest to an attentive watcher, but is absolutely meaningless and valueless to the flat images. It is difficult to believe that a bird sings sweetly, builds a charming nest, and plays the role of a devoted parent, wholly for the enjoyment of the few humans who appreciate this, and not at all for its own satisfaction. If the windows of my mind were as transparent as the open window before me, I might be certain of the answer to this enigma, instead of merely surmising it. And much that is obscure in this mysterious universe might become clear.

I believe that I can explain why the windows of our minds are opaque to so much that impinges upon them. Insulation from the environment is a primary necessity of life. The simplest forerunners of life that floated in tepid primeval seas were probably surrounded by a pellicle, or tenuous membrane, that regulated their exchanges with the water around them, permitting the entry of needed solutes and excluding, to the best of its ability, those that might be harmful; retaining what the protoplast could not afford to lose, while it extruded metabolic wastes. One of the chief differences between a living organism and a dead one is that the former controls its exchanges with the environment and the latter loses all control.

Evolutionary advance has demanded ever more effective insulation. A fish has better insulation than an amoeba, but that of a mammal is still better. Life could not emerge from the water into drying air without increasing insulation. Plants developed a waxy epidermis impervious to water, penetrated by stomata that could open and close, to regulate the egress and ingress of aqueous vapor and other gases. Animals covered themselves with a more or less impervious skin, often well pigmented to shield their tissues from excessive sunlight. The acquisition of homeothermy by mammals and birds would hardly have been possible without additional insulation in the form of fur or feathers to diminish loss of heat and the energy they spend to generate it. Those that achieved the best insulation became so independent of environmental fluctuations that they could remain active in an ambience so cold that all organisms lacking homeothermy become dormant or succumb. Many birds and small mammals have increased their insulation by building snug nests for sleeping. Man's ingenuity has improved the insulation he inherited as a mammal by clothing him with garments that can be thin or thick as the climate requires, by making dwellings that he can warm, and, latterly, by cooling them in the hottest weather by air-conditioning. With these arrangements, he has achieved such independence of the environment that he can dwell in fair comfort in the most extreme climates.

It appears that something similar to physiological insulation has occurred in the psychic sphere. Our minds seem to be enveloped in something corresponding to the semipermeable membrane that surrounds a protoplast, regulating its exchanges with the environment. The senses that are the mind's windows have been selected for utility, admitting the information most useful for survival in a state of nature and excluding much else—to be sensitive to everything that impinges upon us would be distracting rather than helpful. We may ordinarily be insensitive to direct psychic influences for a similar reason. For a predatory animal to be directly aware of the psychic state of his victim—its terror or pain—might be disarming, inhibiting his attack upon it and depriving him of needed food. In civilized life, the disadvantages of perfect psychic transparency might outweigh its advantages. If direct awareness of the feelings and thoughts of the people around us would make deceit impossible, it would also destroy privacy in its most intimate aspect. The social decencies are preserved by our often hiding our secret feelings—our antipathies and resentments, the organic tensions that arise at the most inconvenient times. It would be useless to enjoin silence in a classroom, public library, or gathering if we were directly assailed by the unspoken thoughts of all who surrounded us.

For the advantages of psychic insulation, we pay a price that often seems too high. Were our minds less impermeable to the feelings of the beings around us, perhaps not only of people but even of animals and plants, were we not so dependent upon what they can convey to us by words and gestures, we might not so frequently be devastatingly lonely. Our quest for enlightenment about some of the matters that most interest us would surely be furthered by greater sensitivity to all that the larger world might convey to us—by wider, more transparent windows of the mind. No biologist can doubt that, on the physiological level, improved insulation has been a most important factor in evolutionary advance. Now it has reached the point, especially in man, where further advance may depend upon the breakdown of insulation on the psychic plane.

Since prehistoric times, spiritually sensitive people have been dissatisfied with the narrowness and opacity of the mind's windows. Perplexed and oppressed by the human state, they wished to know more than their five senses revealed to them. They sought communication with unseen beings, including their gods and the spirits of ancestors, and not infrequently they claimed to have received commands or messages from them—as even today certain individuals profess to do. Seekers have scrubbed their minds' windows hard to increase their transparency, with results that are hard to assess. It is most difficult to know the provenance of what enters the mind otherwise than through the senses. Our senses, especially sight, commonly point to the source of the signals they convey. Moreover, at least for our externally directed senses, this source is public, so that its presence can be corroborated by several witnesses. An impression or idea that springs up in the mind with no obvious external prompting comes we know not whence. It may, in fact, be a communication from some unseen being to a mind whose windows are exceptionally transparent, or it may be a fancy or hallucination. This uncertainty hovers over all so-called revelations.

Sympathy and compassion are more widespread and positive indications of the decline of psychic insulation. When our spirits vibrate in harmony with the joys or sorrows of others, it may be that psychic states are communicated directly from mind to mind. On the other hand, all sympathy may be imaginative: from the observed behavior of another being, its expression, actions, and utterances, we form an idea of its psychic state, and this idea incites corresponding emotions. However sympathy arises, it opens our minds to aspects of the lives of other beings that are not directly revealed to us by sensation. From sympathy springs compassion. When the feelings of other creatures tinge our own, we hesitate to make them suffer. The day when a man, or some other animal, was first led by compassion to desist from injuring or killing an intended victim was certainly one of the most momentous in life's onward march. If we could ascertain its date in the remote past, we should mark it in red on all our calendars.

From remote times, man has been interested in the ways of the animals that surround him, especially those of some economic importance. But only recently, largely in the present century, have a significant number of people devoted patient years to the systematic study of free animals in their natural habitats, often foregoing comforts while they pursued their investigations far from the amenities of civilization. This has immensely deepened our understanding of the diversity and complexity of the social systems of animals, their resemblances to ourselves and their differences. It has increased our affection for some of them and our abhorrence or pity for others. Still more recently, imaginative scientists have tried with admirable patience to communicate with animals, to interpret their languages or equivalents and to teach them ours, so that an exchange of information or ideas would become possible. The most promising pupils of these teachers of language to nonhuman animals have been chimpanzees, gorillas, and dolphins. It is still too early to predict how far such studies will open our minds' windows.

In another direction, efforts are made to communicate with the intelligent beings who, in all probability, inhabit at least a few of the planets that circulate around the billions of stars in our galaxy. Messages to them have been included in the cargos of some of the spaceships that are expected to speed beyond our solar system, after reporting on conditions on the outer planets. On vast, dish-shaped antennae turned toward outer space, others have tried to detect meaningful radio signals, which the probable inhabitants of remote planets may be trying to send to us. The difficulties of enlightening communication with beings who may be unimaginably different from ourselves, on planets light years distant, are enormous and may never be overcome. Nevertheless, it is encouraging to notice that modern people, whose ancestors a few generations ago stubbornly insisted that the whole universe was made for man, its only inhabitant with a soul, are opening the windows of their minds more widely, expectantly waiting for illuminating messages to flow in.

Despite these laudable efforts to extend the range of human knowledge, our understanding of the universe is still pathetically limited. We still live in the shade of ignorance about the things nearest to us. That there is a psychic side of Being no one could rationally doubt; his very doubting, a psychic phenomenon, would prove its existence. We are confident that other humans, so similar to ourselves in all observable aspects, have thoughts and feelings more or less similar to our own, but we lack observational proof of this. For positive science, only our senses, directly or with the aid of ever more refined instruments, provide reliable data—all else is conjectural. Nevertheless, that animals, plants, and even minerals have a psychic, no less than a material, aspect is too highly probable to be dogmatically denied. If atoms are wholly devoid of feeling, how does it happen that we, who are made of them, can feel? A whole vast side of reality, indispensable not only for understanding the universe but for the intelligent, compassionate regulation of our relations with the living things that share the Earth with us, remains hidden from us. We must open the windows of our minds still more widely and make them more transparent, perhaps waiting for evolutionary changes that diminish our psychic insulation, before we can hope for full illumination.

Suppose that we could overcome our present distressing limitations and see things as they really are, what would we find? I am convinced that we would discover that we live in a universe that has been striving from its prime foundations to increase the value of its own existence, which includes ours and that of everything around us. For what would be the worth of a universe spread over billions of light years of space, perhaps infinite, if neither the whole nor any of its parts took pleasure in existence? What difference could it make to anybody or anything whether such a universe existed or ceased to be? What would be lost if it were suddenly annihilated? Can we imagine any futility more immense than trillions of atoms vibrating with no trace of feeling, never realizing their ability to create lovely forms and conscious beings; billions of stars dissipating their energy vainly in the void abyss; millions of planets forever barren of vibrant life—a universe thickly interlaced with rays of light that never convey beauty to appreciative eyes or knowledge to eager minds?

Our own unquenchable thirst for a happier, more rewarding and meaningful life, enriched by ever higher values, is a more developed expression of an urge that permeates the very foundations of a universe that refuses to rest in utter barrenness, but tries stubbornly to enhance its existence. It does this by building up the ultimate particles into integrated structures—into patterns that tend to increase in complexity, amplitude, and coherence. This process of harmonization, which pervades our planet and probably all others where physical conditions are favorable, advances in several stages, as is necessary to give existence its highest value. First, it must consolidate its materials into incandescent stars that provide continuing sources of energy, surrounded by planets whose milder temperatures permit the formation of finer structures. A sun and its planets are an admirable example of a harmoniously integrated pattern on a vast scale, so stable that it endures for aeons. Next, it covers such planets, of which Earth is a splendid example, with beautiful forms and colors, including crystals, sunrises and sunsets, rainbows, and the infinite variety of lovely vegetable forms. Plants, and even crystals, may enjoy their existence, but lacking eyes they can hardly appreciate the beauty of the things around them—or their own. Lacking olfactory organs, plants may never sense the fragrance of their flowers. They can neither produce nor enjoy melodies. Accordingly, a third stage was indispensable for the realization of many of the highest values. Animals, often themselves beautiful, with sense organs and minds to perceive the beauty around them, with the ability to produce and to hear harmonious sounds, with the capacity to cooperate, to love, to know, and to cherish all things beautiful and good, were needed to elevate the value of existence.

Without a guiding Intelligence, such animals could be created only by a painful process of trial and error, with many false starts, blunders, and miscarriages. To equip animals with efficient sense organs and perceptive, appreciative minds required an immensely long time, of which the cosmos has no lack. We are the chief beneficiaries of this prolonged, hazardous process, which has caused so much suffering, and we would be unworthy of the splendid endowments in mind and body that nature has given us, if we were not constantly thankful for this high privilege. The best way to show our gratitude is by caring devotedly for whatever embellishes or elevates our lives. Such cherishing appreciation is needed to fulfill the cosmic striving to make existence ever more precious and desirable. When we appreciate, cherish, and try to understand—and help others to do the same—we fill the role that appears most appropriate for us when we survey the whole course of cosmic evolution and our place in nature. Moreover, when we strive earnestly to make our lives beautiful and satisfying by appreciative enjoyment of the many lovely and benign things that surround us, we live conformably to nature's upward trend and can expect its continued support—provided always that we live intelligently and moderately, making no excessive demands upon Earth's bounty.

To play our proper role in the cosmic order, we must keep our windows open, not only those of our dwellings but, above all, those of our spirits. We must permit no hard dogmas or hoary creeds to narrow our vision or trammel our inquiring minds. The more we look for order and beauty in the natural world, the more we shall find, whether we use our unaided eyes, peer through a microscope, or gaze through a telescope. But to perceive sensuous beauty is not enough. We should spare no effort to see beauty in the patterns of life, the mutual adjustments, of the diverse creatures that surround us, and we should not neglect the noble, kindly acts of men. We should remember, too, that, open our eyes and our minds as widely as we can, much will escape us. Except in our individual selves, we have firmly established knowledge of only one aspect of things, the external side, beneath which lurks a psychic aspect to which our windows are still stubbornly opaque. Unless we or our descendants polish them to perfect transparency, the ultimate mysteries of the universe will remain veiled from us.

It would be folly to suppose that while we seek the beautiful and lovable we shall not find much that is hideous and abhorrent. Although to dwell much upon evils and agonies that we can neither remove nor mitigate is to oppress our spirits without benefit to others, it would be fatuous to close our windows tightly to them and pretend they do not exist. The best course is to try to understand how they arose as the inevitable result of a fundamentally beneficent creative process with limitless perseverance, but no evident control by a foresighted Intelligence able to guide and moderate its often excessive intensity. The evil and the ugly may be regarded as by-products, or secondary results, of the cosmic striving to make existence ever more desirable. Nearly everything that exalts and enriches life, and certainly our ability to perceive, to enjoy, and to appreciate, depends upon the existence of harmoniously integrated patterns of atoms, which is what organisms of every kind essentially are. But these patterns arise in such excessive numbers that they compete for the space, materials, and energy they must have to complete and preserve themselves. Clashing together, they thwart, injure, or destroy one another, causing incalculable pain and misery, as is all too evident in the living world.

To view the situation in this light should cause no consternation to us who are endowed with what has been most lacking in the cosmic process—foreseeing minds and the ability to cultivate the high virtue of moderation. If we use these precious gifts wisely and consistently, never losing sight of our proper role in a universe that strives to increase the value of existence, we can bring happiness and fulfillment to our lives by wide-eyed, cherishing appreciation of everything worthy of our love and admiration, with fewer of the sorrows and disgusts that now oppress us. Overcoming the feeling of alienation from the sources of our being that so often dejects modern man, we can cultivate loyalty to a cosmos that is the source of our yearning for a more satisfying or blessed existence, a cosmos that will not fail to support us if we cooperate intelligently, unitedly, and moderately with it.

In the aeonian striving of the universe to increase the value of its own existence by means of creatures that might be regarded as its organs for enjoyment and appreciation, those who delight in wild nature, and above all dedicated naturalists who try earnestly to disclose its secrets, play a special and most important role. By opening their minds' windows to sights and sounds beyond the narrow human sphere that confines the outlook of vast numbers of men, they immensely increase the number and variety of realized values. While they rejoice in the beauty widely diffused over Earth's face, they reveal much more that is hidden from casual view. They trace admirable patterns of organization, and of cooperation among organisms. They witness among non-human creatures many examples of behavior that, when practiced by ourselves, wins our highest praise. They know the exultation of discovery.

Even our distress and indignation at many things that we behold in nature—predation, parasitism, violent conflicts of all kinds, excessive reproduction that leads to widespread starvation—should be regarded as a value that the world process has brought forth in its forward march, a moral value of the highest order. Since the ethical consciousness is evidently an achievement of evolution at an advanced stage, it is a revelation that nature does not rest complacently in its crudities, but is striving, especially through us, to overcome them. Perhaps this is a presage of future mitigation. To suppress or disparage our moral indignation at nature's harshness is not loyalty to nature, or the cosmos, but repudiation of one of the finest things, one of the highest values, that nature has achieved.

In bidding farewell to my readers, I can wish them no greater felicity than that which comes from looking for many years through open windows upon a landscape that has not been ravaged by man's ignorance and greed.

# Bibliography

Abraham, K. F. 1978. Adoption of Spectacled Eider ducklings by Arctic Loons. *Condor* 80:339–40.

Allan, T. A. 1979. Parental behavior of a replacement male Dark-eyed Junco. *Auk* 96:630–31.

Amadon, D. 1967. Galápagos finches grooming Marine Iguanas. *Condor* 69:311.

Baker, H. G., and Baker, I. 1975. Studies of nectar-constitution and pollinator-plant coevolution. In *Coevolution of animals and plants*, ed. L. E. Gilbert and P. H. Raven, pp. 100–40. Austin: University of Texas Press.

Bent, A. C. 1942. Life histories of North American cuckoos, goatsuckers, hummingbirds and their allies. *U.S. Natl. Mus. Bull.* 176:i–viii, 1–506.

Biaggi, V., Jr. 1955. *Life history of the Puerto Rican Honeycreeper, Coereba flaveola portoricensis (Bryant)*. Río Piedras: University of Puerto Rico Agricultural Experiment Station.

Burger, W. 1971. Flora costaricensis. *Fieldiana: Botany* 35:1–227.

Carpenter, C. R. 1934. *A field study of the behavior and social relations of Howling Monkeys (Alouatta palliata)*. Comparative Psychology Monographs, vol. 10, no. 2. Baltimore: Johns Hopkins University Press.

Chapman, F. M. 1935. The courtship of Gould's Manakin (*Manacus vitellinus vitellinus*) on Barro Colorado Island, Canal Zone. *Bull. Amer. Mus. Nat. Hist.* 68:471–525.

Crockett, A. B., and Hansley, P. L. 1977. Coition, nesting, and postfledging behavior of Williamson's Sapsucker in Colorado. *Living Bird* 16:7–19.

Dawkins, R. 1976. *The selfish gene.* Oxford: Oxford University Press.

Euler, C. 1867. Beiträge zur Naturgeschichte der Vögel Brasiliens. *Jour. für Ornith.* 15:177–98, 217–33, 399–420.

ffrench, R. 1973. *A guide to the birds of Trinidad and Tobago.* Wynnewood, Pa.: Livingston Publishing Co.

Foster, B. 1977. Africa's gentle giants. *National Geographic* 152: 402–17.

Goodall, J. D.; Johnson, A. W.; and Philippi B., R. A. 1957. *Las aves de Chile: su conocimiento y sus costumbres.* Vol. 1. Buenos Aires: Platt Establecimientos Gráficos S. A.

Gross, A. O. 1958. Life history of the Bananaquit on Tobago Island. *Wilson Bull.* 70:257–79.

Gundersen, A. 1950. *Families of dicotyledons.* Waltham, Mass.: Chronica Botanica Co.

Hancocks, D. 1973. *Master builders of the animal world.* London: Hugh Evelyn.

Howell, T. R. 1979. *Breeding biology of the Egyptian Plover, Pluvianus aegyptius.* Univ. Calif. Publ. Zool. vol. 113. Berkeley and Los Angeles: University of California Press.

Hudson, W. H. 1920. *Birds of La Plata.* 2 vols. London and Toronto: J. M. Dent & Sons.

Humboldt, A. von. 1852–53. *Personal narrative of travels to the equinoctial regions of America during the years 1799–1804 by Alexander von Humboldt and Aimé Bonpland.* Translated and edited by T. Ross. 3 vols. London: Henry G. Bohn.

Kilham, L. 1977. Altruism in nesting Yellow-bellied Sapsucker. *Auk* 94:613–14.

Kohr, L. 1957. *The breakdown of nations.* London: Routledge & Kegan Paul.

Lemmons, P. 1956. Cardinal feeds fishes. *Nature Mag.* 49:536.

McKaye, K. R. 1977. Defense of a predator's young by a herbivorous fish: An unusual strategy. *American Naturalist* 111: 301–15.

Nolan, V., Jr. 1978. *The ecology and behavior of the Prairie Warbler Dendroica discolor.* American Ornithologists' Union Ornith. Monographs, no. 26. Lawrence, Kans.: Allen Press for American Ornithologists' Union.

Patterson, F. 1978. Conversations with a gorilla. *National Geographic* 154:438–65.

Pfeiffer, J. 1980. Current research casts new light on human origins. *Smithsonian* 11:91–102.

Pinkowski, B. C. 1978. Two successive male Eastern Bluebirds tending the same nest. *Auk* 95:606–08.

Schaller, G. B. 1965. *The year of the gorilla.* London: Collins.

Schumacher, E. F. 1973. *Small is beautiful.* New York: Harper and Row.

Skutch, A. F. 1967. *Life histories of Central American highland birds.* Publ. Nuttall Ornith. Club, no. 7. Cambridge, Mass.: Nuttall Ornithological Club.

———. 1969. *Life histories of Central American birds. III.* Pacific Coast Avifauna, no. 35. Berkeley: Cooper Ornithological Society.

———. 1971. *A naturalist in Costa Rica.* Gainesville: University of Florida Press.

———. 1976. *Parent birds and their young.* Austin: University of Texas Press.

———. 1977. *A bird watcher's adventures in tropical America.* Austin: University of Texas Press.

———. 1980. *A naturalist on a tropical farm.* Berkeley and Los Angeles: University of California Press.

Snow, B. K., and Snow, D. W. 1971. The feeding ecology of tanagers and honeycreepers in Trinidad. *Auk* 88:291–322.

Snow, D. W. 1962. A field study of the Black and White Manakin, *Manacus manacus,* in Trinidad. *Zoologica* (N. Y. Zool. Soc.) 47:65–104.

————. 1968. The singing assemblies of Little Hermits. *Living Bird* 7:47–55.

Todd, W. E. C., and Carriker, M. A., Jr. 1922. The birds of the Santa Marta region of Colombia: A study in altitudinal distribution. *Ann. Carnegie Mus.* 14:1–611.

Wetmore, A. 1927. The birds of Porto Rico and the Virgin Islands. *Sci. Surv. Porto Rico, Virgin Islands* (N. Y. Acad. Sci.) 9, pt. 3:245–406, pt. 4:409–571.

Wickler, W. 1968. *El mimetismo en las plantas y los animales.* Mexico City: McGraw-Hill.

Wiley, R. H. 1971. Song groups in a singing assembly of Little Hermits. *Condor* 73:28–35.

Wilson, E. O. 1975. *Sociobiology: The new synthesis.* Cambridge: Harvard University Press, Belknap Press.

Woolfenden, G. E., and Fitzpatrick, J. H. 1977. Dominance in the Florida Scrub Jay. *Condor* 79:1–12.

# Index

| | |
|---:|:---|
| Designer: | Randall Goodall |
| Compositor: | G & S Typesetters, Inc. |
| Printer: | Vail-Ballou Press, Inc. |
| Binder: | Vail-Ballou Press, Inc. |
| Text: | 11/13 Goudy Old Style |
| Display: | Palatino |